About Franl

An independent, creative force in the astrological community for over a quarter of a century, Frank Clifford has built an eclectic career in astrology, palmistry and publishing:

- As the writer of a dozen books, including a modern classic on hand analysis
- As a columnist and biographer
- As a Sun sign astrologer for numerous magazines
- As a consultant for clients and businesses
- As a publisher of over thirty books and booklets
- As a researcher and compiler of birth data (including a compendium for Solar Fire)
- As a media astrologer–palmist profiled and interviewed on radio, TV and in print
- As an international lecturer and the Principal of the London School of Astrology where, for the past ten years, he has been instrumental in bringing a younger generation to astrology

www.frankclifford.co.uk

FRANK C CLIFFORD

THE

Solar Arc

HANDBOOK

Flare Publications
The London School of Astrology

The London School of Astrology

First edition published in 2018 by Flare Publications
in conjunction with the London School of Astrology
BCM Planets, London WC1N 3XX, England, UK

www.flareuk.com and www.londonschoolofastrology.co.uk
email: admin@londonschoolofastrology.co.uk

A CIP catalogue record for this book is available from the British Library

ISBN: 978-1-903353-51-6 (softcover)
978-1-903353-52-3 (ebook)

To contact the author, please email him at info@flareuk.com
www.flareuk.com

My sincere thanks to Jane Struthers for proofing this book,
to Sy Scholfield for checking all the data, charts and sources,
to Sara Fisk (stf@stf-designs.com) for her beautiful cover,
and to Carole Devine for permission to quote from *Solar Arc Directions*.

Some of the text was first published in *Solar Arc Directions* (2011) and in issues of *The Mountain Astrologer* (USA) and *The Astrological Journal* (UK). My thanks to Tem Tarriktar, Nan Geary, Jan de Prosse (all of *TMA*) and to John Green, Ian Tonothy and Victor Olliver (of the *AJ*) who edited, proofed and published these original pieces.

Dedicated to Mario. Love began with you.

And with love to Helen, Filly and my mother.

And to six other generous blessings in my life:
Sue Smith, Wendy Stacey, Kira Sutherland,
Leticia Trevino, Jane Struthers and Linda Kubota Byrd.

List of Natal, Event and Bi-wheel Charts (A-Z)

Contents

Part I

The Rhythms of Our Lives:
Initial Forecasting Considerations

Be glad of life because it gives you the chance to love,
and to work, and to play, and to look up at the stars and sun.
– Henry Van Dyke

Your success and happiness lies in you.
Resolve to keep happy,
and your joy and you shall form
an invincible host against difficulties.
– Helen Keller

In this opening chapter, I'd like introduce some ideas to consider while preparing to forecast for yourself or a client. And regardless of whether you're using transits, directions or progressions, I'd like to offer a simple method to get to the heart of any forecasting interpretation.

Perhaps it's best to start by saying that this book is about forecasting, not prediction. Rather than using astrological tools to make predictions (firm or otherwise), I believe that we do our best, most helpful work as consulting astrologers when we *articulate the processes* that can take place under various transits, progressions or directions. In doing so, we can help clients to recognize the 'season' they're in and to become aware of (and attuned to) different cycles taking place in their lives.

Our job, I believe, is to help clients become aware of their options and for us to communicate these effectively and ethically to them. Engaging in a dialogue with a client helps to illuminate these options, as well as the client's needs. Then, with knowledge from the astrologer of the themes inherent in the period ahead, the client can *actively participate* in co-creating their future, rather than simply feel that these celestial events are 'happening to them'.

From the moment of our birth – the moment we have a horoscope – all future transits, directions and progressions (and their exact dates of fruition) are set in place. They will occur whether we like it or not! If our Ascendant is at 16° Capricorn, transiting Pluto will have reached that degree in January 2016 and traversed that point back and forth until it moved on in October 2017.

Our birth chart can't avoid such occurrences, and it will continue to be activated long after we're gone (another fascinating area of study). This is perhaps the only predictable, 'fatalistic' aspect that we need to consider in forecasting. But the rest – our own choices, 'fate' and destiny – appears to be negotiable. We can't always stop awful things happening to us or to the people and world around us, but we can engage in our own life processes and honour upcoming transits or directions in our charts. There will be pain, illness, grief and sorrow, but how we choose to *respond* to these feelings – and how we seek to find meaning in these events – is in our hands.

So, our job is to dialogue with clients – to discover where they're at and suggest how they can work constructively with the planets – rather than to 'tell their fortune' or leave them feeling at the mercy of upcoming transits or directions.

Empowering clients – helping them to make the most of their time and talents, rather than sentencing them to 'unavoidable' predictions – can start with a philosophical explanation of how we view forecasting and a responsible use of language. For instance, it's useful to dismiss the idea that planets 'do something' to us ('Saturn and Pluto will be kicking your butt in 2020!').

Some clients elevate astrologers to 'gurus' who are able to 'predict the future'. This may encourage us to make firm pronouncements and prognostications (whether these range from unrelentingly negative or terminally positive, as the late astrologer Donna Cunningham once wrote). Before introducing the power of astrology to an unsuspecting public, every one of us that practises astrology needs a level of counselling skills training. Without training, what can happen is that we recognize the influence we wield, feel seduced by a client's awe or reverence, and then may fail to act responsibly – only intent on impressing them or proving that astrology works.

Alternatively, it's not uncommon for us to feel under attack if clients are sceptical, and this too can prompt reckless, defensive declarations in order to prove ourselves and to validate astrology. This can happen with any astrological approach, but we should be particularly alert if we're employing a rigid doctrine to read natal charts or when combining astrology with another area (such as therapy, reincarnation or karma) where the client may feel more vulnerable.

Here are five considerations for forecasting with the natal chart, followed by a list of keywords for each planet, angle and sign.

1.01 • Think 'Process' Rather than 'Event'

Arguably, forecasting tools describe the processes, feelings and reactions more than the actual events. Knowing which planets, signs and houses are involved gives us a good idea of the areas that might be affected and the type of situation involved, but nothing is certain. And perhaps that's the way it should be.

With hindsight, past events can usually be 'seen' in the chart in meaningful ways, particularly if we have context. Being forewarned of an upcoming event (if that is even possible) may have its uses, but understanding the mood of a period of time (e.g. during a Pluto transit) can be more helpful when it comes to contemplating the meaning of that period in our life and understanding what we're being asked to experience or learn.

Consider the thorny issue of predicting death. Taking a look at the chart of a person who has just been widowed (rather than the deceased themselves), we could find any one of the planets implicated. Why? Because the widow(er) may have all sorts of feelings and circumstances surrounding (or triggered by) the death. The surviving spouse could be shocked, liberated or feel that their life has been turned upside down (Uranus). They might turn to spirits (whether via a medium for guidance or via the bottle for escape) or feel lost or bewildered (Neptune). They might be very aware of their own mortality and start planning for the future (Saturn). As astrologers, we need context: the client's reaction, feeling and motive. The event as a category ('death', 'marriage', 'first-born') isn't enough.

In an article on rectification for *The Mountain Astrologer* (February–March 2018), I wrote this:

The chart will be activated at the time of an important event – but more important than the actual event is the client's *response* to the event. We might presume that the death of a loved one would be Saturn or Pluto in nature, but we need to understand the client's context and responses. What were they going through at the time? Was the death sudden? What did it bring about? What has changed since? We might hear: 'It was a blessed relief for us all – he had been in so much pain', or 'I've now got the funds to travel around the world', or 'It taught me the importance of time and making the very most of what we have left', or 'It's tough; I now carry the responsibility of looking after the rest of the family.' In each case, we should be able to hear the planetary culprit in our client's description – and that planet should be 'seen' in the transits or directions. Sometimes, when the memory is overridden by adult reasoning ('Looking back, it probably wasn't that important'), it's useful to ask the client to describe how they remember feeling at the time.

One client had Solar Arc Saturn come to her Ascendant in Aries when her husband committed suicide. *Saturn did not make this happen!* Following on from the grief, she soon realized how much control her husband had taken in managing their lives and careers (she had no idea even how to write a cheque). She lost her teammate, her greatest supporter. After his death, she had to start taking responsibility for herself (Saturn) and learn to

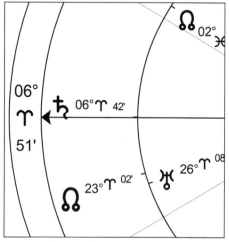

be independent, self-reliant and to go solo (Aries). That's what the Saturn to the Aries Ascendant was about.

Any event or, more importantly, repercussions under such a Solar Arc will have a Saturnian feel to them: it's time in our life to stop, contemplate, take stock and then (ideally) move towards greater responsibility, which in itself leads to growth, maturity and self-governance (Saturn). In Aries, Saturn's issues are concerned with going it alone, starting a new cycle, being self-determining and learning to do things yourself. If such a direction had happened to my client at age thirteen, it's likely to have involved a different scenario but with similar Saturn–Aries lessons (see 1.03).

When using any method of prediction, the timing of actual events can appear to be 'off'. But we need to dig deeper (astrology works but we astrologers often fail to notice astrology in action!) – the event is just one occurrence in a longer, larger process. For instance, a relationship break-up can affect us on many levels and may last for many years (from an early decision to split through to the eventual moving on after the break-up). The precise date of the divorce might not be 'seen' by appropriate transits or directions, but other stages in this process may be of greater importance to the person (and thus more obvious in the chart). So, context is far more important than the actual event.

Here's another example: a marriage date may not be highlighted in the chart by major transits or directions, but the date that coincided with the recognition of falling in love or wanting to spend the rest of our life with that person may be more astrologically significant. Nowadays, marriages and their dates may be chosen for all sorts of expedient reasons.

The astrologer Paul Wright has written of astrology's uncertainty principle: 'The more specific we are in our pronouncements, the less likely we are to be correct ... We lose certainty in translating from principles to particulars and are left contemplating a range of possibilities. This is frustrating for clients, who are almost always more interested in specifics.' (*Jupiter and Mercury: An A to Z*, Flare Publications, 2006, p. 32.) Setting ourselves up as a teller of fortunes rather than a translator of the skies can be problematic in a number of ways.

There is also the bigger issue of whether we should predict at all – and if so, when? 'If I marry her, will it last?' is quite different from 'Will I get the job I was interviewed for?' In the first instance, we can look at the client's natal chart and synastry (chart comparison) with their partner, highlight possible issues and encourage them to make their own decision. In the second instance, with context of what specifically the new job will entail, we can speculate whether the job will be theirs if the transits and directions reflect these specifics.

The more influence a client has over the outcome, the more we should attempt to describe the climate and encourage them to make up their own mind. Astrology then becomes useful in describing the upcoming period and it can be used to elect the best times to take action.

1.02 • Start with the Birth Chart

Although I don't believe that a life event can *only* happen if it's described as potential in the birth chart, a natal horoscope contains many, if not most, of the experiences we are likely to have if we live long enough.

Before we start looking at forecasting, it is essential to consider the nature, motivations and priorities of the person whose chart we're examining. These will most likely be seen in their Sun, Moon and Ascendant complexes, any planets on angles, and any elemental/modal lacks or emphases. We should also consider the main themes and life stories written as 'potential' in their charts (as seen in major configurations and hard aspects). This should be the starting point. How someone works with a transit will depend on what that planet means in their natal chart and their earlier experiences of it (the planetary 'memory', which is discussed on pages 27–9).

Here's a quick outline of my seven steps to highlighting key themes of the chart as well as defining planetary strength that I wrote about in *Dialogues* and *Getting to the Heart of Your Chart*:

i Elements and Modes
Is there a dominant or missing element or mode? These reveal the psychological balancing act of motivations (elements) and personal style (modes) in a person's life. When these are 'weighted' (using nine chart points: the Sun to Saturn, the Ascendant and MC; with extra weight assigned to the Sun, Moon and Ascendant), they reveal how and where our basic nature may be in or out of sync. When there's an imbalance of the elements or modes in the birth chart – be that a preponderance (three or more points) or lack (zero or one point) – it shows up as a fundamental factor in our psychological make-up.

ii Key Archetypes and Areas
Is there an emphasis on a sign or house in the horoscope? Signs are archetypes of the human experience and symbolic of a particular stage in life's journey. A sign emphasis will bring to prominence the sign's key traits, responses, scripts, 'birthright' and life situations that we are likely to encounter. A house that is emphasized

(i.e. heavily tenanted by planets) will show the mundane and psychological areas of life in which our main dramas are likely to play out. For an emphasis, we should expect at least three points in a sign or house, or at least two of the Big Three (the Sun, Moon and Ascendant) placed there.

iii Angle Orientation

The four angles represent a highly personal compass, showing how we view, negotiate and interact with our immediate and broader environments. They are also the badges we wear: our identity, meet-and-greet badge (Ascendant); our advert for (or label we assign to) an 'other' (Descendant); our social status or professional CV badge (MC); and our family coat of arms (IC).

Consider whether the compass's orientation (by element or mode) matches the nature of the inner planets. When we look at the two axes (particularly the two 'public persona' angles, the Ascendant and Midheaven) that make up the structural foundation of the chart, are they of a particular mode? Perhaps all the angles are in fixed signs. Maybe all four elements are found on the angles.

Noting the orientation of our compass is key to understanding our stance in personal, relationship, social and family settings. It shows how easily we can utilize our planet/sign talents in the world around us. Is our compass (environment) in harmony with the personal planets and key themes of the chart? Or do we need to reconcile our inner nature (as shown by the personal planets) with the conflicting demands of our environment (as seen by the angles)?

Make a note of any joint rulerships: the angles may have planetary rulers in common (as they do when the mutable signs are on all four), and these rulers may be in aspect, making this an important feature of the chart.

iv Character, Temperament and Personality

Consider the Sun, Moon and Ascendant – follow their trails and look for repetitions (e.g. shared elements or modes, or links to a particular planet, sign or house).

Arguably the most important positions in the horoscope, the Big Three are very reliable entrance points into the chart when we begin interpretation as they are the areas we engage with most frequently. How do they work together? Are they dominated by one element or mode? What do they have in common and where may there be conflicts of interest? Often the Sun, Moon and Ascendant rulership trails can lead to the discovery of a key aspect or focal point in a horoscope.

- The Sun – core character: our fundamental mission, individual role, life purpose and vocation; what we're in the process of becoming; our essence and inner identity; our type of 'heart'.

- The Moon – behavioural traits: our habits; our fundamental relationship needs and impressions; innate responses to everyday life; our 'backpack' of emotional experiences that have been stored since childhood; our feeling nature and vulnerable side; who we are 'behind closed doors'; our hidden agenda.

- The Ascendant – personality characteristics: our approach to life; our meet-and-greet function and the role(s) we play to navigate our journey; mottoes for survival and interaction; first impressions made and received; our overt agenda.

v Major Dynamics, Life Stories, Challenges and Talents
Highlight the major aspects in the chart and run with these. Aspects show a dialogue and a flow of energy between planets (or between planets and angles). These help us to zoom in on the main life stories and the fundamental dynamics, talents and challenges within the personality. The three major aspects to consider are the conjunction, square and opposition. (I only consider trines in this early assessment when the orb is very tight – under 2–3°.)

- The conjunction is a focal point in the chart; a powerful merging of energies that do not act alone. It's a script/dynamic that is obvious to others but may not be so easy to see objectively in ourselves.

- The square is an area that requires action, effort, striving and stretching. It's a script/dynamic manifesting as a challenge that 'builds character'. The square is a tension that creates achievement, mastery and excellence.

- The opposition represents a face-off between conflicting parts of our nature – those that are most often seen in relationship patterns. It is a see-saw script/dynamic demanding that we integrate parts of ourselves through relationships, rather than disowning or projecting them.

vi Key Life Themes and Obsessions
Is there a major aspect configuration? Planets that interlock by forming geometrical configurations, such as the T-square, Grand Trine or Yod, usually dominate the birth chart and overshadow other placements. T-squares in particular reveal the major life challenges and themes – the areas in love and work that we get obsessed with and that take up much time and focus. The actual aspects (e.g. the three trines of the Grand Trine) define the *nature* of the dialogue, while the planets (and their sign and house placements) describe the players involved in the creative tension and activity.

vii The Life's Work
Is there a signature (planet/sign/house theme) or a pivotal aspect/ feature that's central to the action? Make a note of major themes or a key aspect that ties up much of the chart.

Here, we are looking for repetitive statements and patterns – what we might call signatures. It is often said that a major statement will be written/expressed in at least three ways in the birth chart. For example, a horoscope may have a Pisces Ascendant, plus a Sun– Neptune conjunction which is opposed by the Moon in the 12th House. These three factors (particularly important because the Big Three are involved) would suggest a Neptune/Pisces/12th House emphasis, which I would term a Neptune signature.

Most planets have rulership over two signs and houses. When we spot a Venusian emphasis, is this a Venus/Taurus/2nd House or Venus/Libra/7th House signature? Or perhaps there's a mix, e.g. Libra is on the Ascendant and the Sun is conjunct Venus in Taurus in the 7th. I would still see this as a Venus signature, but would clarify which of the signs and houses are involved.

When there is more than one planetary signature (e.g. Venus and Neptune), consider these to be a bit like a planetary pairing by aspect (i.e. Venus conjunct Neptune). There may not be a dialogue/ aspect between these two planets in the horoscope, but the main themes and thrust of the birth chart (and life) are of the nature of both planets. When those two planets also happen to be in aspect to each other, the theme is strengthened.

By spotting a planetary signature, we uncover a key part of the life story/character. We can then go deeper and assess the 'condition' of that planet to pinpoint themes, life issues and needs.

The method above is not about reducing the chart and avoiding its complexities. It's a technique that can help us get to the very heart of what the chart, person and their life are truly about.

Planetary Strength

When examining the birth chart, there is another important consideration: planetary strength and influence. It is important to address the issue of 'good' and 'bad' placements and consider what constitutes a strong or influential planet. Our assessment is important if we wish to isolate key players (the driving forces in our chart) and look for the signatures/repetitions mentioned above.

I tend to avoid using words like 'dignified', 'exaltation', 'fall' and 'detriment' in natal astrology – they can obfuscate interpretation or lead to the incorrect assumption that some planet-in-sign positions are 'good', 'bad' or 'weak'.

The more charts we read, the more we realize that both successful and unfulfilled people have every possible planet-in-sign combination. People accomplish extraordinary things with so-called 'debilitated' positions, while people with planets in 'pristine condition' can choose paths, or encounter limiting external factors, in which these 'advantageous' placements languish or stagnate.

A planet in its sign of rulership (e.g. Mars in Scorpio or Venus in Libra) shows an ability to carry out the job it is naturally inclined to do. That's why planet and sign were linked by ancient astrologers. Here, planet and sign share an affinity; they speak a similar language. The manifestation (effect) is straightforward and without a conflict of interest. But that's as far as it goes. Every planet-in-sign combination has a range of expression and possibility – with talents, strengths, problem areas and weaknesses. Combinations that aren't traditionally 'strong' simply do jobs differently or have an unconventional agenda.

I think that we fail as astrologers when we don't recognize the potential inherent in a 'foreign' placement. Consider how capable

Mars in Libra can be in times of war: a cool-headed strategist with peace on the agenda who excels in the art of negotiation. A study of leaders with Mars in Libra reveals a track record of dynamic leadership. The placement is an important alternative to 'natural' Mars expressions in hot-headed Aries or volatile Scorpio. Aries and Scorpio may be the signs of war (Mars), but we might need other signs to do specific jobs at particular times. Planetary strength is less defined by its placement and more by an *awareness* of the strengths and weaknesses inherent in that sign placement.

With that in mind, let's consider how to spot a planet that plays an influential role in the chart. Such a planet is one that dominates, receives singular recognition or is set apart from the others. It is a leader in the chart, a dominating force in the person's life stories, traits, encounters and experiences. Once an influential planet has been identified, the style and specific nature of its impact (its anticipated expression and manifestation) can be seen in the planet's position by sign, house and aspect. (The same applies to a planet that isn't influential – we can see which areas and talents may be insufficiently used and help clients to address these.)

Influential by Isolation

- A planet as a 'handle' of a Bucket-shaped chart shows what we 'hold on to'. It is often a focus of activity (a *raison d'être*) to the point of compulsion and at the expense of other planets. It can either result in an extraordinary accomplishment or act as a millstone or an 'excuse' for neglecting other areas of our life.

- An unaspected planet is one that can function autonomously and in an all-or-nothing manner.

- A 'leading' planet is the first (in sign order) in a series of planets after much unoccupied space. It is a driving force, a front-man.

- A singleton by hemisphere (less so by element or mode) is a stand-out planet. This is particularly noticeable when above or below the Ascendant/Descendant axis, where it represents the only planet that is either 'seen' externally (above) or hidden beneath the surface (below). Sometimes there are two, and their combination tells a story as well.

Influential by Integration

- A heavily aspected planet becomes a key figure because it is in dialogue with much of the chart's action.

- The dispositor of a stellium or the ruler of two angles becomes an 'ambassador' – a representative with influence that describes the impetus behind much of the chart. (Stick to traditional rulerships, saving modern rulerships – the outer planets – to show links to wider, societal or generational themes.)

- The focal planet ('apex') in a T-square becomes a powerful, principal point of release and a 'solution' to the dynamics of the configuration.

Influential by House or Zodiacal Position

- A planet conjunct one of the chart's four angles and/or in a Gauquelin Zone (especially around the Ascendant or Midheaven, or behind them in the cadent Placidus 12th or 9th House respectively). This is where the planet is at its most prominent and its characteristics most noticeable in our life and to those we encounter.

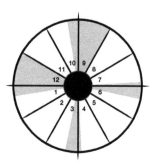

- At 0° or 29° of a sign. At 0°, a planet acts out the most obvious and familiar traits, but there's a fresh, raw, unstudied quality or naïveté. At 29°, there's a knowingness (and skilful mastery) of the sign's dynamics and the planet may exhibit the sign's most challenging, extreme facets. (More on these later.)

1.03 • Look for Context, Awareness and Levels of Manifestation

As I've already mentioned, to attempt a forecast we must seek out some personal context from the client. What is their perception/awareness? On what level are they chiefly operating (e.g. spiritual, financial, psychological)? At what age and stage are they in life? How active are they in the area being triggered in the forecast?

For instance, a Solar Arc direction or transit linked to the 6th or 10th House could manifest quite differently if the person has retired or hasn't yet started school. Transits/directions to our 10th House can describe our children's careers once we've retired or perhaps our new role as grandparent. When young, transits/directions to our 10th House can reflect what's going on in our parents' professional lives that might (consciously or otherwise) shape our own ideas around success and formulate early ambitions. (As Noel Tyl is fond of saying, 'The angles belong to the parents when young.')

A Saturn direction for someone aged twelve might coincide with boarding school, studying to take tough exams, or the loneliness of emerging adolescence. At forty, it could trigger a review of major life commitments up to that date and may coincide with a number of big decisions (divorce, change of work, settling down). At eighty-five, it might herald a period of chronicling the past, making new commitments, broken bones, the deaths of contemporaries, frosty winter nights with limited finances to pay for heating, and so on.

A performer with transiting Uranus on the Midheaven could move suddenly from obscurity to prominence, but for another, in a career that's already been established, such a transit could coincide with a *reversal* of fortune (Uranus), a fall from position.

Ultimately, the *nature* of the planet will be seen, and much depends on the choices made and the events that have transpired in the life up to that point.

Transits, progressions and directions can manifest on several levels (inner, outer, social, psychological, spiritual), and often these will be simultaneous. It's also worth remembering that people who enter our lives under a certain planet's transit are usually of that planetary nature/significance to us. During a major Pluto transit to a planet or angle, we'll encounter Pluto in as many areas of our life that we are aware of. Pluto will appear at work, in relationships with family, in other people's accounts of their lives, in our dreams, in the movies we watch and the conversations we overhear. So, a big question is: what's the level of the client's awareness, activity or interest in the areas being impacted?

An ambitious Aries client arrived at my office determined to know how astrology could help her plan her PR business and make her a fortune. At the time, there was little in her chart that reflected the big career advancements she was hungry for. Instead, I thought her transits and directions indicated a time to develop her interpersonal skills, and pursued this with her. Natally, Uranus rising in Libra manifested as her having a provocative manner with people, and it seemed from our dialogue that her approach was making her more enemies than friends. But she wasn't interested in hearing about anything personal or psychological, so I did my best to adapt to what she needed, even if the chart said 'Wait' (not a word an Aries likes to hear or say). She surprised me by returning a year later and wanting to look at these facets of herself. Sadly, it had taken an unprovoked, Uranian attack (an unstable woman she didn't know suddenly threw a cup of scalding hot coffee into her face) for her to consider looking internally.

1.04 • Play Detective

It's essential to ask for information and then make connections. What happened the last time transiting Saturn squared the client's Sun? What does a particular planet bring up? *Who* is Saturn for the client in their life now? Here are two examples.

Saturn was due to enter a client's 4th House by transit. The client spoke of a sick parent who might need to move in and live with them, and asked me if this would happen. This already sounded like a 'Saturn moving into the 4th' type of event, but I was waiting to 'hear' Saturn in the description of what would happen if the parent moved in. The nature of Saturn in the 4th became clearer when the client said their parent's stay would be indefinite, the parent would need round-the-clock care, and that it would put a strain on my client's home life, space and finances. Saturn is linked to time, limits, heavy impositions – it seemed likely that this transit would manifest in that way.

Another client I saw had been stealing from his employer. Transiting Saturn was approaching a conjunction to his Sun – a time of reckoning and reviewing one's path/journey. He continued stealing, was caught and, at the exact hit, Saturn 'appeared' as the magistrate setting a date for trial. He later 'did time' and 'went straight' (both Saturn associations).

Essentially, it's vital to honour the transiting planet (to do something productive); with Saturn, if we don't align with a moral compass or find discipline within ourselves, we may be subjected to Saturnian discipline from others.

One of the most important ways to help a client is to listen to them describe their current situation, draw a parallel between two areas of their life, and help them to identify the similarities. A client might not be able to see a Pluto theme of intimidation or manipulation with someone at home, but they might be able to articulate how their boss treats them this way at work. Through dialogue, they're more likely to see their domestic relationship in a clearer light.

We might also hear, 'I'm so Scorpionic that Pluto transits don't affect me as much as they do others.' That may be true, but however much we think we 'know' a planet, it will always teach us more about ourselves and our world. And the planet we're least familiar with is often the one that will have the most impact when it transits/directs.

I want to chuckle when astrologers say, 'I know what that Uranus transit will be about.' Well, if they could predict it, it wouldn't be Uranian in nature! In fact, I often apply a sort of 'reverse psychology' to certain planets, particularly Uranus. When Uranus is about to aspect a planet, I'm on the alert to hear the client describe what has become stale, outdated, limiting and inhibiting. These are the very things Uranus loves to wake up and shift – and so often does. Ask yourself why this part of the chart needs Uranian energy.

A few years ago, a client arrived who had Uranus transiting over her Aries Moon – twice before the consultation, with a final hit due soon after we met. She revealed that the first time Uranus hit, she'd been caught speeding and lost her driving licence (perhaps only Uranus could speed up turbo-charged Aries). Feeling restless, she had also started an extra-marital affair with a neighbour. The second time, after a domestic dispute, her husband had been found at the bottom of the stairs with his head bashed in. She'd been arrested but freed when there was no evidence of her criminal involvement. The remainder of our session was spent looking at how she could avoid making this a hat-trick of negative events …

One final thing you'll notice: when clients have outer-planet transits or directions that wake up their charts and lives, it's not uncommon to find the client running to Saturn – or rather, what it represents: to seek refuge in anything that appears to offer solace, security and anchorage. For example, Neptune directs to the 4th House cusp and, wishing to escape the feeling of insecurity this might bring, a client gets married, buys a house and takes on a 25-year mortgage. All this, perhaps, at a time when they should be going with the flow in a very different, Neptunian way.

1.05 • Define and Connect

Let's take a transit of Saturn to natal Mercury in Sagittarius. Constructing a possible interpretation can be complex if we start by taking too many parts of the chart into consideration (house rulerships, numerous aspects, etc.). I've found it useful to break down the parts involved so as to understand the natal chart and the energy of a particular transit. I teach a simple four-step approach that I call 'Define and Connect' – it helps students to consider the possible ways a transit, progression or direction may manifest.

i Define the activator

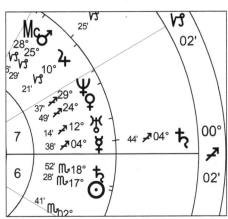

In the example, the transiting planet (outer wheel) is Saturn, moving through the 7th House.

This is the energy in the forecast. What is Saturn's astrological meaning? What is its function? What does it represent in us and in the world around us? And what could it be bringing to that house?

ii Connect this planet to the natal chart

Natally, Saturn is in Scorpio in the 6th House. It conjoins the Sun and rules the Midheaven.

Examine the natal position to get a picture of how the planet behaves, responds and functions in this particular chart. This is the 'memory' – a storehouse of lifelong associations – triggered every time this planet activates something (or is activated). Pinpoint the 'memory' and you've identified the heart of the forecast: the personal relationship/history the client has with this planet.

iii Define the planet/angle being activated/aspected

Mercury is being transited.

What are its principal astrological functions, meanings and associations? In general, what does this planet represent in us and in the world?

iv Connect the activated planet to the natal chart

Natally, Mercury is in Sagittarius in the 7th House. It rules the Ascendant, conjoins the Descendant and widely conjoins Uranus.

This is the area of the person's life that is being revisited, opened up for some insight/learning, and is in the process of being transformed. Again, identifying what this natal placement means in the client's life (past and present) is key to understanding what's undergoing change. On a psychological level we must ask: what is being brought forward for the client to explore?

When we are given some context, we can usually understand the area in which the event will play out, and the types of situation the planet in question can 'give birth to'. But arguably it is more the astrologer's job to:

- Pinpoint the cycle/planetary period
- Articulate the processes taking place
- Speak in a way in which the client can understand and apply this information

There are too many external variables (culture, gender, society, education, time in history, etc.) to assume that the chart provides all the details and answers to our future. With forecasting, much depends on our ability to understand the client's natal horoscope; in this we can see their life story (particularly in their major placements and configurations) and patterns of behaviour, viewpoints and a range of reactions to various situations (essentially the Moon and Ascendant complexes).

Whichever predictive techniques appeal, the true measure of any forecasting work is whether:

- The tools perform reliably and consistently
- The astrologer is able to convey the period ahead clearly and ethically

Astrology is like a language waiting to be communicated, and all astrologers need to have a good astrological vocabulary, a means of gathering together the information and an ability to articulate the forecast to the client.

Any approach to prediction must be open to some adjustment or revision, since every chart and dialogue with a client teaches us something new and enriches our understanding of astrology 'in real life'. Ultimately, techniques are never as important as the clients – we must endeavour to tune in to their needs, their context and their reality.

Forecasting is arguably primarily a process of Mercury and Jupiter. We act as an intermediary between cosmos and client, look for patterns, synthesize them and then express these in consultation (Mercury). But we may also seek to transcend the technique and use the dialogue to connect to a bigger picture: to explore the meaning and significance of someone's life (Jupiter). When working with clients, we often have the chance to discover the wider, Jupiterian narrative that has been woven into the life as a result of these Mercurial patterns, and then we can embark on this explorative journey with our clients.

1.06 • Keywords for the Planets, Angles and Signs

Here are some verbs and associations to describe the energies of the planets, followed by some keywords about the angles and ideas linked to the journey, issues and talents of the twelve signs.

☉ The Sun
... illuminates, focuses, spotlights, makes aware, brings to prominence/attention.

Our journey, vocation, purpose, fathers, leaders, authorities.

☽ The Moon
... needs, feels, attaches to, connects, digests, responds, intuits, nurtures.

Our emotional responses, daily rituals, eating habits, mothers, home, public mood.

☿ Mercury
... articulates, negotiates, links, finds patterns, translates, analyses, rationalizes.

Our thought processes, communication, writing, expression, opinions, finding patterns, siblings.

♀ Venus
... unites, harmonizes, persuades, beautifies, values, compares, gratifies.

Our relationships, popularity, pleasure, self-worth, values, tastes, attitude to women and female stereotypes.

♂ Mars
... strives, desires, fights, activates, motivates, enthuses, competes with, wins, achieves.

Our desires, energy, driving force, independence, conflict, attitude to men and male stereotypes.

♃ Jupiter
... broadens, inflates, opens up, explores, invests belief in, blesses, edifies, educates.

Our approach to travel, exploration, beliefs, higher learning, abundance, opportunities, growth, expansion, excess, fame.

♄ Saturn
... limits, controls, delays/denies, inhibits, fortifies, crystallizes, teaches, masters.

Our burdens, fears, reality, learning from trial and error, mastery, commitments, results from hard work/discipline.

♅ Uranus
... liberates, awakens, disrupts, deviates, shocks, detaches, splits, breaks, reverses.

It is linked to shocks, catalysts, sudden changes, reversals, discoveries, breaks for freedom, flashes of insight.

♆ Neptune
... dissolves, sensitizes or numbs, resigns, transcends, enchants, palliates, confuses, distorts, deceives, longs for.

It is linked to anything without boundaries, addictions, chaos, escapes, visions, spirituality, higher creativity.

♇ Pluto
... buries or brings to light, strips away, humbles, eliminates, erupts, empowers, cleanses, evolves.

It is linked to non-negotiable transformations, rebirths, evolutions, obsessions, extremes, mass influence.

The angles of the horoscope are not energies but four compass points – directions through which we channel our planetary energies.

Ascendant
Environment, physical body, approach to life, first impressions, expectations, open agenda.

Descendant
Relationship dynamics, interactions, projections, contracts.

Midheaven/MC (Medium Coeli)
Reputation, status, social/public success and persona.

IC (Imum Coeli)
Roots, personal/family history, inner world, hidden motivations.

♈ **Aries**
Initiating, daring, winning, trailblazing, asserting individuality.
　Not coming first; being left out.

♉ **Taurus**
Ownership, security, sensuality, faithfulness, principles.
　Getting stuck; being pushed/rushed.

♊ **Gemini**
Questioning, learning, duality, youth, avoidance.
　Not being heard or understood; committing.

♋ **Cancer**
Home, mother, emotional security, protection, the past/roots.
　Not letting go; being dependent/cared for.

♌ **Leo**
Self-expression, identity, father, confidence, children, courage.
　Not being recognised; being ridiculed.

♍ **Virgo**
Perfectionism, usefulness, health, aloneness, order.
　Not being valued; descending into chaos.

♎ **Libra**
Balance, fairness, partnerships, decisions, people-pleasing.
　Not being treated equally; encountering injustice.

♏ **Scorpio**
Intimacy, trust, intensity, crisis, secrets, regeneration.
　Not going deep; fear of betrayal.

♐ **Sagittarius**
Freedom, travel, speaking up, faith, exploring meaning.
　Not being believed; being curtailed.

♑ **Capricorn**
Duty, responsibility, control, time, the status quo, hard work.
　Not being respected; being overlooked.

♒ **Aquarius**
Differentness, original ideas, tolerance vs. bigotry.
　Not being treated humanely; being pigeon-holed.

♓ **Pisces**
Art, music, mysticism, sacrifice, devotion, addiction.
　Not being considered; being blamed.

Part II

The Sun as Our Guide

I believe in God like I believe in the sun, not because I can see it,
but because of it all things are seen.
– C. S. Lewis

So why are we basing a whole system on the Sun? Astrologer Noel Tyl, who has spent many years using, teaching and promoting Solar Arc directions, writes in *Synthesis & Counseling in Astrology: The Professional Manual* (Llewellyn, 1994, p. 204):

> The Sun's light reaches out to illuminate all planets in its system, and all the planets come to light through the horoscope in terms of that Sun's energy. Similarly, the birth imprint personalizes what happens in life within development as the entire birth pattern reaches out to illuminate its potentials within the passage of time.

> This extremely important hypothesis – that the entire birth pattern, the whole person, shown symbolically within the horoscope, is involved with change – is a primal premise in astrology, but it eluded facile mathematical measurement for thousands of years.

In a birth chart, the Sun reveals our calling, our life purpose, the reasons why we've been born. Part of an astrologer's job can be to remind clients of who they were born to be, to illuminate their life path – in effect, to help them follow the Sun (the sign and house position and any aspects) in their horoscope.

The Sun is not about a set of adjectives that reveal personality traits (Cancerians are 'caring', Geminis are 'versatile'); rather, it shows what's at the heart of our nature, our core character. Astrologers know that we feel alive when we 'follow our bliss' and live out the main mission of our Sun sign and its aspects in the natal chart. Engaging in our Sun sign – even just a little bit every day – makes our heart sing.

The Sun is a key to us all obtaining healthy self-esteem and to following a path of integrity. The sign in which our Sun is placed says a great deal about our vocation in the deeper sense – what we are 'called' to do during our time on this planet. Our Sun sign describes a life journey, a way of living. It is the leader, the conductor, the centre and the heart of our horoscope.

Of course there are not just twelve types of people in the world, but each of the twelve Sun signs is a *particular archetype* with a *specific journey* attached to it. Each one of us is asked ('called') to embark upon this journey (along with lots of other 'life lessons' or situations, as shown in the rest of the chart). In doing so, we have an opportunity to connect with our core essence, our life force, our calling.

Despair, it is said, comes from choosing to be someone other than ourselves. If we don't engage with our birthright, we can languish in the worst traits of the opposite Sun sign.

Aries and Libra are opposites
Taurus and Scorpio are opposites
Gemini and Sagittarius are opposites
Cancer and Capricorn are opposites
Leo and Aquarius are opposites
Virgo and Pisces are opposites

Coming back to these basic ideas is helpful when considering a forecasting method such as Solar Arc directions, which is based on the Sun's movement through the zodiac. Our birth chart describes the motivations, challenges and passions behind our choices. Solar Arcs reflect the progress we make through the zodiac and through life on our way to fulfilling our potential.

So, to start thinking about the ultimate goal and 'heart of our chart', here's a quick guide to each of the signs and their missions, as well as some of the pitfalls when we choose (consciously or otherwise) not to follow our path but instead to wallow in the worst of our opposite Sun sign.

If you know the signs of your North Node and Midheaven (MC), the following descriptions should also be relevant in helping you understand your spiritual purpose (the journey from the South Node to the North Node) and your path from the IC to the MC, which shows moving from early influences to then influencing the world around you.

♈ Aries, the Ardent Pioneer

The Early Opportunity
Encountering conflict, unfairness, being put second or feeling left out has prompted you to stand up and be counted, to recognize your own needs, fight for what's right, and face fears of disapproval.

The Life Work
You are born to enthuse people with your boundless energy, unbridled enthusiasm and hope. Yours is a spontaneous, dynamic and adventurous spirit. You have an independent nature and you lack the patience to wait for group decisions or to work in a team, so it's important to be in a position of autonomy and to learn to motivate yourself and blaze your own trail. Avoid waiting for others to approve of you and don't expect them to provide maintenance. Instead, sprint ahead of the pack, show courage, fight for the underdog, dare to break new ground and put yourself first without apology.

♉ Taurus, the Principled Rock

The Early Opportunity
Being pushed around or having people want what you own has helped you learn to say 'no', to attach yourself to strong principles and develop a stubborn resistance to the influence of others.

The Life Work
Yours is a powerfully determined energy, and it's important for you to have a strong idea of what you stand for. Your sign is the 'rock', the constant upon which others can rely. Productive and sincere, you do your best work in a steady environment of loyalty and integrity, where change is rare and ideally on your own terms. Helping others to build strong foundations and sustain their enterprises are two of your talents, but don't forget to ensure your own security and safety, too, and enjoy the sensual pleasures in life without being ruled by them.

♊ Gemini, the Quick-witted Communicator

The Early Opportunity
Facing misunderstandings or people who can't/won't relate to you has encouraged you to clarify information, to untangle mixed messages and become the communicator and interpreter you were born to be.

The Life Work
Eternally curious and restless, your ideal work environment is one that keeps you interested and able to move freely. You need stimulating work that doesn't bog you down with too much routine or responsibility, and one that offers options to indulge your many eclectic interests. A natural salesperson, trader or agent, your talent is to simplify complex ideas and convey these with clever clarity. An agile wit, you always offer people 'the other viewpoint' and introduce ideas they hadn't considered. But stay with the facts and don't get attached to 'one right way' of doing something.

♋ Cancer, the Tender Caregiver

The Early Opportunity
Living through emotionally bleak or isolating times has helped you to seek the right kind of support system, to create your family of choice, move away from co-dependent situations and release emotions buried by your family.

The Life Work
Your protective, sensitive spirit and almost psychic empathy are ideal in work situations that need strong emotional kinship and lessons of tough love. It is essential for you to be part of a family at work – a tribe of like-minded people who offer each other nourishment – rather than you ending up being bitter about playing carer–counsellor to all and sundry. Your past will always be an important part of your present, and your talent is helping you (and others) reconnect to your heritage and treasure your history – without it hardening your nature or ruling your actions.

♌ Leo, the Divine Child

The Early Opportunity
Feeling early pressure to 'be someone', living up to others' expectations or dealing with a domineering bully has given you a chance to separate your needs from those of others, to emerge from their shadow and assume control over your own destiny – to be your own boss.

The Life Work
Your work must reflect your individuality and need for self-expression. You were born to shine and to stand apart from the crowd. Even if you choose to do this in a quiet way, your journey is to discover your creative potency and express the forceful energy that lies inside you. But rather than it being 'all about you', the challenge is to allow others their time in the spotlight and encourage them to find their own vision. In short, you were born to be a generous mentor.

♍ Virgo, the Skilful Discriminator

The Early Opportunity
Dealing with chaos, inequalities or a lack of discipline in those around you has sharpened your ability to discriminate, to discover what is healthy for you, to leave the safety zone of the mind and to develop a relationship with your own pleasure.

The Life Work
Your journey involves learning your trade and perfecting a skill that will enable you to play an essential role in any work situation. Your sign is the industrious craftsperson of the zodiac – your job is to get to the heart of the matter, avoid chaos and ensure that the overall machine runs efficiently. Yours is a service-orientated spirit that has a plan to make the world a better place. But it's important not to downplay your vital role – otherwise others may do so, too, leaving you feeling undervalued or victimized.

♎ Libra, the Impartial Tactician

The Early Opportunity
Finding yourself surrounded by conflict early in your life or being forced to make life-changing decisions from seemingly impossible choices has developed your diplomatic, mediation and decision-making skills.

The Life Work
You were born to become a strategist, an expert at negotiation, with an ability to charm others into submission. You're most effective when bringing an objectivity to situations and when building bridges between opposing factions, rather than provoking opposition or being manipulative. Always good at teamwork, you shine when addressing imbalances of power or when you're in environments where a rational, fair and civilized approach is needed to solve complex solutions or resolve conflict. Two running themes in your journey are to fight for justice and to abandon the disease to please.

♏ Scorpio, the Powerful Alchemist

The Early Opportunity
An exposure to the sordid, traumatic side of life or the power games that others play has given you a knowingness and rare psychological insight that can enable you to reinvent yourself and exhibit strength in the face of crisis.

The Life Work
Your journey is a deep exploration of the darker sides of human nature. Your sign has remarkable courage and willpower to face aspects of yourself and the world around you that would scare most other signs. An unflinching investigator of life's mysteries, your path is to psychologically examine power, taboos and the forbidden – all in a search for intimacy, trust and a deep union with a few chosen people. Staying in a comfort zone or focusing only on the sexual or financial will never truly satisfy this most complex of signs.

♐ Sagittarius, the Eternal Student–Teacher

The Early Opportunity
An early injustice in which you've spoken up and not been believed may have prompted a lifelong desire to tell your truth, to shoot down pretence, highlight hypocrisy or to blow apart corruption. Narrowness or bigotry around you prompts you to reach for a grander vision of life.

The Life Work
Your sign is born to aim high and explore the possibilities beyond the simple facts. You know that the journey is much more interesting than the arrival, and your voracious appetite for knowledge can turn into a quest for the meaning of life and the purpose of your existence. You need work where you can ignite others with your vision and optimism and, by separating yourself from results or expectations, you'll avoid feeling disappointed when others won't or can't match your enthusiasm and generosity.

♑ Capricorn, the Master of Distinction

The Early Opportunity
Adversity, a lack of support or a tyrannical figure in your life may have delayed initial progress, but it has spurred you on to aim to achieve great things on your own and to believe that patience and application will result in a highly satisfying type of success later on.

The Life Work
Your sign is born to rise above initial hardship or delays, to endure a long apprenticeship, take on responsibilities and attain a position of respect and authority. Your journey is a monument to hard work, backbone and individual achievement. Like fine wine, you mature well, often making your greatest contribution in the second or third chapters of your life. But always attend to your reputation, avoid becoming the type of tyrant you fought against, and retain a moral code that is beyond reproach.

≈ Aquarius, the Iconoclastic Individualist

The Early Opportunity
If early events or a lack of role models confirmed the inner feeling that you didn't fit in, don't adopt the role of people-pleaser and deny your own needs. Instead, use any past feelings of alienation to embark upon the road less travelled, define your own rules and become your own role model of leadership.

The Life Work
You were born to tear up the rulebook and topple traditions, stereotypes and hierarchies. Yours is an innovative spirit able to provide a clear, original perspective in your work. You do your best in areas where differentness and originality are valued strengths. You're a catalyst who should dare to adopt a different stance, to help the group understand that everyone is both equal and special, and avoid letting your own ego needs dominate your actions.

⋈ Pisces, the Spiritual Samaritan

The Early Opportunity
Resisting the control and undue influence of others has led to you trusting your own intuition more, acknowledging your survival instinct, forming a stronger sense of self and recognizing your talent for acceptance and forgiveness.

The Life Work
Your sign's key aptitudes are compassion, intuition, sensitivity to suffering, and altruism. You do your best work when dedicating time to healing those in need or improving conditions for others – rather than plotting an ambitious path for yourself or trying obsessively to control 'the small stuff'. Your artistic, spiritual or poetic energy allows the people around you to see the interconnectedness of all life, provides them with a glimpse into the world of spirit and reminds them that we are all in need of empathy, kindness and support.

Introducing Solar Arc Directions: Key Principles

The sun does not shine for a few trees and flowers,
but for the wide world's joy.
– Henry Ward Beecher

So now, we're at the key part of the book where I'll introduce this powerful and accurate method of forecasting.

Over the years, there have only been a few books and full-length articles written on this subject – luckily these have been written by some highly experienced astrologers. In my library, I have books by Noel Tyl and Carole DeMott Devine and I have quoted them when they say it better than I could!

When I first wrote on this subject (for my mini-book *Solar Arc Directions*, in 2011), my aim was to write an instant, accessible pocketbook guide – a very Aries way of getting to the point fast. The booklet proved very popular and a useful companion to students at the lectures and workshops I was giving on the subject.

I have presented my work on Solar Arc directions in over a dozen countries and I never tire of teaching its methods and then exploring the charts of those in the class or seminar. Their stories truly reflect astrology in action and usually attendees are amazed at how the biographical descriptions are reflected by the Solar Arcs occurring in their lives.

I love teaching this subject because it's a method that's quick to spot, easy to use and, in my experience, very accurate. Adopting this forecasting tool has given me a way to spot life events and pivotal moments quickly. Solar Arc is accurate, reliable, straightforward and simple – so simple that these measurements can be made at a glance.

This new volume, which incorporates the best bits of the mini-book with many more case studies and guidelines, is designed to help you become familiar with this exciting method, to spot the important years of a life quickly from a natal chart and, with many famous examples, see how directions can reveal and describe the unfolding of major developments and life events. My aim is to show you how to add Solar Arc directions to your predictive toolbox and integrate them into your practice. You'll be glad you did.

In my forecasting work, I use Solar Arc (SA) directions, transits (TR) and the lunar phases. I began using Solar Arcs because I'd sometimes find significant events in a person's life that couldn't be explained by their transits, which were either absent or insubstantial;

I needed a second tool that could pinpoint and explain these events. Using Solar Arcs gives me a head start and great advantage with clients. I have also found that Solar Arcs are excellent at the beginning of a consultation – when asking questions about key life dates – to test the accuracy of the client's birth time.

Here, in a dozen or so DIY steps with various examples, is all you need to know to get started with – and get the best from – Solar Arc directions.

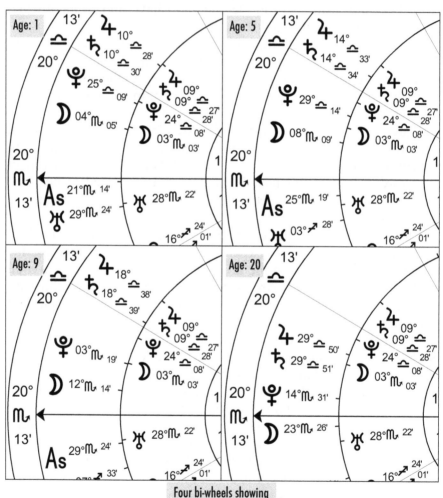

Four bi-wheels showing
part of the chart directed
1, 5, 9 and 20 years

3.01 • A Day for a Year

Simply put, one rotation of the Earth's axis (which takes a day) is said to symbolize one rotation of the Earth around the Sun (a cycle that takes a year). In both cases, we have a view from Earth of the complete zodiac in that time period.

Firstly, each day, the Sun, planets and the backdrop of signs all appear to rise at the astronomical point we call the Ascendant, culminate at the MC, set at the Descendant and anti-culminate at the IC. This diurnal (daily) movement is completed in 24 hours, and during this time, when viewing any one of these four points, we'll see the entire zodiac.

Secondly, from our viewpoint, the Sun appears to move approximately one degree (i.e. 60 minutes of arc) forward through the zodiac each day, taking a year to pass through the zodiac.

With Solar Arc, this 1° of arc (space) a day represents a year (twelve months) of time, and this is the speed at which everything in the Solar Arc-directed chart moves per year. For every year of life, the Sun's movement each day after birth is calculated. How far the Sun has moved at the age in question (e.g. at age ten, the Sun would have moved approximately 10°) is then *added to all the planets and house cusps* so they all move at the same rate. For instance, in the diagrams opposite (the outer wheels are set for the 1st, 5th, 9th and 20th birthdays), we can see how each and every planet and angle has moved approximately one degree for every year.

Our job is to then consider and interpret the aspects (e.g. conjunction, opposition) that the newly directed planets (in the outer wheel) make to the original, natal chart (inner wheel plus the house cusps, which extend to the outer wheel). In the natal chart example (all four inner wheels, opposite), Pluto is at 24° Libra and the Moon at 3° Scorpio. By age 9, Pluto has directed to 3° Scorpio (24° Libra plus 9° = 3° into Scorpio). So the owner of this chart would have <u>Solar Arc Pluto conjunct natal Moon</u>. By then, the Solar Arc Moon has also moved nine degrees and is positioned at 12° Scorpio, on its own way to making aspects to the natal chart (inner wheel).

To interpret a direction, we would consider keywords and the symbolism of the directed planet/angle and its effect on the natal planet/angle (taking into account the age, awareness and context).

3.02 • One Degree or Solar Arc?

The two most common types of directions in current use are:

- One Degree: the positions in the birth chart are all moved forwards by exactly 1° for every year of life (regardless of the exact daily motion of the Sun). For example, to plot the directed positions of a chart of someone aged thirty-two years and six months, move the entire chart forwards by 32°30' (half a degree = half a year).

- Solar Arc: again, using the one-day-equals-one-year principle, the planetary positions and angles of the birth chart are directed forwards by the actual distance (arc) the Sun has transited each day after birth, which is usually very close to (but not exactly) 1°. (It ranges from 57' to 1°01'.)

On the face of it, there appears to be little difference between these methods but due to the fact that the daily rate of the Sun differs slightly throughout the year, there are likely to be notable discrepancies the older one gets.

On the opposite page, there are two bi-wheels (in each, the natal chart is the inner wheel, the directed positions for the 40th birthday are in the outer wheel). The top is calculated using the One Degree method, while the bottom bi-wheel uses Solar Arc. Every planet/ angle has moved approximately 40° but notice how the degrees and minutes in the top's outer bi-wheel differ slightly from the bottom's.

The One Degree method is one that Noel Tyl objects to: 'The simplification of using the mean motion of the Sun actually did away with the individualized Sun, the individual measure of life energy and developmental potential linked to the different rate of movement of every person's Sun. Mathematically, everyone was "evened out".' He recommends only using this One Degree approximation when estimating how far the chart has directed at a given age and then doing precise Solar Arc measurements by computer to bring the approximation into clearer focus.

In this book, we will be looking at the second type, Solar Arc, which I too find superior to the rough-and-ready One Degree method.

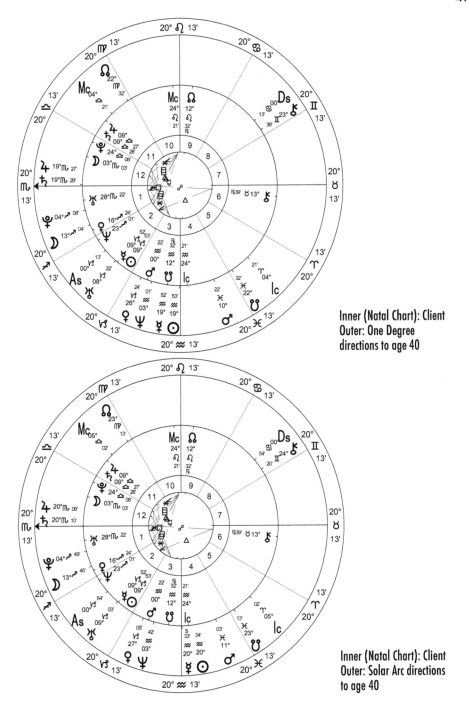

Inner (Natal Chart): Client
Outer: One Degree
directions to age 40

Inner (Natal Chart): Client
Outer: Solar Arc directions
to age 40

3.03 • Solar Arcs or Secondary Progressions?

How do Solar Arcs differ from Secondary Progressions? Day-for-a-year Secondary Progressions take the ephemeris as their guideline (e.g. the planetary positions in the ephemeris thirty days after birth equate to the progressed positions at thirty years of age), so each planet will progress at its own rate. During those thirty days, the Moon would have moved through the entire zodiac, while the outer planets may have only moved by 1° at most. Planets in the ephemeris also speed up, slow down, go direct, stationary and retrograde, and form new aspectual patterns with each other – and therefore so do planets in the progressed chart.

When I was training to be an astrologer, progressions rarely seemed to produce results. I began to seek a predictive tool that could offer me a clear demonstration of astrology in action – something I could work out quickly while glancing at the horoscope. It must have been a fellow Aries who prayed, 'Lord give me patience … but hurry!' When I discovered Solar Arcs for myself (in fact, like a good Aries, I thought I *had* discovered them – period!), I ran with them when I saw how useful they could be in tracking life events.

Whereas progressions take the actual planetary positions and speeds recorded in the ephemeris as their guide, the method of Solar Arc is symbolic. The whole horoscope moves forward (planets, house cusps, angles, even retrograde planets)[1] at the daily rate of the transiting Sun (approximately 1°/60' of arc) for every year of your life. Everything in the chart moves approximately:

- 60' (1°) of arc in twelve months
- 30' of arc in six months
- 5' in one month
- 1' in approximately one week

We'll revisit this soon. Although not as widely used by astrologers as Secondary Progressions, Solar Arcs offer many advantages to those of us using them with (or, preferably, as a substitute for) progressions. Sometimes I get carried away when I explain this to students. At one venue, I blurted out that progressions didn't seem to show life events as well as Solar Arcs did, only to be told rather patronisingly by the organiser (who used progressions exclusively) that progressions were for those astrologers more attuned to 'soul work' and exploring the psyche. Pffff! But maybe she was right, in part. Perhaps progressions are linked more to the inner psychological climate (in a subtle, lunar way) and directions reflect key life stages and concrete events (in a more dynamic, solar way). Or maybe Solar Arcs just work better.

Over the page, there are two bi-wheels for the chart we looked at earlier (in each, the natal chart is the inner wheel). The top, outer wheel is calculated using Solar Arcs for the 25th birthday, while the bottom outer wheel uses Secondary Progressions for the 25th birthday. You'll notice some major differences – in the bottom bi-wheel (Secondary Progressions), the social and outer planets (Jupiter to Pluto) have not moved far, while the Moon has moved through most of the zodiac and is set to return to its position at age 27. (Most planets/points will be in different positions in the two charts – except the Sun and Midheaven/MC, which stay the same in both systems).

---

1 Solar Arc directions can also be moved backwards. These are known as Converse directions. These are essentially the same as regular, forward-moving directions except the planet/angle doing the directing is swapped (instead of point A reaching point B, point B goes back to point A – the Ascendant can be directed forwards to Mercury in the 1st House at age seventeen, or Mercury can move back to the Ascendant by Converse direction at age seventeen).

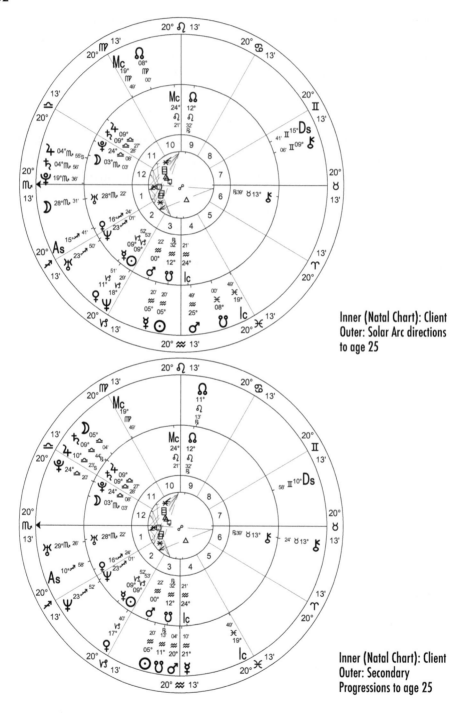

Inner (Natal Chart): Client
Outer: Solar Arc directions
to age 25

Inner (Natal Chart): Client
Outer: Secondary
Progressions to age 25

3.04 • Natal Aspects Between Planets/Angles Remain the Same

With Solar Arc, every planet/
angle moves forwards at the
same daily rate – even if that
planet is retrograde in the natal
chart. So, all the planets in the
natal chart remain in the same
aspectual relationship to each
other in the Solar Arc directed
chart. In other words, directed
planets move forwards and make
aspects to natal planets/angles
but they will not change their
relationship with each other. A
Moon–Saturn conjunction (with

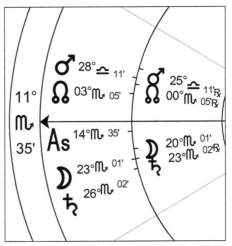

an orb of 3°01' – see inner wheel above) will always be conjunct by
Solar Arc by that same orb because both planets are directed at the
same speed through the years. In other words, you can't ignore natal
aspects – they'll be present in the natal and Solar Arc charts.

This is where directions differ greatly from progressions. The
progressed Moon moves very fast (between 12–15° per progressed
year – covering much more ground than the directed Moon),
while progressed Neptune and Pluto barely move more than a few
degrees during an average lifetime. With directions, there is much
greater outer planetary movement and during an average lifetime
the outer planets (along with every other planet/angle) can direct
through three or four signs and three or four houses. There is also
no likelihood of a planet slowing down and moving retrograde as it
can do in the progressed chart. With progressions, the inner planets
are given more importance (the progressed Moon is a particularly
important timer/trigger), but with directions, every planet/angle has
(potentially) the same importance/weighting. Note, however, that
the Sun and the MC move at the same rate in both the Solar Arc
method and the progressed chart, and thus will each be on the same
degree in both systems.

As noted in the last section, the charts opposite demonstrate the
differences between Solar Arcs and Secondary Progressions.

3.05 • Once in a Lifetime Happenings

Whereas transits are part of larger cycles, showing 'trends' and life developments, and reflecting the waxing and waning (and repetition) of cyclical aspects of our lives, each Solar Arc direction (e.g. SA Mercury conjunct natal Venus) occurs only once in a lifetime and many specific aspects will never occur if the planets/angles are too far from one another.

For an exact aspect to reoccur (e.g. a conjunction), we would need to live to a grand age of 360 years! Even exact sextiles (60°) to the same planet/angle would only occur again after approximately 120 years. Repetitions of the minor aspects (such as the semi-sextile or semi-square) are possible in a lifetime (from approximately age 60 and 90 respectively) but with Solar Arcs we use conjunctions, oppositions and squares first and foremost; trines and sextiles are used less frequently.

Incidentally, if you have – or wish to have – a good understanding of these two minor aspects, look at what happens around age 30, when every planet in the chart is semi-sextile its natal position by Solar Arc; and at age 45, when each planet semi-squares itself.

So, being essentially one-off occurrences, Solar Arc directions can be seen as key stages ('saddle points') in our lives, symbolizing *the unfolding of the chart* as it is directed forward by the rate of the Sun (itself a symbol of life development and its unfolding). The Solar Arc directions in our lifetime (particularly the conjunctions, oppositions and squares) show the milestones on our journey towards the discovery of *who we are meant/were born to be*, and towards *fulfilling our life purpose(s)*. As we saw in Part II, this is, in essence, the solar principle.

Carole DeMott Devine (on page 11 of *Solar Arc Directions: How to Read Life's Roadmap*, L.A.B, 2000) writes that Solar Arcs show 'turning points in the life because they indicate times when we must address the issues we were born to resolve. The natal chart shows these issues clearly, but what we do about them is entirely up to us.'

3.06 • The Natal Aspect Grid Reveals Early Solar Arcs

Solar Arcs that occur early in life are also very useful to consider during a consultation when pinpointing and understanding patterns ('scripts') formed in childhood.

To understand which Solar Arcs occurred in childhood, look at the aspect grid found on most chart print-outs (see below). Most astrologers set an 8° orb for conjunctions, oppositions and squares in their software, so the grid will automatically show all the early Solar Arcs that take place up until the age of eight.

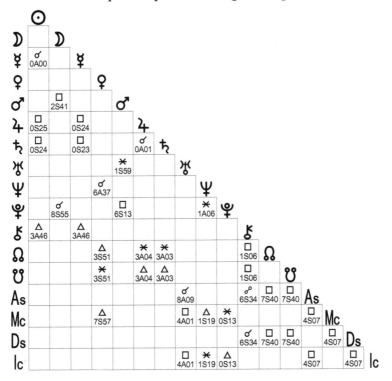

As the earliest Solar Arcs we encounter are found in our natal aspect grid, if we truly want to know how our natal Moon conjunct Pluto works in our lives, look at the orb between the two planets (almost 9° in the wheel above). This translates to the age in our life when the two planets got together by Solar Arc. This is a useful tool to help clients understand a repetitive theme or issue they may have. They, of course, live with this natal aspect every day of their lives, but there will usually be a significant event at the exact age when these two planets met by Solar Arc. Even those planets in orbs considered too wide for natal interpretation (e.g. Moon at 1° Virgo, Neptune at 13° Sagittarius) will come together by aspect at a specific age (in this example, by square at the age of twelve) and make an impact of that nature. For instance, if a client is discussing feeling exhausted by co-dependency issues (Moon–Neptune) or a perpetual need to rescue others (Moon–Neptune), then it might be useful to look at the year in their life when the Moon and Neptune first aspected each other by direction. This may be the year when an event triggered the behavioural pattern or 'script'. The way to use this in consultation is to hear the client 'speak' the appropriate planets and see when these first met by Solar Arc.

So, if you want to understand how someone's Moon–Pluto conjunction works in their life, for instance, ask them what happened during the year when these two planets were exactly conjunct by Solar Arc. The client may not be immediately aware of an event, but it's worthwhile describing the aspect/issue and leaving them to ponder the significance of that age in understanding it. Carole DeMott Devine suggests that planets that direct very early in childhood are most likely to be 'deeply buried and an instinctive response' (p. 25).

Devine (pp. 10–11) reminds us to 'always go back to the natal chart to see what life script lesson is being addressed. Even if a grand square [cross] were [directing to a natal] grand trine, the natal configuration of the grand square is the primary concern. If the grand square is speaking of a painful childhood with direct ramifications on the native's ability to earn a living, then every time that grand square contacts *anything* in the chart, there is another opportunity to heal that particular problem ... Being able to address these issues at the right *time*, however, is invaluable. We are supposed to address and heal particular dramas in a timed sequence, and that is what solar arc provides – a timing device ... It may have been somewhat inaccessible to these particular dilemmas before that time if there was no natal contact between them ... It is like making a discovery that you can learn how to handle the problems you have at that time from within your own store of wisdom, which, of course, was always there.'

3.07 • Aspects and Orbs

With Solar Arc, the conjunction and major hard aspects (square and opposition) between the planets (and four angles) are the most significant. These are energetic aspects that tend to 'manifest' as concrete life events and dynamic turning points. Consider the trine, sextile and 'minor' aspects as secondary. In this book, I'm not considering midpoints, but many astrologers do (e.g. directions to the ASC–MC midpoint or to the important Sun–Moon midpoint, which Noel Tyl links to major turning points in relationships). Here's a quick summary of aspect meanings:

- **Conjunction** (0°): a powerful merging of energies; a prominent, focal time; the beginning of a cycle
- **Semi-sextile** (30°): gradual efforts to build and manifest
- **Semi-square** (45°): friction; indecision; on-the-job training
- **Sextile** (60°): a bridge of opportunity requiring commitment
- **Square** (90°): an obstacle appearing as a challenge to act, strive, manifest and master; fight or flight; no guts, no glory
- **Trine** (120°): fast and flowing; right place/time opportunities
- **Sesquiquadrate** (135°): unexpected detours or disruptions
- **Quincunx** (150°): ill at ease, off-kilter situations requiring adjustment; niggling issues suddenly demanding our attention
- **Opposition** (180°): key exchanges/encounters with others; being offered the opposite or foreign view; a major difference demanding awareness, resolution and balance

Watch for developments, tensions or releases that occur around age 30, 45 and 60, when each directed planet/angle either semi-sextiles (30°), semi-squares (45°) or sextiles (60°) its natal counterpart.

I use a 30' orb either side of exactitude; this correlates to six months of time each side of the exact SA aspect to the natal point, although events often occur when the orb is much tighter. One whole degree (twelve months) is a wide time frame, but orbs are about the *gradual realization of a process*. Events themselves may happen in a split second but, looking deeper, there are usually meanings, feelings and associations that have been building up beforehand that also last beyond any particular 'event' or moment of time.

3.08 • The Speed of the Sun

I often say, 'If you can count, you can do Solar Arc.' It's a very simple method: start by counting the degrees between any two planets. This number translates to the year of our life when Planet A (earlier in the zodiac) Solar Arc directs to Planet B's position in the natal chart. When one planet conjoins (or makes any aspect) to another, that's when those planetary energies 'meet' and play out in our lives.

Solar Arc is a cumulative rate (i.e. if we were born on 1 February, we add the daily rate of the Sun on the next day and so on to every point in the chart, for every year of our life). But the Sun moves at different speeds during the year. This information can be found in *Raphael's Astronomical Ephemeris*, published annually by Foulsham, and usually appears on pages 26–28. These speeds differ very slightly from year to year. Let's examine the Sun's daily motion (i.e. its speed in degrees, minutes and seconds) on the first day of each month of 2018.

1 January: 1°01'08"	1 May: 0°58'13"	1 September: 0°58'03"
1 February: 1°00'52"	1 June: 0°57'29"	1 October: 0°58'59"
1 March: 1°00'12"	1 July: 0°57'12"	1 November: 1°00'02"
1 April: 0°59'11"	1 August: 0°57'23"	1 December: 1°00'49"

The Sun is at its slowest in late June/early July (approx. 0°57'12") and at its fastest at the turn of the year (approx. 1°01'11"). Noel Tyl offers a way to remember this: the Sun's rate is slow in the hot, balmy summer (when we take life at a more leisurely pace) and the Sun's rate is fast in the cold winter (when we need to speed up to keep from freezing). Well, it's a helpful analogy for those of us in the Northern Hemisphere who (if we're lucky) experience some kind of summer between June and August. (And, to be clear, the speed of the Sun is the same regardless of the hemisphere in which we were born.)

The Sun's pace is exactly 1° per day only in early March and late October/early November. It is possible, then, that those born at other times in the year have directed horoscopes that have either lost ground (especially May–August births) or raced ahead of their age (especially December–January births). For example, if we were born with the Sun in Gemini, Cancer or Leo, the Sun moves more slowly (57' a day), so by ten years old the cumulative daily motion of the Sun means that the Sun has lost up to 30 minutes of arc (half a degree) from what we might expect – i.e. by age ten, everything has been directed 9°30' instead of an estimated 10°. By age fifty (when, by the One Degree method, everything has moved forwards by 50°) it is possible to have lost almost 2°30' of arc (i.e. the Solar Arc chart has only moved forwards by 47°30').

The Sun in Sagittarius, Capricorn or Aquarius moves faster than 1° a day, so at age fifty, the chart will be directed further than estimated (about 50°50').

To reiterate this point: those born with the Sun in Sagittarius, Capricorn or Aquarius will reach 50° of arc faster (and at an earlier age) than someone with the Sun in a 'slower' moving sign (Gemini, Cancer or Leo).

Over the page are the directed charts at age fifty of two people, one who was born in June (slow arc, top chart) and the other born in January (fast arc, bottom chart). Notice how far each planet and angle has moved in each chart in those fifty years.

If you're like me, you'll want to look at the natal chart, count the degrees between any two points, and make a rough, quick estimate of the age at which they'll manifest in someone's life; then you'll need to take these seasonal speeds into consideration. By Solar Arc, 1° equals one whole year of life, so keep the month of birth in mind and let your astrology program calculate the fine detail.

The following table is useful for estimating how far planets/ points have moved over a particular period of time:

1° = 1 year of life	40' = 8 months	20' = 4 months
55' = 11 months	35' = 7 months	15' = 3 months
50' = 10 months	30' = 6 months	10' = 2 months
45' = 9 months	25' = 5 months	05' = 1 month
		01' = 7–8 days (roughly 1 week)

Phew, that's the only maths we have to do in this book, I promise!

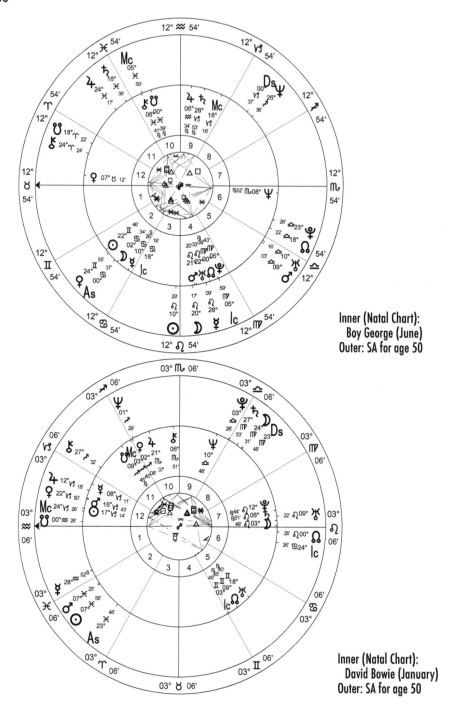

Inner (Natal Chart):
Boy George (June)
Outer: SA for age 50

Inner (Natal Chart):
David Bowie (January)
Outer: SA for age 50

3.09 • Double Whammies and Natal Aspects with Tight Orbs

Since planets maintain their relative positions to each other as they direct through the zodiac, this brings up an important point: if we have natal planets/angles in very close aspect, the planets or angles concerned will be activated at the same time (either when they direct to a part of the horoscope or when a planet/angle directs to them).

For instance, when a Moon–Uranus conjunction with a tight orb of 0°34' (natal chart, right) is directed, both planets will come into contact with a third (natal) planet within seven months. This third planet will be aspected by one directed planet, followed by another some 34' of arc (seven months) later.

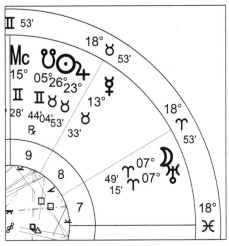

For example (see the bi-wheel below), the directed Moon conjuncts natal Mercury. Uranus (which is 34' behind the Moon) will conjunct Mercury roughly seven months later (34' of arc).

The same 'double whammy' occurs when any planet directs to make an aspect to this natal Moon–Uranus conjunction, but it will hit Uranus first, then the Moon, because Uranus is earlier in the zodiac.

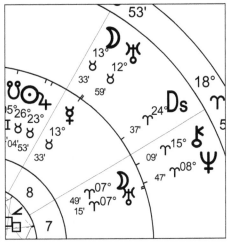

When we have a number of Solar Arcs in one year, this suggests it is a pivotal year in our lives. Dramatic years of life often coincide with a deluge of directions.

3.10 • Rectification

Transits move backwards and forwards over a planet or angle (sometimes with up to five hits within a 1° orb from the furthermost, outer planets), and this process can last a few years. If the astrologer is looking to forecast, it is often difficult to pinpoint when an event (if any) will manifest during this period by looking at the transit alone. This is where one-off, forward-moving directions can help, particularly if the orb is tightened to less than 30'.

Solar Arcs have a steady consistency to them and can coincide with events within an orb of 30' (six months) or less but they still describe the theme(s) of a year (30' either side of exactitude for a twelve-month period). To narrow down an event further – to the nearest month – we must look at inner planet transits (particularly those that trigger a direction or outer planet transit) and the progressed Moon.

To test or fine-tune the birth time from an estimated recollection (e.g. 'between 3:00 and 4:00 p.m.'), we must use directions to and from the four angles, which are the most time-sensitive, fastest moving parts of the chart. Then, check for corresponding events and reactions. If apt events are 'out' by a year, then it's likely that the angles are 1° off, too. A few minutes' difference in the birth time can change the angles by one degree and represent a whole different year in our life.

Here's an example from my article on rectification in *The Mountain Astrologer* (February–March 2018):

One client, 'Daniel', gave me a window of time that meant his chart had 28° Libra to 2° Scorpio on the Ascendant. With piercing blue eyes and a request for 'complete, absolute confidentiality' as we started, he appeared *on the face of it* to have Scorpio rising. Seeing Neptune in the 1st House at 20° Scorpio (between 18° and 22° away from the Ascendant degree possibilities), I asked him what he recalled in his life around age 18–22 (by Solar Arc, these are the possible ages at which the Ascendant would have directed to Neptune). He had been at university for most of that time, and he couldn't recall anything in particular, except … his grandmother had died when he was eighteen. This is not an event I would associate with the Ascendant directing to Neptune, but he added that, the following year, he'd felt her presence and had, despite his 'practical [Taurean] nature', received 'survival evidence' from a medium that 'prompted a strong, searching interest in spiritualism and the afterlife'. Now, that sounds more like the Ascendant to Neptune

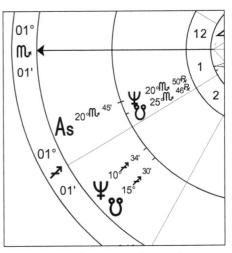

in Scorpio! I spent some further time asking questions about more recent Solar Arcs, again in an attempt to hear the right planet speak.

Some years back, when I first began teaching Solar Arcs, a student in class offered her chart to see if we could fine-tune her birth time. 'Cathy' was pretty certain she had rectified it correctly (and with the Sun conjunct Mercury and Mars in Taurus, I wasn't going to argue – or perhaps change her mind). She had decided that her Ascendant was 15° Pisces because a transit from Uranus at 15° Pisces had coincided with a big emotional explosion.

It's worthwhile beginning by looking at the planets near the angles. Sometimes if you look at planets too close to an angle, the client won't remember that far back into their childhood and they will come up with a blank. It's advisable to start with a planet and angle that are 7° to 17° away from each other. This doesn't always work, but often there's a description (or most importantly, their *perception*) of an event that links to the planets and angles involved.

In this example, the Ascendant that the student was happy with was 15° (15 years) away from Jupiter in Aries in the 1st House. Jupiter in Aries in the 1st House indicates great enthusiasm or pushiness, an enterprising outlook, being on a crusade or an interest in being the first (Aries) to travel, learn or experience something. A Solar Arc from the Ascendant (indicating one's surroundings, body or personality) to this Jupiter would suggest that her environment or outlook changed that year and she was enthused by some great belief or adventure. Perhaps she had travelled for the first time and experienced freedom and independence (symbols of Jupiter in Aries). The fact that the Ascendant is in Pisces (a sign ruled by Jupiter) adds weight to this being an important time.

When I asked if Cathy remembered anything of that nature, she said a simple 'No!' (It took me a while to learn that this is Taurus's first response to most things!) Did she recall learning a new language or feeling very positive about her future? 'No.' Then after a pause, she told the class. 'Nothing happened at 15, but at 17 I became a born-again Christian and tried to convert everyone around me.' The class erupted with mirth – what an apt expression of the Ascendant in Pisces entering Aries and conjuncting Jupiter there! This suggests the Ascendant is a few degrees earlier, say 13° Pisces, so it would take an additional two years/degrees to have reached Jupiter.

Next, I looked at Saturn in the 7th House in Virgo. This would imply encountering criticism from others, a stern teacher or even an event in the parental marriage that brought chaos, worry or illness (Virgo). According to her rectification, the Descendant would have directed to Saturn at age 11. Again, there was no event. But she said that at age 13, she was sent to an all-girls boarding school (very Saturn) and the other girls abused, teased and tore her apart verbally (Virgo). It was a lonely, unhappy time in her life.

We didn't have the time to test other, later Solar Arcs to the angles but, from those two vivid examples, it was looking likely that the birth time was slightly earlier. But her mind was not to be changed and I heard later that she absolutely hated the idea of Solar Arcs!

On the right, there are bi-wheels using Cathy's own rectification (left) and mine (right) for both events at age 17 (top) and 13 (below). You'll see how the two degrees of difference in the charts changes significantly the Solar Arcs by two years.

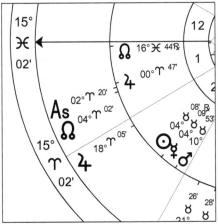

Inner (Natal Chart):
 'Cathy'- her rectification
Outer: SA for age 17

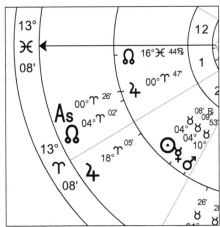

Inner (Natal Chart):
 'Cathy'- my rectification
Outer: SA for age 17

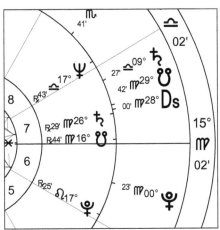

Inner (Natal Chart):
 'Cathy'- her rectification
Outer: SA for age 13

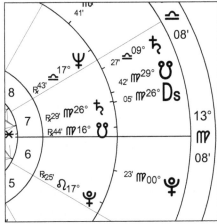

Inner (Natal Chart):
 'Cathy'- my rectification
Outer: SA for age 13

3.11 • Solar Arcs ... At a Glance

When using a computer to calculate Solar Arcs for a particular moment, there's no need to set up the directed chart for an exact *time* – the date or the first of the month will suffice – because the directed chart moves so slowly (roughly one minute of arc in a week). In addition, there's never a need to change the place of birth or adjust any time zones.

There is no point in reading a directed chart on its own, as a constructed Solar Arc chart will look very similar to the natal chart; planets will be found in the same houses and with the same aspects to each other, but in different signs. On the other hand, a Secondary Progressed chart can be analysed on its own.

When looking for key Solar Arcs from a natal chart, I often begin by looking at planets that are close to each other (within, say, 60°) and counting the degrees between them. It certainly helps to remember that there are 30 degrees per sign and 60 minutes of arc in each degree.

It can be a little daunting to think of checking every possible planetary combination, but spotting planets that will conjunct in a lifetime is the best way to start, or taking one planet and seeing the major aspects it makes as it travels through a sign. After a while, you'll start seeing that the planets in the horoscope are, in reality, all in some relationship to each other by a particular number of degrees.

As we already know, the degrees that separate any two planets correspond (approximately) to the year of life when a merging of those two planetary energies manifests and the potential is realized. Remember that, with directions, it's always the planet at the earlier degree that will conjunct the planet positioned later. From the moment of our birth, the horoscope is fixed and set to unfold in a particular order of Solar Arc directions that is unique to us.

A Heavy Habit
Let's use the birth chart of the former political leader Charles Kennedy. He was born in late November when the Sun moves approximately 1°00'40" (slightly faster than the One Degree method), so over the years the Solar Arc directions will have moved

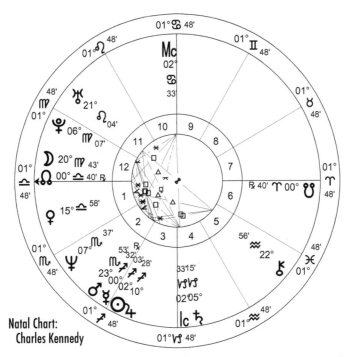

Natal Chart:
Charles Kennedy

slightly further in degrees than his age (e.g. at age sixty, the directions will be around 61° further than their natal positions). It is useful to keep this in mind.

To train the eye, start with a planet near one of the four angles. There are two planets either side of his Ascendant (ASC). Let's start with the Moon, which is at 20°43' Virgo. The Ascendant is 1°48' Libra. There are just over 11° between the two points. So, moving all of the positions forwards, we would say that just after his eleventh birthday, Charles had SA Moon conjunct natal ASC, i.e. his Moon directed towards his Ascendant at that particular age. (His SA Ascendant at this age would also have moved 1° for every year of life, and would be standing somewhere around 12° Libra.) At age eleven, there was a meeting of planetary energies, and we can expect some Moon–Ascendant symbolism (in the form of an event or process) to have taken place.

What about Venus? It stands at 15°58' Libra. If directed onwards through the zodiac, Venus will never reach the Ascendant in Charles's lifetime, but the Ascendant *will* reach Venus by Solar Arc. But at what age? The Ascendant is 1°48' Libra and Venus is 14°10' ahead of it in the zodiac. So, just after the age of 14, Charles will have SA ASC conjunct natal Venus.

Here, for simplicity, we are making a rough estimate based upon One Degree, but a computer will tell us the exact date that the directed Moon moved on to the Ascendant and when the Ascendant directed to form a conjunction with Venus.

Neptune stands at 7°37' Scorpio, just shy of 36° away from the Ascendant (the distance from 1°48' Libra to 7°37' Scorpio). So, SA ASC conjunct natal Neptune will occur at around the age of 36.

It is possible to find the arc between each of the planets and angles and work out when they would meet (conjunct) each other. Some, of course, will never form a conjunction during a natural lifetime, but we should also be looking at other aspects such as the square and opposition.

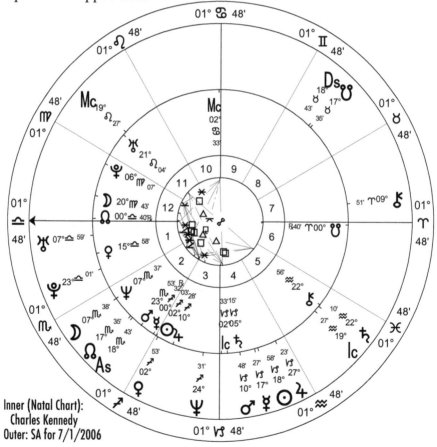

Inner (Natal Chart):
Charles Kennedy
Outer: SA for 7/1/2006

Let's look at the differences between One Degree and Solar Arc for the directions on **7 January 2006** (the bi-wheel opposite). On this date, Charles was 46 years, 1 month and 2 weeks old. By the One Degree method, everything would have moved 46°07' (46 years = 46°, 1 month = 5', 2 weeks = approx. 2'). But by Solar Arc, everything has moved almost 46°55'. Not much difference, it seems, but, in terms of accuracy, those 48' equate to almost 10 months in real, calendar time.

On 7 January 2006, Charles Kennedy resigned as Leader of the Liberal Democrats, two days after admitting that a serious drinking habit (much rumoured in the press) was affecting his health, productivity and reputation. By Solar Arc, the Moon had reached an exact conjunction with his natal Neptune. The important point to remember is that the active planet – the one directing and on the move – is the planet that brings its energy and symbolism (based on its basic meaning as well as natal set-up) to the natal planet. It acts as the verb that affects or comes into contact with a particular aspect of our character (as seen by the natal planet's placement). For example, the Sun 'illuminates', 'spotlights', 'highlights'; the Moon 'instinctively feels the need to …' and 'takes care' and 'comforts'; Mercury opens a door of communication to 'express', 'connect', 'find patterns' and 'formulate'. (See pages 30–2 for more keywords.)

Natally, Kennedy's Moon (habits/dependency) is in the 12th House (secrets/undoing/the uncontrollable and unruly areas of ourselves that can run riot) in the sign of Virgo (health/efficiency). It rules the MC (reputation) and the 10th Equal House (EQHS). Neptune (alcohol/addiction/scandal/resignation) is in the 2nd House and rules the 6th House (both 'Earth' houses related to the body and work routine/health respectively). Interestingly, his political party had spent much of the past five years concealing his battle with the bottle. Kennedy had sought professional help in 2002 when Solar Arc Neptune squared his natal Moon – his addiction (Neptune) had reached crisis point (square), which brought an attempt (square) to get healthy and to restructure his daily life (Moon in Virgo).

Another Solar Arc is fast approaching: SA Saturn conjunct Chiron in Aquarius in the 5th. Drinking is a major part of socializing for MPs in the Commons. This direction could suggest sobering up (Saturn) and the end of partying (5th) with his peer group (Aquarius) – fun (5th) that had caused him much harm (Chiron).

Apart from a few inner planet 'triggers' to his natal and directed charts, there were no outer planet transits (using tight orbs) at this time. This is a reminder for us to have more than transits in our toolkit, and to always look at the natal chart to understand the key traits, motivations and needs of the person themselves.

Kennedy remained involved in politics but lost his seat in Parliament during the 2015 General Election. It was a difficult year. His father died on 5 April, Charles lost his seat on 7 May (with transiting Saturn conjunct his Sun), and then he died suddenly on 1 June (transiting Saturn on his Mercury), from a haemorrhage said to be the result of his alcoholism. Looking at his Solar Arcs for **7 May 2015** (bi-wheel below), SA Saturn was 1°40' Pisces – square to his Sun (father, vocation) in Sagittarius and moving into the 6th House.

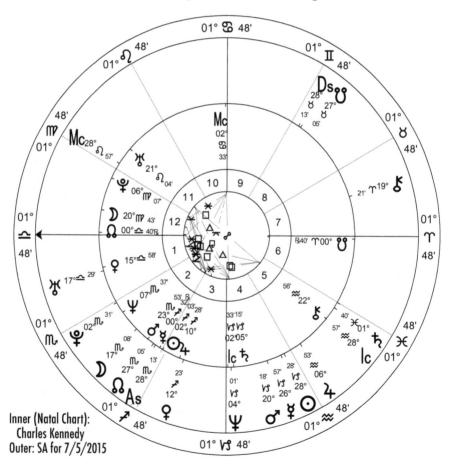

Inner (Natal Chart):
Charles Kennedy
Outer: SA for 7/5/2015

I've never seen any consistent and reliable astrological indicators of death (which is just as well), but a planet moving into the 6th is also quincunx (150°) by Equal House the rising degree – both the house and aspect speak of a (sometimes urgent) need to address our health.

As well as aspects from the directed chart to the natal chart, consider the importance of planets that move into a new house of the horoscope. Here, the birth time needs to be accurate and we'll also have to decide on a system of house division! I've used Equal houses for many years and find that they work very well for natal and forecasting work, but try some out and use whichever house system works consistently for you and the charts of friends and family.

Remember that the directed planet/angle is the *energy* of the forecast – it's on a mission – and the planet/angle being aspected is the part of life being opened up for transformation. But in practice, it's the merging of the two planets/angles involved that provides the clearest sense of what's occurring in the life. (And the combination is also more important than the actual aspect – conjunction, opposition, etc. – involved, too.) These events could take many forms (we know that external, educational, cultural and social factors affect how we express our horoscope's potential) – but they will always be of the nature of the planets involved. And, as I've stated, the key to interpreting Solar Arcs is to start by understanding the natal chart and the specific range of meanings of the planets/angles currently involved in the action.

3.12 • With Transits; Synastry

It is said that a Solar Arc direction (like a progression) waits for a trigger from a transiting planet before an 'event' occurs, but I've seen countless dramatic (and highly descriptive) Solar Arcs occurring at times of significant events for which there has been an absence of corresponding, meaningful transits (or progressions and lunations, for that matter).

It is possible, though, to connect events and periods in the life by linking transits to the natal chart with later transits to the directed chart. For example, the Saturn Return occurs at 29 but transiting Saturn catches up with SA Saturn some two to three years later. This 'Shadow' Saturn Return repeats issues that emerged during the Saturn Return but they are of a different quality (sign position) and usually in a different area of life (house position). It's a second chance to complete the unfinished business of our late twenties. I'll be addressing this later. (I named these 'Shadow Transits' and they met with some resistance in the US when I first wrote about them – some students had been taught never to combine directions with transits. But it's nice to see that some astrologers are testing and working with these now.)

Solar Arcs are also fascinating in synastry (the astrology of relationships). When our planets (or angles) Solar Arc direct to the positions of planets in others' natal charts (and vice versa), these are key times in our relationships with them. Sometimes it's the first meeting. For instance, every new client that's ever come to see me (in the last 25 years!) has had a natal or Solar Arc planet within a degree of a key planet in my own chart. The specific planets involved describe the purpose of the visit, along with the kind of interaction the client and I will have. I don't make it the most important area of the consultation (it's about them, not me!), but it's always interesting to spot and reflect back on after they've left.

3.13 • Power Degrees in a Solar Arc Planet's Journey

When we interpret Solar Arcs, we're usually looking at aspects from the Solar Arc directed planets/angles to the natal chart – from the outer wheel to the inner wheel – as well as when planets direct into a new house of the natal chart. But there are two other considerations that relate to the Solar Arc directed position itself. Firstly, when a planet has directed to 0° of a sign (where it remains for a whole year). Secondly, when a planet has directed to the final degree (29°) of a sign (through which, once again, it'll take twelve months to travel). I have written extensively on these two degrees that bookend each sign (see the bonus chapter towards the end of this book), but here are some ideas on both instances.

The First Degree
By Solar Arc, planets take thirty years to travel through a sign, so sign changes are eventful, transitional times. As a planet enters a new sign (known as an ingress), it automatically enters a new element and mode, and this indicates a new attitude, style and motivation. For instance, Venus directing from Libra to Scorpio means there is a shift from cardinal Air to fixed Water.

It would be too simplistic (and not very helpful) to note that Venus has moved from its sign of rulership (Libra) to detriment (Scorpio). It is no less 'good' or 'bad', but the environment Venus is now in has changed considerably. It has moved into new and different territory, and it is our job to explain this constructively to our client (ethics aside, it won't be leaving Scorpio for another thirty years so we'd better have something helpful to say about it).

This change of landscape is particularly noticeable during the first twelve months as the planet moves through the first degree (0°). The natal planet has the opportunity to speak a different language (new sign) and to connect with new 'people' in the horoscope (the ruler of that sign or any planets posited).

I would go as far as to say that a planet moving through the whole first degree (0°) indicates a year of getting to know and beginning to experience the essence of that sign (and the messages of natal planets placed there). In some ways it's a portent – a signpost indicating much of what we can expect for the next thirty years condensed into the first twelve months. My astrologer–friend in Brazil, Fernando Guimaraes, suggests the first degree is like an 'operatic overture' – an introduction that sets the mood for what follows. The experience is heightened during this first year, and the remaining twenty-nine years are eventful in this respect only when that planet aspects other planets/points along its journey. Additional information about the 'first degree experience' will come from the house in which 0° of this sign falls.

In addition, I've noticed that when a planet enters a new sign it connects and 'speaks' to any planet or angle in that sign – regardless of the degree. For example, if our Sun moves by Solar Arc into Capricorn, it will begin to 'illuminate' (a solar verb) any planet/angle we have in that sign. It may take years to reach the exact degree of that planet/angle in Capricorn, but its entry (particularly the first year when at 0°) will mark a time when our Capricorn planets are beginning to undergo change (the specifics of that change will be reflected in the Solar Arc planet, the house involved and any planets already in that sign natally).

Summary: a major shift and new script; an augury, setting the mood of the period to come; an 'operatic overture' – an intense period in which we are swamped by images of this new sign and experience issues around it.

The Final Degree: Poised for Change

A planet that has directed to the final degree (29°) of a sign will often bring to the fore crisis-driven issues that are specifically related to that sign–planet combination. During that year, we tend to experience the most challenging characteristics/themes of the sign, particularly if it is relatively 'foreign' to us or if we have not taken care to understand/integrate its essence. After all, this degree recalls the cumulative effects of that planet/angle's (and our) experiences through the sign.

This final degree appears to have a sting in its tail: although we are poised for change, we have to attend to areas ruled by that sign before we are able to move on. I started to see this with clients who felt (or were rendered) impotent in some way with regard to the areas/themes linked to the sign. These could be crisis times when they felt they were in the dark. As the closing of a chapter, there was the anticipation of transition, of stepping into the unknown and a sense of urgency to wrap things up (or a last chance to get it right) 'before it's too late'.

Consider the Taurus–Scorpio polarity. Both are signs of potency, linked to the processes of attachment and accumulation, as well as the exploration of physical and emotional pleasure and possession. One client had her Ascendant ('surroundings', 'horizon', 'environment') directed to the end of Scorpio in her 2nd House and experienced huge financial instability (a Scorpionic crisis and near wipe-out). Before her Ascendant left Scorpio it made a trine (by Solar Arc) to her Moon and, under additional aspects and transits, she experienced the release (trine) of her elderly mother passing away. The following year, the directed Ascendant moved into Sagittarius and immediately conjunct Jupiter, offering a major relocation plus financial opportunities from abroad.

Another client divorced as Venus directed towards the end of Taurus (in her 12th House). At the final degree, she had to pay her spouse a large sum of money in a divorce settlement – one that she felt was unfair and unjustified. Although this did not force a financial crisis, it did limit her future options. (Venus is less to do with 'money' than being concerned with the perks, luxuries and privileges that extra money can bestow.)

Sometimes these pivotal years are last-minute repeats of old patterns, which serve as reminders to let go of particular behaviour patterns. But when the planet (or angle) crosses over to the next sign, there's an awareness of switching our approach, and we may encounter a fresh opportunity to experience a new quality of that planet. As it's the end of a thirty-year era, it often coincides with an intense twelve months (the final degree) that 'pack a punch' – a time when exaggerated manifestations of that sign appear as life events.

Known as the anaretic degree or 'degree of fate', the final degree is often given a negative spin. Astrologer Richard Swatton reminded me that, according to some traditional bounds and dignities by term, the malefics rule the final degrees of all the signs. Some horary practitioners observe that the querent can do nothing to affect the outcome; it's simply too late to have control over a situation.

Whereas the planet/angle at 0° is taking initial steps on the road ahead to envision, discover and create its journey, the planet/angle at 29° senses inevitability, irrevocability and finality – the end of a familiar path. But a planet at the final degree has a 'knowingness' about it; it's a seasoned player, very skilled in that sign, having earned its stripes. Positively, that which has been mastered – skills that have been acquired – can be put to good use in these twelve months. This is where the last degree can truly come into its own. It can be a year of distinction and wrapping up a long period of endeavour.

Summary: the end of a familiar path/chapter; poised for change; what has passed cannot be undone; a period of crisis – experiencing exaggerated or intense manifestations of the sign; mastery; finishing off long-term projects.

The Middle Degree

Planets or points at the middle degrees, from 14.5° to 15.5°, appear to be truly entrenched in that sign's *raison d'être*. It can be advantageous to learn as much about the planet-in-sign combination as possible during this stressful time. When in a cardinal sign (Aries, Cancer, Libra, Capricorn), the planet/angle is fully engaged in the process of moving forward and can encounter challenge and conflict around the sign's main themes. In the middle of fixed degrees (Taurus, Leo, Scorpio, Aquarius), the planet is at its most permanent, solid and durable, but sometimes becomes stagnant or stuck in the sign's key areas. When mid mutable (Gemini, Virgo, Sagittarius, Pisces), it is at its most versatile and diverse but also precarious, scattered and prone to fluctuation and instability. It is a changeable, unsteady period when goalposts shift in areas linked to the sign.

3.14 • Shadow Transits: A Hidden Forecasting Tool

I had always wondered what the difference would be between a transit to a natal position and a transit to a Solar Arc directed position. Is one more important? Is it a case of either/or? When I asked around, the reply was, simply and unsatisfactorily, 'Ah yes, that's interesting.' And the matter was left dangling. When asked, some astrologers felt that these two types of transit should never be mixed, and only Melanie Reinhart had a viewpoint (on transits to natal and progressed planets) that answered some of my questions. Melanie saw the period between, for example, a transit over natal Uranus and progressed Uranus as an intensification and elongation of the transit process, where it stretches the trail and 'echoes' the theme through that period of time.

I soon discovered that not only is the transit to the directed position (what I named a Shadow Transit) as important as the original transit-to-natal event, it also has a strong link to the themes that came up and developed under the original natal chart transit. But some students, when hearing about this, think, 'Another set of measurements to consider! Isn't it complicated enough?' Yet, rather than adding a whole new system into the mix, we're looking at repetitions and their connections. In my practice, Shadow Transits have become a very useful tool and enabled me to discuss a past event with a client in order to help them draw parallels and gain some insight into the process currently unfolding under the Shadow Transit. (Generally, I use 1° either side for transits.)

As an astrologer with a Gemini Ascendant, it's my experience that if you can help the client to link patterns that occur in different areas or times in their life, they're able to step back and look objectively at their situation and see those patterns clearly at work.

Repeating Themes
Since 2004, I have worked with Shadow Transits and have found that they *repeat* themes, events and feelings that transpired during the original transit to the natal horoscope. I believe that the event gives us another chance to tidy up unfinished business, another stab at an opportunity or a further possibility to recognize a pattern from the past – and to make different choices, if necessary.

For example, when I first wrote this section for my original work on Solar Arc (on **23 June 2011**), I had just finished a phone consultation with a client, **'Natalie'** who had TR Neptune (outermost wheel, below) conjunct her SA Descendant at 0° Pisces. She was attempting to be in relationship with a man who was uncertain about his sexual orientation (and was more interested in pursuing his first opportunity with a man). He was, simply put, unavailable.

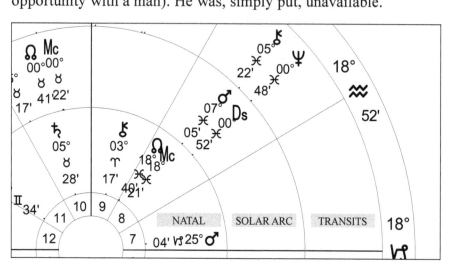

My client felt that they had a very important link and attempted to forge a further bond by starting a committed relationship. As we spoke about this, I mentioned several dates in 1992–3 when TR Neptune had been conjunct her natal Descendant. At this time, she was immersed in a one-sided, devotional relationship trying to 'save' a man who was non-committal and troubled on a number of emotional levels. During the consultation in 2011, my client was able to see the link and its importance in several ways, and realize that this was a 'second chance' to revisit and examine her own compulsion to rescue or pursue the unavailable. In her words, she didn't want to 'drown again' (her words, Neptune) in a less-than-ideal situation. (With a heavy emphasis on the Water signs in her chart, there is a strong natal theme of dependency in relationship.)

Knowing what happened during the transit-to-natal period enables us to understand themes that might be revisited when that transiting planet finally catches up with the SA position. Of course, the length of time it will take to do so depends on the transiting planet, so it may not happen in our lifetime. The Shadow Transit will bring up the same issues (planet/angle) but with a different emphasis (sign) and usually in another arena (house).

The Shadow Saturn Return

Part of the reason I started researching this idea was because clients were coming (or returning) to see me at age 31–32 with the same issues they'd had at their Saturn Return (at 29). This often came with the cry, 'You told me it would all be over two years ago!' Inaccurate and a little unfair, but …. This 'repetition' was happening long after the planet had moved beyond a reasonable orb of influence. I started to realize that the Saturn Return isn't over till the Shadow Saturn Return, which occurs two to three years later, has been completed.

When transiting Saturn completes one lap of the zodiac and returns to its natal position, we experience a special Saturn transit: the landmark, coming-of-age Saturn Return. But in those 29 years, Solar Arc Saturn has directed forward roughly 29 degrees ahead of the natal Saturn (and usually into a new sign and a new house). It will then take the transiting Saturn in the sky a further 2.5 to 3 years to catch up with Solar Arc Saturn, which by then would have moved another 2.5 to 3 degrees (1 degree for each year). This is the Shadow Saturn Return. Here are some examples.

Publishing

I was able to look at **my own Saturn Return** (in Gemini in the 12th near the Ascendant) and make this connection, too. I had been publishing my own and others' astrology books from the age of 24, but at 27 I signed a contract with a major publisher to produce my first book on palmistry (not surprisingly, Gemini is highlighted frequently in the charts of hand-readers).

The writing process had been a joy, but the editing proved to be a struggle. I had been greatly looking forward to the editing process (my work being shaped and moulded by the sort of editor a writer dreams of) but discovered that the book didn't really have an editor, just a proofreader, who managed to add a few hundred mistakes of her own to the manuscript! I rectified as many of these as I could spot and hoped the publisher would incorporate these corrections in time for the printing.

When the book was published during my once-only Saturn Return hit in May–June 2002, it contained even more errors. I was livid at the shoddiness of the work and how it would reflect on me. By speaking out and being unhappy with the mistakes I had encountered, I became regarded as a 'difficult' author. The publisher corrected most of the errors in the second print run later that year, but I took the opportunity to sign with another publisher when the chance arose.

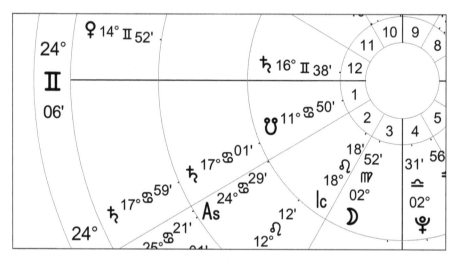

I wrote a second palmistry book, and the editing process was again stressful, as I seemed to be the only one who wanted the book to be as error-free as possible! It was published during my Shadow Saturn Return (arriving on my desk in **July 2004**, above tri-wheel).

I doubt very much that the Saturn/12th House 'lesson' of letting go of the control-freak side of my character was fully learned during either transit because the experiences made me realize that I needed greater control over my work and reputation (Saturn is co-ruler of my Midheaven). After all, an author's name, not a proofreader's, is on the cover.

A Betrayal

In her early thirties, **'Anna'** arrived for an astrology–palmistry consultation in April 2005, during the transit of Saturn conjunct SA Saturn (her Shadow Saturn Return). Natally, Saturn was in Gemini in the 8th House (by Placidus and Equal Houses) and formed the handle of a bucket pattern. Saturnian issues of privacy and respect, emphasized by the planet's 8th House position, assumed even greater importance with her natal Moon in Capricorn and a Scorpio Ascendant. Treading carefully, and before discussing her current situation, I asked Anna what had happened during her original Saturn Return. She explained that her partner had had an affair and hurried back to confess all, leaving Anna to deal with the knowledge of a betrayal and the burden of a remorseful confession.

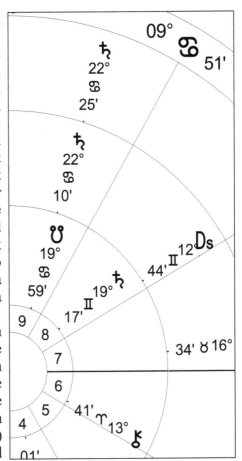

Arguably, given Saturn in Gemini in the 8th House, one message of the Saturn Return might have been to voice (Gemini) deep or volatile feelings such as betrayal (8th House) to process (mutable) this experience (Saturn) and communicate (Gemini) a range of Saturn/8th House issues. In *The Twelve Houses* (Flare, 2007), Howard Sasportas writes, 'The 8th House yields the opportunity to reexamine the connection between present relationship issues and those problems encountered with the mother and father early in life ... The ruins and rubble from childhood are excavated in the 8th House ... The gift of the 8th House is greater self-knowledge and self-mastery, freeing us to continue our journey renewed, less encumbered by unnecessary baggage.' But my client had said nothing to her partner at the time and, in her words, 'just buried it'.

Now, in April 2005, she sat with me in my office undergoing the final leg of her Shadow Saturn Return, which was occurring one sign and house on: in Cancer in the 9th House. I asked her if there were any links between the events of her first Saturn Return and her current situation, possibly with a 9th House (travel/education) or Cancerian (home/family/motherhood) theme. There were. She and her partner were still together and had been discussing whether to start a family, but my client had gone abroad (9th House) for a holiday on her own in August 2004 (the first hit) and had begun an affair with another man. When she returned, she kept silent about the holiday romance. When asked if anything occurred during the second hit (January 2005), Anna replied, 'I went back and spent another week with him.' I mentioned that the final hit would happen in **mid-May 2005** (tri-wheel, previous page), just a few weeks away, and Anna smiled nervously. She had already booked another trip for a week during that period. The Shadow Saturn Return brought up the same issues but with a different emphasis (sign) and in another arena (house).

We spent much of the remaining time discussing the possibilities of exploring and articulating her natal Saturn in Gemini in the 8th. It is in such circumstances that the astrologer feels privileged to be engaged in a process that is meaningful and empowering to both parties; it is not a matter of 'getting it right' and impressing clients with accurate past dates. When a dialogue is opened, it is more pertinent to ask, 'Where do we go with this information now?'

Other Examples

My client files are packed with fascinating examples of these links. Often, at the time of a Shadow Transit, the same person reappears in our life or a similar situation arises that forces us to confront an area of our horoscope once again.

One client/student with TR Neptune to natal Jupiter in Capricorn had, under the heavy weight of expectation (Capricorn), quit (Neptune) before taking her final exams at university (Jupiter in Capricorn). At the time of our consultation, TR Neptune was conjunct SA Jupiter in Aquarius. She was training to be a professional astrologer but shied away from taking the final exams. When made aware of this link between transits to her natal and directed charts, she realized how important it was to stick with her investment, and I'm delighted to say that she ended up passing her exams and qualifying as an astrologer.

Another client, 'Larissa', had TR Uranus on her SA Mercury at 15° Pisces. I asked her what had happened the first time around (when TR Uranus had conjoined natal Mercury at 10° Aquarius in the 2nd House). Back then, out of the blue (Uranus), an eccentric architect friend (Mercury in Aquarius) had offered her workspace in his building for a minimal fee. At the start of her art career, this had helped Larissa's finances enormously. Now, during the Shadow Transit, the charitable friend had come back into the picture with another building space and another offer – this time free of charge (Pisces).

And another client had TR Pluto conjunct her Moon–Neptune–IC in Scorpio when her father was dying of cancer. Part of the stress during this time was keeping his illness secret from her mother, who was herself incapacitated. When TR Pluto moved to 0° Capricorn in early 2008, it was now sitting on my client's SA Moon in the 5th House. Under this transit, she began a difficult separation from her long-term partner. During the consultation, she said, 'This situation has been even more painful than losing my father to cancer.'

When trying to anticipate how a transit to a Solar Arc directed planet is working in a client's life (possible themes, experiences, areas of life and events), I now track the date of the original transit to the natal chart and ask, 'What happened back then?' More often than not, the client recalls an event that has a direct link to current circumstances. But the new aspect will usually be in a different sign or house, so there's a twist in the interpretation. It may be a repeat, 'here we go again' experience but in a different setting with different players. It's the same visitor at the door, but in a different costume.

Try it out yourself. Play detective and look at your Shadow Saturn Return or other transits (not just conjunctions) to Solar Arc positions. With the benefit of hindsight, we can make useful, meaningful links between past and present conditions that can empower our clients, and ourselves, to make informed choices about our lives.

In Part IV: Case Studies, you'll find examples in the stories of Margaret Thatcher, Jordan Chandler, Marion Jones, Bob Geldof and others.

3.15 • What We've Learned So Far ... in a Nutshell

1 With Solar Arc, one degree (60 minutes) of arc equals approximately one year of time (so 5 minutes of arc equals one month). The natal planetary positions and angles are directed forwards by the actual distance the Sun has transited each day after birth; this is usually very close to 1° but there are slight seasonal variations (up to 1°01' at the turn of the year, as slow as 0°57'–0°58' from May to August, and very close to 1° in March and October/November).

2 Everything in the chart is directed forwards at the same rate. A Solar Arc chart will look the same as a natal chart except that every point will have moved forwards approximately 1° for every year of life (i.e. the aspects in the chart remain but the chart moves forwards through the signs and houses); very 'tight' natal aspects (with an orb under 1°) give rise to 'double whammies', where an aspect combination (e.g. Sun square Mars) directs to hit a natal position in the same year.

3 With all points moving approximately 1° a year, no Solar Arc direction (using the five major, Ptolemaic aspects) can be repeated in a lifetime; directions are one-off occurrences, saddle points in our lives.

4 Starting off, it is best to focus on the conjunction, square and opposition, allowing a half-degree orb either side of exactitude (this is equivalent to six months before and after the exact hit). Study your own chart retrospectively by looking at key events in your life and see how the symbolism of a direction describes the events and, in particular, the feelings, actions and repercussions associated with these events. Or you may prefer to take one planet at a time and track the aspects it makes during particular years in your lifetime.

5 It is possible to fine-tune (rectify) the horoscope by using directions to and from the four angles to test possible alternative birth times.

6 A planet or angle directing from a sign (29°) into a new sign (0°) is an important period of change; so are directions over house cusps, but the birth time must be accurate in order to see the latter.

7 There are powerful links between a transit to a natal position (e.g. TR Saturn to the Sun) and the same, later transit to the Solar Arc position (e.g. TR Saturn to the directed Sun). The Shadow Transit is a second chance for us to work on issues that transpired in the original transit, except that the SA aspect usually occurs in a different sign and house, adding a slight twist to the interpretation. One we all share is the Saturn Return at age 29, followed by the Shadow Saturn Return at around age 32, when we get another opportunity to implement key life choices.

3.16 • What to Look For: Solar Arcs in Seven Steps

1 Start your Solar Arc journey by noting any aspects made by planets/angles in the outer wheel (the Solar Arc positions for a given date) to the planets/angles in the inner wheel (the natal chart). I begin by looking for directed planets/angles in the 1st House and seeing if any natal planets/angles are at the same degree. Then I move on to the 2nd House, and so on.

2 Pay particular attention to conjunctions (0°), squares (90°) and oppositions (180°) which coincide with the most important life events and developments. Conjunctions are the most obvious merging of planetary energies and their symbolism. Oppositions often manifest as new dynamics in relationships, while squares appear in the form of obstacles that require a great deal of energy to surmount. Use an orb of 30' (half a degree either side = six months of time) before and after the exact aspect.

3 Look for when a planet or angle moves into a new sign. It's important to remember that each sign is made up of 30° (from 0°00' to 29°59'). By Solar Arc, it takes a planet (or cusp) thirty years to travel from the start to the end of each sign. The year when it travels through the first degree of a sign (0°00' to 0°59') is a new phase in the life – an intense twelve months when we get to know the directed planet in a new sign. It's a portent of things to come and the issues we need to deal with. During this initial year, this directed planet also 'speaks' to any natal planet in that sign, regardless of its degree, unleashing the potential of that planet.

4 Consider the year when a planet or angle reaches the final degree of a sign (29°00' to 29°59'). This is a year when some of the most challenging facets of that sign demand attention and mastery. It's the end of a familiar path, heralding twelve months of 'crisis' associated with that sign.

5 Look for when a planet or angle moves into a new house (an accurate birth time is necessary). This will mark a period when the planet shifts focus into a different area of your life. A planet will

stay in an Equal house for approximately thirty years (or longer/ shorter with unequal houses) but don't expect it to be 'on' all the time. Its main effects will be seen when:

- it enters that house
- it makes an aspect to a planet/angle in that house
- it aspects (from that house) a planet/angle in another house (e.g. by square or opposition)
- a transiting planet hits this directed planet

I've been using Equal houses for many years now, and this gives me a tool to differentiate between the 10th House and the Midheaven, and the 4th House and the IC. These differences show up most vividly in forecasting about work/job (Equal 10th House) and home/house (Equal 4th House) matters, and exploring deeper psychological principles around how we see ourselves in the context of society (MC) and our family (IC) – where we've come from (IC) and where we're going (MC). (For more details, please see my mini-book *The Midheaven: Spotlight on Success*.)

6 Note the period when a planet/angle directs to the middle of a sign (14.5°–15.5°). These will be years when the planet is fully entrenched in the meanings of the sign. For instance, a planet/ angle directing through mid Virgo is a time when there is much fixing, processing and tidying up, plus work, routine or health matters may be in a precarious state.

7 Use Solar Arcs along with one or two other forecasting tools (I would recommend transits and New and Full Moons rather than another method of progression/direction). You'll get a well rounded view of key stages in the life journey (directions) and major phases in our life cycles (transits). And consider using transits to Solar Arcs (Shadow Transits).

Part IV

Case Studies

People are like stained glass windows: they sparkle and shine
when the sun is out, but when the darkness sets in
their true beauty is revealed only if there is a light within.
– Elisabeth Kübler-Ross

In this section, I have selected over forty charts and life stories
that interest me and I've researched a key date or two for each
example. Rather than simply listing the Solar Arcs as 'proof' or
interpreting every direction in a cookbook fashion, I wanted to tell
the person's story and look at the natal chart, too. I hope you'll
find these profiles interesting and I hope they'll encourage you to
engage in further research.

Although most of the birth data are from official sources (e.g. birth
certificate, hospital records, etc.), at times I have noted where I
think the birth time might be slightly different because of Solar Arcs
and corresponding life events.

4.01 • Madam Cyn's Painful Past

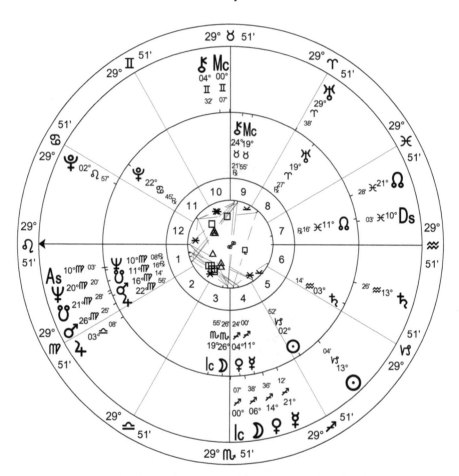

Inner Wheel (natal chart): 24 December 1932 at 21:00 GMT
in Bognor Regis, England (50N47, 0W41).

Outer Wheel: Solar Arc directions to 24 December 1942.

Data Source: From her to Frank Clifford.

Let's begin by looking at the chart of **Cynthia Payne**, the late, headline-grabbing hostess and brothel owner. Payne has a chart that suggests a flair for self-publicity: 29° Leo rising and a conjunction of Mars and Jupiter in the 1st House trine the MC. The Moon is in Scorpio in the 3rd (a need to talk about sex), while MC ruler Venus is in party-loving Sagittarius in the 4th. As a 5th House Capricorn, sex and entertainment (5th) were her business (Capricorn). With her Ascendant conjunct fixed star Regulus, she had personal associations with prominent people.

Cynthia was born in December, so the Sun's speed is slightly fast. **On her tenth birthday**, everything in the chart has moved forwards approximately 10°12' of arc. Take a look at the outer wheel (directions) and compare it to the inner (natal chart).

Soon after Cynthia's tenth birthday, her gentle, undemanding mother passed away. In the chart, Cynthia's SA Ascendant (which represents her surroundings and horizon) was conjunct Neptune in the 1st House, suggesting her overwhelming feelings of bewilderment and loneliness. Just when she needed tenderness the most, the ten-year-old was left in the custody of a remote father, and her affection was rebuffed. It was a confusing time (SA Ascendant to Neptune); Cynthia had great trouble concentrating and learning in the classroom, and was soon underachieving at school (note that natal Neptune is squared by the planet of schooling, Mercury, in Sagittarius).

It was a busy year of Solar Arcs. Elsewhere, the MC/IC axis (parents, direction) moved into mutable signs (changeable times); SA Chiron opposed Venus in the 4th, suggesting the pain of losing her beloved mother; and SA Pluto opposed Saturn, perhaps reflecting the non-negotiable demolition (Pluto) of parental security (Saturn) and being forced to live with a cold father. In Cynthia's words, 'The wrong parent died.'

Payne would later run a discreet bordello in her home for prominent businessmen, lawyers, vicars and MPs. That home was raided on 16 December 1978, when SA Mars in Scorpio squared natal Saturn (the law), SA Pluto reached Neptune (the exposure of scandal), and the SA Sun squared her MC/IC (reputation, home). Nicknamed 'Madam Cyn', her trial, imprisonment and campaigns for changes in sex laws kept her in the news for years, and her life story inspired the films *Wish You Were Here* and *Personal Services*.

4.02 • Personal Grief on a Public Stage

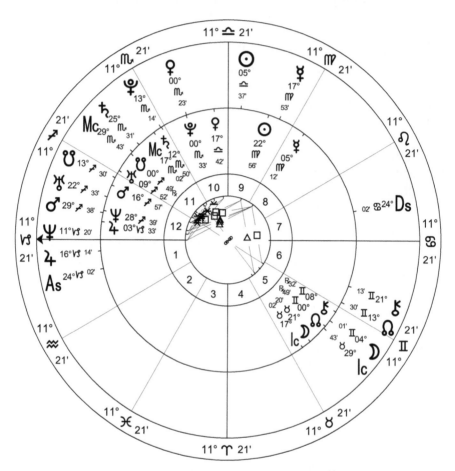

Inner Wheel (natal chart): 15 September 1984 at 16:20 GDT
in Paddington, London, England (51N32, 0W12).

Outer Wheel: Solar Arc directions to 31 August 1997.

Data Source: Palace announcement in newspapers on date; copy on file.

Additional Data: Prince William, 21 June 1982 at 21:03 GDT in Paddington,
London, England (51N32, 0W12). Data in a letter from Buckingham Palace;
copy on file.

Here, we have another Solar Arc involving Neptune and the Ascendant. At the time of his mother's death on **31 August 1997**, **Prince Harry** had no major transits or progressions to his natal chart, yet we note a few highly influential and meaningful directions.

Firstly, Neptune was one minute from a conjunction to his Ascendant. We can speculate, as he approached adolescence, that this must have been a highly disorientating time for the young prince. In addition to his own sadness, he encountered an unprecedented wave of national grief and mass mourning (Neptune) that swept the UK. Natally, Neptune originates from the 12th House in Sagittarius and squares the Sun in Virgo. Someone with the Sun square Neptune may not have the clearest sense of who their father is, what they were born to do or what their role should be; William and Harry have been labelled, rather unkindly, 'the heir and the spare'.

At the time of his mother's death, Solar Arc Uranus was four months away from an exact square to his Virgo Sun. Harry's subsequent 'searching for himself' and provocative behaviour provided much tabloid fodder and may have had much to do with SA Neptune–Ascendant and SA Uranus square Sun, as well as a natal Mars–Uranus in Sagittarius. (In addition, SA Mars had directed to a crisis degree – 29° Sagittarius – which could also symbolize his mother's car chase and violent crash in a foreign country.)

Twelve months before, his parents' divorce had been finalized (SA Pluto approaching Saturn, the demolition of the family anchor). At the time of the crash, the rulers of Harry's MC and IC (the axis showing the parental influence on formative years and the subsequent emergence into society) met by Solar Arc: Venus (having just plunged into Scorpio) formed a conjunction to Pluto at 0° Scorpio. This was no bountiful Venus–Jupiter direction! It was the violent death of his beloved, radiant mother who was in full bloom and developing independence. (Harry's Venus rules his IC and disposits his Moon in Taurus.) His natal MC in Scorpio is indicative of a 'heavy' life direction that is marked by a major transformation (often the death of a mentor/parent). Note, too, that the MC had directed to the final crisis degree of the crisis sign, Scorpio.

His brother William's chart showed Mars fast approaching Pluto by direction (both planets rule his MC) and his directed Ascendant at 11° Capricorn (Harry's rising degree) at the time of their mother's death, perhaps bringing the brothers much closer at this time of loss.

4.03 • That's What Hits Are For

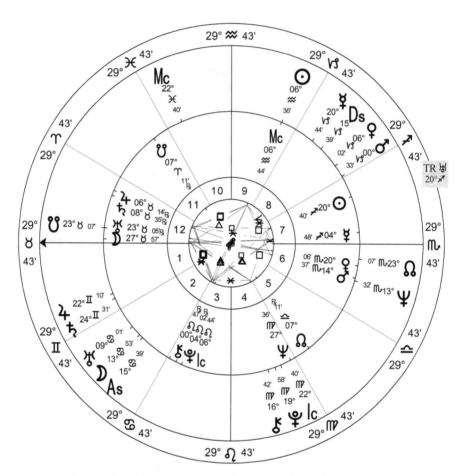

Inner Wheel (natal chart): 12 December 1940 at 15:08 EST
in Orange, New Jersey, USA (40N46, 74W14).

Outer Wheel: Solar Arc directions to 18 January 1986.

Data Source: Birth certificate, as quoted in *The Gauquelin Book of American Charts.*

A Solar Arc direction to/from the Midheaven (MC) can sometimes coincide with a major shift in our reputation or social status. It can indicate the beginning of a new success in our lives, a period of renown, respect or recognition. If it occurs early on in life, it is often linked to our parents' own accomplishments. Jupiter directed to my MC when my father was in the news for winning the biggest (Jupiter) personal injury payout in UK history (in Equal houses, my Jupiter is in the 8th). It was also a time when I began studying at a school in which Eastern philosophies and languages were a major part of the curriculum, another reflection of Jupiter to the MC.

After two decades of hits and winning fame by singing the songs of Burt Bacharach and Hal David, the classy chanteuse **Dionne Warwick** (once known as the 'Black Pearl') became a key fundraiser for AIDS research. The recording that raised money and gave Warwick her biggest hit was entitled 'That's What Friends Are For' (Aquarius MC), a Grammy Award-winning collaboration with Elton John, Stevie Wonder and Gladys Knight.

The song reached the summit of the US charts the week ending **18 January 1986**, when her directed Sun (natally in Sagittarius) was conjunct her MC in humanitarian-themed Aquarius (TR Jupiter was at 7° Aquarius when it was recorded, and TR Uranus conjunct Dionne's Sun when it hit #1). SA Sun made a square to natal Jupiter (in Taurus) – much awareness and funds were raised by her efforts. With SA Pluto approaching a square to her natal Sun, this led to a new role as the United States' Ambassador of Health in 1987 and spokeswoman (Sagittarius) for various AIDS-related charities.

Natally, the Sun is sesquiquadrate (135°) Jupiter, suggesting a sudden shift (sesquiquadrate) of vocational focus (Sun) towards fundraising (Jupiter in Taurus). And during this time, Jupiter was making a sesquiquadrate to Dionne's Midheaven by Solar Arc (reflecting this shift of gear).

As a combination, the friendly, accessible signs of Sagittarius and Aquarius are concerned with envisioning a more ideal future, as well as opening channels of communication to reach out to humanity, erode prejudice or break down barriers. Warwick was one of the first female singers of colour in the pop charts. And although her promotion of The Psychic Friends Network in a range of infamous infomercials received some ridicule, it was another example of this combination of signs and her life-long interest in esoteric matters.

96

4.04 • The MTV President

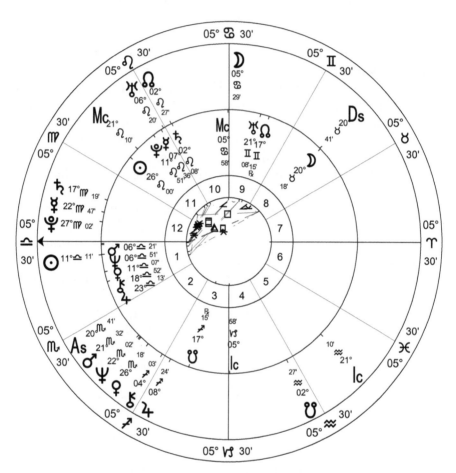

Inner Wheel (natal chart): 19 August 1946 at 08:51 CST
in Hope, Arkansas, USA (33N40, 93W35).

Outer Wheel: Solar Arc directions to 20 January 1993.

Data Source: A note from Clinton's mother to Shelley Ackerman; copy on file.

The chart for a president's inauguration is important, but the president's birth chart itself reflects the America that he comes to represent during his term in office. The America during the Nixon and Bush Junior administrations was as paranoid and divisive as its leaders' Mercury–Pluto aspects, while the Venusian- and Neptunian-tinged charts of charismatic presidents Clinton and Kennedy reflect the scandal-hungry American public of the 90s (fed on details of the former's salacious love life), and America's early 60s idealism (encapsulated by John and Jackie's Camelot).

In addition, the transits and directions under which a president is elected say much about his term of office: its themes, effectiveness and the public's response. **Bill Clinton** was sworn in on **20 January 1993**, when Solar Arc Moon in Cancer was directing into the 10th House and fast approaching his MC. The natal Moon (ruling the MC and 10th) is in Taurus in his 8th House. At the same time, the directed Sun was conjunct Venus in Libra in the 1st, Venus moved to square his Sun (Scorpio to Leo) and the Descendant reached his natal Moon. In addition, his directed chart was semi-square his natal.

Venus speaks of the popularity contest of an election, while the Moon reflects the people and the public mood (interestingly, when his wife lost her bid to become President in November 2016, Clinton's SA Moon was at the final degree of Cancer and SA Saturn was conjunct his Venus – it was the abrupt end of a political era).

The Venusian–lunar directions of 1993 were indicative of times ahead – of the informal, charming and likeable man, the hip MTV President who played saxophone, his health care reform plan, the economic expansion and a federal surplus, the election slogan of 'Putting people first', and the promotion of women to key jobs in his Administration. (In addition, when he won the election on 3 November 1992, TR Jupiter was conjunct his Ascendant–Mars–Neptune in Libra, and TR Pluto had just crossed over the directed positions of these three points, which were now at 20–22 Scorpio.)

But looking at his natal chart and directions, it is not surprising that his terms of office were tainted by revelations of his sexual misconduct, or, more to the point, his denials of extra-marital affairs, and the witch-hunt to remove him from office (note that Venus is natally conjunct belligerent Mars and scandalous, boundaryless Neptune). Clinton was, of course, later impeached for obstruction of justice but was acquitted.

4.05 • Internally His

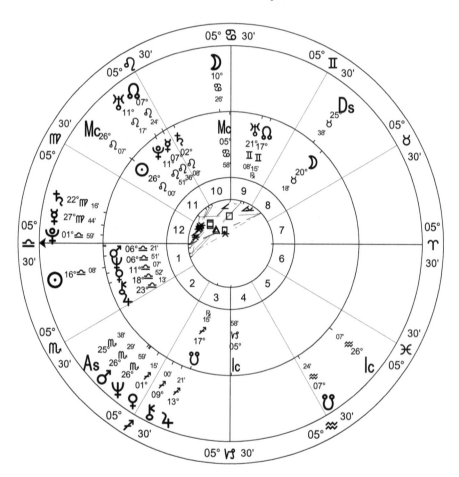

Inner Wheel (natal chart): 19 August 1946 at 08:51 CST
in Hope, Arkansas, USA (33N40, 93W35).

Outer Wheel: Solar Arc directions to 26 January 1998.

Data Source: A note from Clinton's mother to Shelley Ackerman; copy on file.

In **Bill Clinton's** chart, Mars–Neptune are tightly conjunct in Libra (with Venus nearby) and within a degree of a square to the MC. And with Mars–Neptune conjunct Venus, this trio of planets is suggestive of personal magnetism, insatiability and serial adultery – three traits that could shape his reputation (the square to the Midheaven).

Clinton's tight (less than one degree) link-up between Mars, Neptune and the MC means that every time his MC directs over a planet, it is infused with the symbolism of Mars–Neptune, and the exactness of the aspect means that all three parts of the chart are activated simultaneously. For instance, Clinton's **Whitewater** company was incorporated on **18 June 1979** (chart on right), when his SA MC reached Mercury in Leo

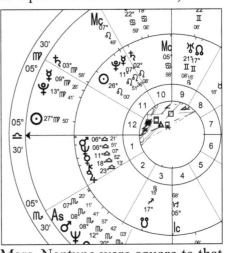

(and in doing so, the Ascendant–Mars–Neptune were square to that Mercury). The scandal erupted soon after his 1992 election, when the SA Moon crossed the MC and squared natal Mars–Neptune.

The Sun coming to the 10th House (by Equal, i.e. square to the Ascendant–Descendant axis) can be a pivotal time in a politician's career, as can the directed 10th House to the natal Sun. But when there's a Solar Arc between the Sun and the MC, it can be linked to a reputation-changing time in the person's life. In the previous bi-wheel (page 96), when Clinton became President, the Sun is five degrees (years) away from squaring the Midheaven. So what could be more monumental and memorable than becoming President?

When Clinton's SA MC reached his Leo Sun (with SA Mars–Neptune squaring it), it wasn't a high professional moment in his life. It was *the* defining moment of his presidency – and it couldn't help being tinged by Mars–Neptune. It was **26 January 1998** (bi-wheel, opposite) – five days after a scandal broke – and Clinton went on record to deny an extramarital affair with a young White House intern named Monica Lewinsky. The rest is a sordid, sorry tale overshadowing the politician's promise – one that would influence his wife's political ambitions years later.

4.06 • The Patsy's Decline

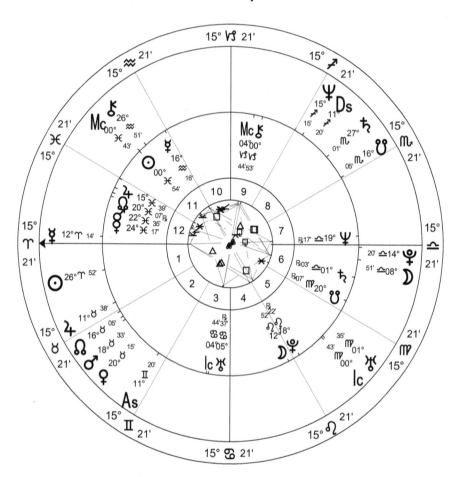

Inner Wheel (natal chart): 20 February 1951 at 08:40 GMT
in Giffnock, Scotland (55N48, 4W18).

Outer Wheel: Solar Arc directions to 27 June 2007.

Data Source: Birth certificate, as quoted by Caroline Gerard and Paul Wright.

Opposite Page: Inner (same natal chart as above)
Outer: Solar Arc directions to 11 May 2010.

British Chancellor **Gordon Brown's** long wait to take over Tony Blair's mantle as Prime Minister came to an end on **27 June 2007** (bi-wheel, opposite), after much speculation of a Blair–Brown 'inside deal' to pass over the reins of power. The timing was very apt for Brown: SA MC was conjunct his natal Sun at the time he became leader. But at 0° Pisces, it felt as though he was being set up to play the patsy (Pisces) for the Blair years and the illegal war on Iraq.

A year later, in late July 2008, some MPs openly called on Brown to resign. This so-called 'Lancashire Plot' occurred when Solar Arc Pluto directed to his Descendant. At the time of Brown's **11 May 2010 election defeat** (bi-wheel below), MC ruler Saturn was at 29° Scorpio and the Sun was at 29° Aries (and TR Pluto on his MC) – classic 'script-changing' directions revealing the end of a major phase in his life.

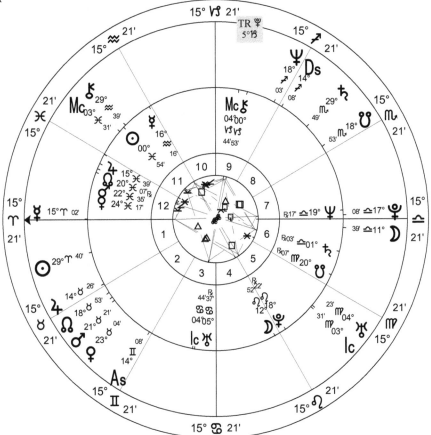

4.07 • The Return of Pat the Rat

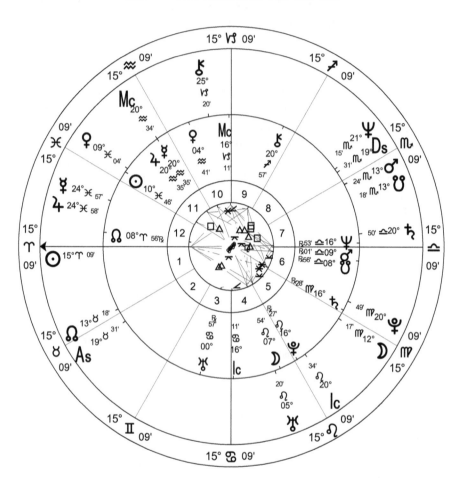

Inner Wheel (natal chart): 2 March 1950 at 08:30 AEST
in Tamworth, New South Wales, Australia (31S05, 150E55).

Outer Wheel: Solar Arc directions to 1 October 1984.

Data Source: From her to Frank Clifford, quoting her father.

Actress **Belinda Giblin** captured a million Australian hearts in the 1970s as sexy secretary Kay Webster in the TV soap opera *The Box*. A number of films followed (*Petersen, End Play*), and there was a small but significant role as a devious wife in the internationally-distributed film *The Empty Beach* (released November 1984).

In **October 1984**, the SA Sun crossed Belinda's Ascendant in Aries, and the SA Midheaven directed to conjoin her exact natal Mercury–Jupiter conjunction. For an actress, these Solar Arcs could speak of emergence, prominence and publicity – being noticed, speaking up or appearing in the newspapers. At this time, Giblin was asked to replace Rowena Wallace, the lead actress who played the infamous 'Pat the Rat' in the drama series *Sons and Daughters*. With the Sun directed onto her Aries Ascendant, it put Belinda in the spotlight (Sun), and the role became the TV sensation of the year. Her role as a scheming, quintessential soap opera 'bitch' (Aries) was front-page news in every Australian tabloid: her professional name (SA MC) was big (Jupiter) news (Mercury). And although many high-profile theatre roles followed, it is this TV role that is most associated (MC) with this talented, energetic actress.

What happened in **mid 2005** (chart, right), when Mercury–Jupiter (some twenty degrees behind the Sun) directed over her natal Ascendant? Belinda, who had begun teaching acting, began to diversify and she created a successful parallel career as a **corporate trainer** and executive coach (SA MC was conjunct the natal Sun, too). She began using her acting skills to help teach CEOs how to communicate effectively (Mercury–Jupiter).

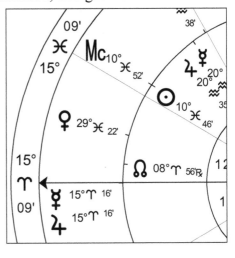

Mercury–Jupiter originally spoke of enormous tabloid attention and a TV role that would make her internationally recognized, but the combination was later linked to teaching and enthusing others and helping executives (Jupiter) articulate themselves (Mercury) – two sides of this versatile planetary pairing.

4.08 • Mel Gibson's First Mutiny

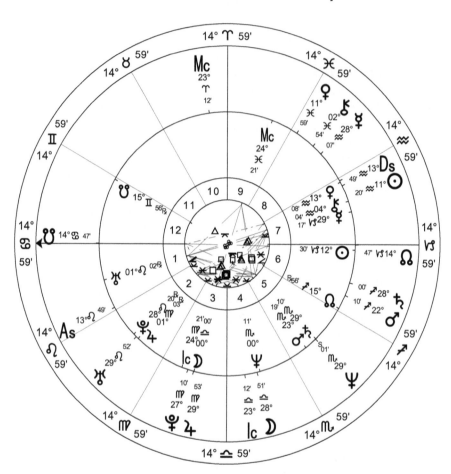

Inner Wheel (natal chart): 3 January 1956 at 16:45 EST
in Peekskill, New York, USA (41N17, 73W55).

Outer Wheel: Solar Arc directions to 4 May 1984.

Data Source: Newspaper announcement, as quoted in the biography
Mel: The Inside Story by Wensley Clarkson; copy on file.

And on to another Australian actor. In **Mel Gibson's** chart, we can see that Jupiter is at 1° Virgo (in his 2nd House of money and resources) and it is 29° away from the Moon at 0° Libra (in his 3rd House of communication). So, at around the age of 29, Gibson would have had Solar Arc (SA) Jupiter conjunct natal Moon.

At 29, we should expect to see an event in his life that has the astrological meaning of Jupiter – expansion, travel, opportunity – affecting the area of his life linked to the Moon. For an actor, the Moon is linked to rapport with an audience, and the Moon has associations with, among other things, imagination, instinct, intuition and water. (And, of course, there's a pivotal transit around the age of 29, too: the Saturn Return.)

Jupiter reached Gibson's Moon by Solar Arc in mid-1984 when his nautical film with Anthony Hopkins, *The Bounty*, was released (**4 May 1984**) and when he was finishing production of his first Hollywood film, *The River*, which premiered that December. Both films promised more than they delivered (Jupiter) but the latter was his first Hollywood film and opened many doors (Jupiter), making Gibson a sought-after acting commodity (the Moon often describes how an actor has his finger on the public pulse). Note, too, the watery/lunar film themes when his Moon was activated.

Natally, Pluto is positioned at 28° Leo in the 2nd House (this out-of-sign conjunction suggests the potential for enormous earning power, and is shared by Bill Gates). Pluto is approximately three degrees earlier than Jupiter, so three years after SA Jupiter conjunct his natal Moon, SA Pluto made a conjunction to that Moon. With Gibson now a Hollywood actor, you might have expected to hear about a powerful money deal (Pluto in the 2nd) that would affect his personal popularity (Moon, the ruler of his Ascendant) and make him a bankable star (Pluto–2nd). And perhaps it would also trigger the start of a partnership (Moon in Libra at 0°).

In fact, Solar Arc Pluto exactly conjunct his natal Moon in late February 1987, and this was days before the release of *Lethal Weapon* (6 March). The film was the first of a series of highly-successful 'buddy cop' partnership (Libra) movies that made Gibson an international star and hugely wealthy. The four *Lethal* films he made (between 1987 and 1998) grossed $955 million.

Actors often win jobs that are already 'written' in their charts; roles that appear to have been scripted for them. Through their

4.09 • Mel Gibson's Fall From Grace

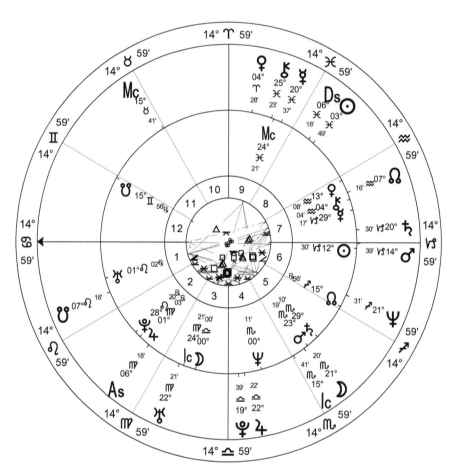

Inner Wheel (natal chart): 3 January 1956 at 16:45 EST
in Peekskill, New York, USA (41N17, 73W55).

Outer Wheel: Solar Arc directions to 29 July 2006.

Data Source: Newspaper announcement, as quoted in the biography
Mel: The Inside Story by Wensley Clarkson; copy on file.

acting roles, they can use the various 'characters' shown in their horoscopes in ways that the rest of us can't. Acting provides them with an opportunity to play out key themes and dynamics as well as Solar Arc directions in their charts. When **Mel Gibson** filmed *Mad Max* (in November–December 1977), SA Uranus in Leo had reached a square to natal Mars (which is conjunct Saturn in Scorpio). The film was set in a dystopian, apocalyptic future (Uranus) where law and order are beginning to break down (Uranus) due to energy (Mars) shortages (Saturn). *Mad Max* is a story of murder and vengeance and Gibson played the leather-clad, post-apocalyptic survivor (all are descriptive of Mars in Scorpio).

With Pisces on his natal MC, Gibson has a reputation as a chameleon – he is able to convey a myriad of emotions and roles. (Pisces is also linked to religion and addiction, and Gibson struggled privately and publicly with alcohol for many years.) Many of his films have had Pisces themes. He's played a man paranoid about the 'system' (*Conspiracy Theory*); a man with child-like vulnerability (*Tim*); an advertising executive who hears women's voices (*What Women Want*); a former priest convinced of extraterrestrial life (*Signs*); a desperate father searching for a lost child (*Ransom*); and a drug dealer trying to go straight (*Tequila Sunrise*). His most controversial project was as director of *The Passion of the Christ*, which began shooting in November 2002, when his Solar Arc Sun left Aquarius after 30 years and moved into the first degree of Pisces (a sign linked to Christianity, crucifixion and 'fishermen'). Gibson's natal T-square of Mercury opposite Uranus both square Neptune can suggest speech that is both provocative and misinterpreted. When the film was released (March 2004), SA Mars was on his Sun.

With a Capricorn Sun on his Descendant, the Moon in Libra and Cancer rising, the focus is on the anchors of relationship and family. Gibson found stability and structure (Capricorn) through his religious 28-year marriage. But when SA Mars (natally in Scorpio) reached 14° Capricorn, he made some anti-Semitic remarks while being arrested for DUI. This led to much negative publicity and, due to the drinking, he and his wife separated the following day (on **29 July 2006**). It began a five-year divorce battle (Mars) which would be one of the costliest in Hollywood history. (By transit, Saturn was at 13° Leo opposite natal Venus in the 7th, and Pluto was at 24° Sagittarius, making a square to his MC–IC axis.)

4.10 • Kylie Minogue's Loco Year

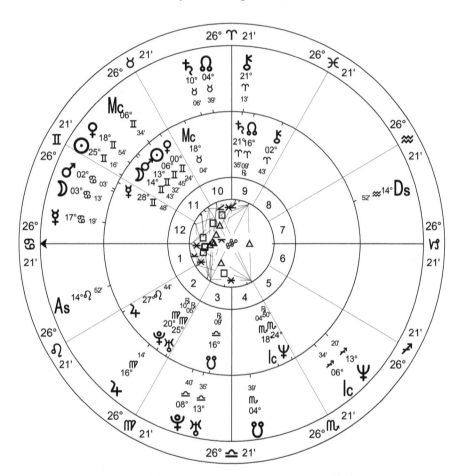

Inner Wheel (natal chart): 28 May 1968 at 11:00 AEST
in Melbourne, Victoria, Australia (37S49, 144E58).

Outer Wheel: Solar Arc directions to 1 October 1987.

Data Source: From a magazine article by Val Hopgood in *Women's Weekly
Magazine* (May 1997). Same in *Kylie Confidential* (2002) by Sean Smith.

One international export that everyone cherishes is petite pop titan **Kylie Minogue**, a marketing marvel with a talent for reinvention. This is aptly described by MC ruler Venus at 0° Gemini opposite Neptune, and five planets in Gemini (two of which square Pluto).

After some early bit parts and joining the Australian drama series, *Neighbours*, in 1986, Minogue's success went through the roof in 1987: a Logie for *Neighbours*; the top-selling Australian single of the decade ('The Loco-Motion' in July, when TR Jupiter moved into her 10th House); and a recording contract with music producers Stock, Aitken and Waterman (October 1987), which led to enormous pop success in the UK. It's no surprise that in late 1987/early 1988, her Solar Arc Midheaven (reputation, status) was on her natal Sun in Gemini – crowning her dual (Gemini) high-profile career as an actress and singer. In addition, the SA Sun was making a square to Uranus; it was an exciting, whirlwind time. The bi-wheel opposite is set for **1 October 1987.**

Later, Kylie's work with Nick Cave (released October 1995) gave her career a new credibility and diversity. Solar Arc Saturn – the planet of respect and gravitas – was on her MC in Taurus, and her SA MC was approaching her Moon in versatile Gemini.

Appropriately, when SA Mercury (her Sun-sign ruler) moved to 0° Leo (the sign in which her Jupiter is positioned), she had the greatest commercial success of her career: 'Can't Get You Out of My Head' (September 2001); it also coincided with a time when the SA Ascendant crossed over Jupiter in Leo in the 2nd.

Kylie's career came to a halt on **17 May 2005** (bi-wheel, right) – an enforced 18-month retirement following a diagnosis of **breast cancer**. Solar Arcs for this event (and others) suggest her birth time is a few minutes earlier: SA Pluto would have been square to the Ascendant, and SA Ascendant at 0° Virgo. (TR Saturn was approaching her Ascendant, TR Neptune square her MC, and TR Pluto conjunct SA IC.)

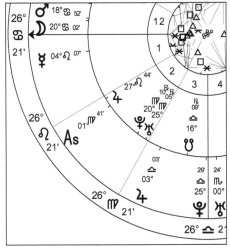

4.11 • Didn't She Almost Have it All?

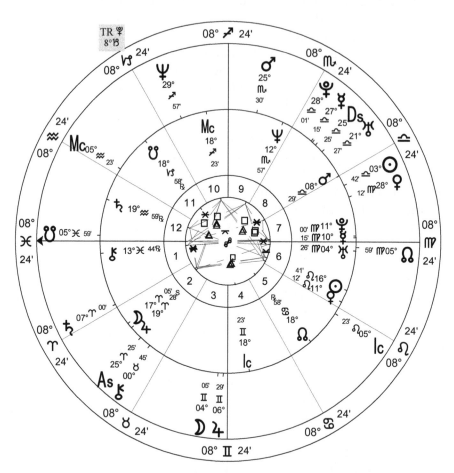

Inner Wheel (natal chart): 9 August 1963 at 20:55 EDT
in Newark, New Jersey, USA (40N44, 74W10).

Outer Wheel: Solar Arc directions to 11 February 2012.

Data Source: Birth certificate, as obtained by Kathryn Farmer; copy on file.

On **11 February 2012**, singer extraordinaire **Whitney Houston** was found dead in The Beverly Hilton hotel. She was 48. The Los Angeles coroner concluded that she had died from a cocaine overdose and a massive heart attack, which resulted in the accidental drowning that took place in her hotel bathtub. Whitney was on a comeback trail and, although fans were supportive, the press were quick to note how her voice had deteriorated and many felt that her return was too soon and too rushed by her record company.

Interestingly, at the time of Whitney's death, transiting Neptune was back at 0°18' Pisces, where it had been at the time of Amy Winehouse's passing on 23 July 2011. An outer planet at 0° gives us some major hints and warnings of what the transit will bring in the years ahead. Both singers had shaped their generations and had fought very public, on-going battles with addiction.

There were physical 'warnings' in her chart: SA Moon was square to Uranus in Virgo in the 6th (a need to change one's bad habits and health), and Chiron had moved to 0° Taurus in the 2nd House (suggesting that the body, particularly the throat, is prone to 'wounding' and in need of extra care). Pluto was also involved in two sesquiquadrates: one to Chiron and one from the Ascendant.

It was the end of the Houston era, which ran the gamut from elegant, sophisticated glamour to seedy, drug-induced stupors. SA Neptune had reached 29° Sagittarius in her 10th House. It had started so promisingly thirty years before, as SA Neptune ingressed into Sagittarius (her MC sign) in 1981. That November, an 18-year-old Whitney – beautiful and talented but already using drugs recreationally – had become one of the first African-American models to grace the cover of a national magazine (*Seventeen*). She seemed to have it all.

Although I've never seen an astrological aspect that could be an irrefutable or definitive significator of death (or its prediction), TR Pluto was squaring Whitney's Mars in the 8th House – a transiting period that would suggest a fight for survival. (Of course, it could also be symbolized by 8th House money conflicts, lawsuits or sexual obsessions, among other things.)

Astrologers observe that charts 'live on' and are activated at times of significance after the person has died. It is the charts of those who are left behind to grieve and deal with the loss of a loved one that tend to show transits and directions associated with death.

4.12 • Bobby Brown Buries His Daughter

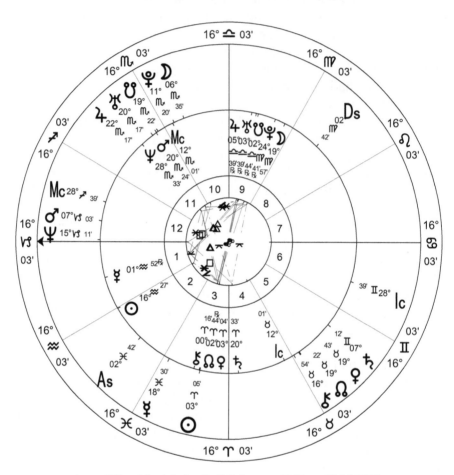

Inner Wheel (natal chart): 5 February 1969 at 05:21 EST
in Boston, Massachusetts, USA (42N22, 71W04).

Outer Wheel: Solar Arc directions to 1 August 2015.

Data Source: Birth certificate, as obtained by Frank Clifford
(same for Bobbi Kristina Brown).

Opposite Page: Inner: Bobbi Kristina Brown, 4 March 1993 at 11:38 EST in
Livingston, New Jersey, USA (40N48, 74W19). Outer: SA to 11 February 2012.

Activity in the chart of Whitney's 18-year-old daughter, **Bobbi Kristina Brown**, is also telling. **At the time of her mother's death** (bi-wheel on right), TR Neptune's ingress into Pisces would be profound for a girl with the Sun, Mercury and the MC in this sign. Solar Arc Pluto had reached 14° Sagittarius, exactly squaring her Sun in Pisces. It must have been an extremely dark and overwhelming time for the

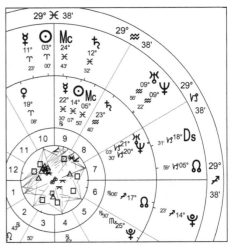

inconsolable girl. Her SA Mars (natally in Cancer in the 1st) was at 29° Cancer (being squared by TR Saturn at 29° Libra), suggesting the end of her role as caretaker for her mother (and vice versa).

Transiting Uranus was approaching a conjunction with Bobbi's SA Sun at 3° Aries and Whitney's SA Sun at 3° Libra. Interestingly, Bobbi's father Bobby Brown has natal Venus at 3° Aries opposite natal Uranus at 3° Libra – these planets had Solar Arc directed to 16° Taurus–Scorpio in square to his (and Whitney's) natal Sun, tying in the charts and the tragic event. At the time of his ex-wife's death, his Sun had directed to 29° Pisces (and his Ascendant to 29° Aquarius) – for father Bobby, it was truly the end of an era.

On 31 January 2015, Whitney and Bobby's daughter was found unresponsive in a bathtub, in an event eerily similar to the circumstances of her mother's death. Bobbi Kristina was placed in a medically-induced coma and died on 26 July 2015. The event and subsequent passing of his daughter were devastating to **Bobby Brown**. During those six months, TR Pluto was hovering near his Ascendant, and TR Uranus was square both and then conjunct Saturn in the 4th. By Solar Arc, Chiron had just moved into the 5th (children) and squared his Sun (role as father).

Bobby's SA Uranus was conjunct natal Mars, and his SA Sun reached 3° Aries (see above) and conjunct 5th House ruler Venus when daughter Bobbi was laid to rest on **1 August 2015** (the date used for the bi-wheel, opposite). Both SA Pluto and SA Neptune were within one degree of the MC and Ascendant, respectively.

4.13 • No Longer in Vogue

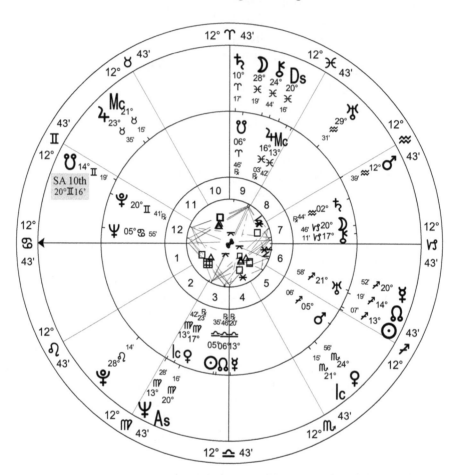

Inner Wheel (natal chart): 29 September 1903 at 22:30 LST (-0:09:20)
in Paris, France (48N52, 2E20).

Outer Wheel: Solar Arc directions to 1 April 1971.

Data Source: Birth certificate, as obtained by Marc Brun.
Date and place confirmed by Sy Scholfield.

Who could forget **Diana Vreeland**, the legendary, formidable *Vogue* editor and arbiter elegantiarum – and recall her famous parrot-colouring make-up and her cigar-store-Indian face? Vreeland's luminaries are the classy, chic combo of Libra–Capricorn, and Neptune–Ascendant and Jupiter–MC in Pisces reveal the influence she had as the 'High Priestess of Allure' and 'Empress of Fashion'.

Growing up, she found her father undemonstrative, while her free-spirited mother hunted rhino and treated Diana as the family's ugly duckling. After a nomadic childhood, they settled in New York when Diana was 10. The young girl found solace in dance and was later entranced by the emerging fashions of the Roaring Twenties. She married Thomas Reed Vreeland on 1 March 1924 (as SA Descendant conjunct her Saturn, and SA Uranus conjunct Descendant). She was devastated by his death on 3 August 1966 (SA Saturn opposite Sun).

Vreeland wrote her first 'Why Don't You' column for *Harper's Bazaar* in August 1936 ('Why don't you … wash your blond child's hair in dead champagne, as they do in France?' she once advised at the height of the Great Depression). Her message was pure Jupiter–MC aristocratic hauteur (in Pisces opposite Venus in Virgo): 'Fashion must be the most intoxicating release from the banality of the world.' Always an original (Uranus and Pluto form a Grand Cross with Venus and Jupiter), she was ferocious in her determination to give readers something 'they never knew they wanted'.

'Exaggeration is my only reality,' said the eminently quotable visionary with Jupiter on a Pisces MC. 'The bikini is the most important thing since the atom bomb,' she declared. For Vreeland, fantasy was a pulse that kept fashion alive. She shaped fashion consciousness (her Ascendant conjuncts the USA's 4 July Sun) and put the famous in her magazines. Mannequins like Lauren Bacall and Twiggy became personalities, and personalities like Streisand and Cher became mannequins.

Vreeland moved to *Vogue* as editor-in-chief in January 1963. It coincided with the birth of 1960s hedonism, which indulged her extravagant nature. She was fired suddenly in **spring 1971** (as SA 10th hit Pluto, SA Sun squared MC, SA Neptune opposed MC, SA Mercury in the 6th opposed Pluto, and TR Saturn conjunct SA MC); broken, she was down but not out. Twelve months later (SA Mercury conjunct Uranus), she rose from the ashes and took on a new role at the Metropolitan Museum of Art's Costume Institute.

4.14 • Fashion Killer

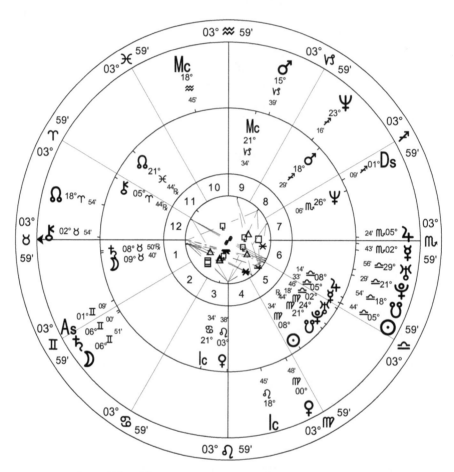

Inner Wheel (natal chart): 31 August 1969 at 21:41 PDT
in National City, California, USA (32N41, 117W06).

Outer Wheel: Solar Arc directions to 15 July 1997.

Data Source: Birth certificate, as quoted by Lois Rodden.

Additional Data: Gianni Versace, 2 December 1946 at 06:00 MET in
Reggio di Calabria, Italy (38N06, 15E39). Data from birth certificate,
as quoted by Grazia Bordoni.

The shocking, high-profile murder of celebrity designer Gianni Versace at the hands of **Andrew Cunanan** occurred around 08:44 on **15 July 1997** outside Versace's South Beach mansion in Miami, with Venus rising in Leo exactly opposite Jupiter setting in Aquarius. Both victim and killer were born with Mars out of bounds at 18° Sagittarius and the following interaspects:

Versace	**Cunanan**
Ascendant 27° Scorpio	Neptune 26° Scorpio
Chiron 2° Scorpio	Descendant 3° Scorpio
Eris 5° Aries; Neptune 10° Libra	Chiron 5° Aries; Mer–Jup 5-8° Libra

In addition, Cunanan's Sun is on Versace's MC at 9° Virgo. This is particularly apt: their names/reputations have been inextricably linked since the crime, which occurred seven weeks before the Solar Eclipse at 9° Virgo (coinciding with the deaths of Princess Diana and Mother Teresa). The SA Sun of Versace's life partner, Antonio D'Amico, had directed to 9° Pisces at the time of the murder.

Cunanan was on the 'Ten Most Wanted' list, having just murdered a handful of ex-lovers and other men before he reached Florida. Biographers have suggested Cunanan was a narcissistic sociopath who pursued older, wealthy men for the privileges of high society to which he felt entitled (note MC ruler Saturn conjuncts the Moon and Ascendant in Taurus, and squares Ascendant ruler Venus in Leo).

Eight days after Versace's murder, Cunanan committed suicide in a Miami house boat, surrounded by police and the world's media. In July 1997, TR Jupiter retrograded back over Cunanan's Solar Arc MC, and Solar Arc Sun had reached the degree (5° Libra) of his natal Mercury–Chiron opposition. Additional transits and Solar Arcs – including TR Saturn at 20° Aries square MC–IC, and SA Chiron–Mercury aligning with his ASC–DSC axis – suggest his birth time could be a few minutes earlier than stated on his certificate.

Versace's sister Donatella has natal Mercury opposite Saturn in Scorpio, both square Pluto, and 3rd House ruler Moon square Mars in Gemini (which can reflect her powerful brother and his untimely murder). At the time, SA Saturn (ruler of her MC) was at 29° Sagittarius in the 8th conjunct her North Node, and TR Pluto was square SA MC. Exactly a year later, having taken over the House of Versace, she mounted her first couture show as SA Saturn moved into Capricorn (where her MC is placed).

4.15 • Entering The Twilight Zone

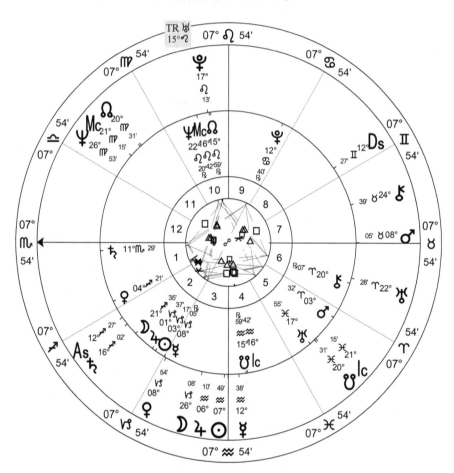

Inner Wheel (natal chart): 25 December 1924 at 03:07 EST
in Syracuse, New York, USA (43N03, 76W09).

Outer Wheel: Solar Arc directions to 24 November 1958.

Data Source: Birth certificate, as obtained by Glen Olson; copy on file.

The Twilight Zone was a seminal show on American TV, considered the most influential sci-fi anthology series of all time. Its 156 eerie episodes fused science-fiction, fantasy and metaphysics with a brand of paranormal and psychological horror.

The show was created and hosted by **Rod Serling**. The information from his recently traced birth certificate produces a chart with Saturn rising in Scorpio, and Neptune on the MC – both apt placements considering the themes of his best known show. Interestingly, Serling has no planets in Air, his chart being mainly Fire and Earth. His Sun is conjunct both Jupiter and a retrograde Mercury in Capricorn – descriptive of his adventurous, creative explorations. (Mercury retrograde is found so often in the charts of gifted thinkers and wordsmiths that we can surmise that this position reflects an ability for divergent thinking.)

When Serling moved into television writing, he became known as the 'angry young man' of Hollywood – a pugnacious writer clashing with his bosses, censors and sponsors (note the Mars–Saturn signature, which includes three Capricorn planets in square to Mars in Aries). Before *The Twilight Zone*, his Mercury in Capricorn (disposited by Saturn rising in Scorpio) had already 'shown up' in the titles of his two Emmy Award winning teleplays, *Patterns* (1955) and *Requiem for a Heavyweight* (shown on 11 October 1956, as transiting Uranus reached his 10th Equal House cusp).

A time travel TV pilot, 'The Time Element', was Serling's pitch for a sci-fi series. Serling knew that through allegory he could explore social and moral issues (Capricorn) and slip past the 1950 TV censors (Mercury opposite Pluto). It aired on **24 November 1958** (with transiting Uranus conjunct MC, and Solar Arc Pluto conjunct MC) to overwhelmingly positive reviews and CBS got in touch and commissioned *The Twilight Zone*. When Pluto directs over the MC, it can transform the public life and overshadow past and future accomplishments. With Scorpio rising and Mercury opposite Pluto, the series became a cult and engulfed Serling's life and reputation.

The first season (from 2 October 1959) coincided with Saturn entering Capricorn and heading over Serling's Jupiter–Sun–Mercury conjunction, along with Neptune transiting over his natal Ascendant. Saturn can coincide with times when a lifetime of hard work pays off, while for a writer Neptune transits/directions can reflect a dream manifesting or selling a vision to the masses.

4.16 • When John Met Paul

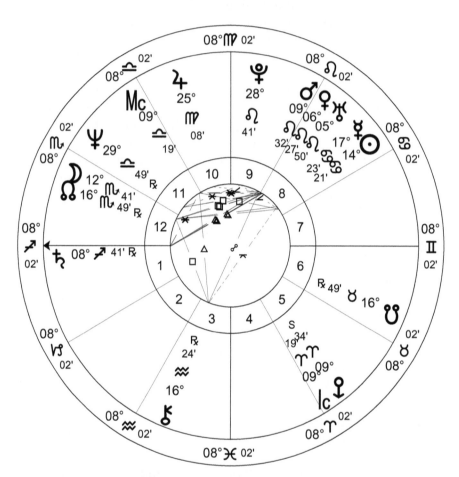

Wheel (meeting chart): 6 July 1957 at 18:48 GDT
in Woolton, Liverpool, England (53N23, 2W52).

Data Source: A speculative time from a highly detailed biography by
Jim O'Donnell, *The Day that John Met Paul.*

The charts of first meetings, weddings, company launches – anything – can later be transited and directed, showing developments linked to the original 'birth' of that event.

On **6 July 1957**, 15-year-old **Paul McCartney was introduced to John Lennon** in the hall of St Peter's Church in Woolton, Liverpool. McCartney impressed Lennon with his guitar-playing and was invited to join John's band, the Quarrymen. Three years later, this band would be renamed the Beatles and go on to change pop music forever.

Astrologer Paul F Newman wrote a fascinating article, 'Lennon Meets McCartney' (in *The Astrological Journal*, May 2007), which focuses on the meeting chart's angular Saturn, lists the Saturn-inspired titles that dominate the Beatles' catalogue, and analyses the pair's composite horoscope. But here, I'd like to look at the meeting chart's creative and fractious elements, and consider key transits and Solar Arcs to it.

Lennon and McCartney's musical marriage is, of course, one of the most celebrated in music history. John once said, 'Paul was the first love of my life, Yoko was the second.' The chart is steeped in imagination, inspiration and innovation: an emphasis on Water signs (and houses); the Sun as the leading planet (conjunct the asteroid *Lennon* at 15° Cancer); and Venus–Mars–Uranus in the sign of Leo.

But what happened when the fun (Leo) stopped, and the scales tipped (MC in Libra)? Two events are said to have hastened the relationship's demise: Lennon meeting Yoko Ono (7 November 1966, when TR Neptune conjunct SA Moon at 21° Scorpio) and the death of Beatles manager Brian Epstein (on 27 August 1967, ditto). In the chart, MC ruler Venus is trapped between a fertile conjunction of prickly Mars and explosive Uranus in proud Leo, and all three planets square the Moon in jealous Scorpio (interestingly, John and Paul had initially bonded over the early deaths of their mothers).

Eris (a minor planet linked to strife) is on the IC and would suggest deep-down feelings of envy or resentment, as well as McCartney's later struggles with Lennon's warrior widow, Yoko Ono. (The chart's Pluto–IC line goes through Ono's birthplace of Tokyo.)

Although I'd rectify the time to a few minutes earlier, this meeting chart still responds remarkably well to forecasting and also makes links to the charts of the duo's wives. Yoko Ono's Ascendant

4.17 • An Autograph, a Gun and a Tragedy

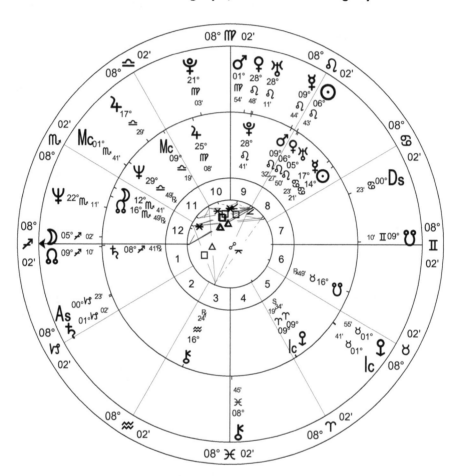

Wheel (meeting chart): 6 July 1957 at 18:48 GDT
in Woolton, Liverpool, England (53N23, 2W52).

Outer Wheel: Solar Arc directions to 8 December 1980.

Additional Data: Yoko Ono, 18 February 1933 at 20:30 JST in Tokyo, Japan
(35N42, 139E46). Data from Ono to Roger Elliott.

Mark Chapman, 10 May 1955 at 19:30 CST in Fort Worth, Texas, USA (32N44,
97W19). Data from hospital records, as obtained by Darrell Martinie.

is 8° Libra (and the asteroid *YokoOno* is at 9° Sagittarius near the chart's Saturn and her natal Moon at 11°), while Linda McCartney (24 September 1941) has her Venus at 11° Scorpio. Cynthia Lennon (10 September 1939) has a Moon that's most likely in early Leo (and Jupiter at 6° Aries). Even Heather Mills (12 January 1968), McCartney's 'trouble and strife' from 2002–8, is in there: her Venus is at 12° Sagittarius, while her Saturn at 6° Aries is on the meeting chart's Eris and IC.

The Beatles' first single was released on 5 October 1962, when transiting Neptune hit the chart's Moon at 12° Scorpio. On 31 December 1970, with SA Neptune conjunct that Moon (and SA Jupiter at 8° Libra), McCartney moved to dissolve (Neptune) the Beatles' partnership. For much of 1970, as the members broke up from the band and began their own independent projects, transiting Uranus (separation, breaks) crossed the meeting chart's MC.

When **Lennon was gunned down** outside his Manhattan residence just after 22:50 on **8 December 1980**, TR Jupiter and Saturn were conjunct at 7°–8° Libra (conjunct the meeting chart's MC) and SA Chiron was squaring Saturn. The meeting chart's Solar Arc Ascendant had moved to 0° Capricorn. (As I think the original 1957 meeting was a few minutes earlier, I would speculate that the murder took place as SA Ascendant stood at 29° Sagittarius, which then led to a 'change of script' when it moved sign for the first time into the solitary, 'hard reality' sign of Capricorn.)

Mark Chapman, the assassin, has natal Mercury at 8° Gemini and his relocated Ascendant in Manhattan is 8° Sagittarius (both link to the meeting chart and Lennon's horoscope). Chapman's Sun–Saturn opposition sits across the meeting chart's nodal axis, too. Widow Yoko Ono, who'd had TR Uranus on her natal Ascendant when the Beatles broke up, now had TR Uranus at 27° Scorpio on her Solar Arc Ascendant (a Shadow Transit) when her husband was gunned down in front of her. TR Jupiter–Saturn crossed her natal Ascendant.

Lennon had been back in creative mode, and the chart's Leo planets were being activated: SA Sun was at 6° Leo conjunct Venus, with SA Mercury at 9° Leo conjunct Mars (Mercury–Mars is personified in the autograph hunter with a handgun), SA Jupiter square Mercury in the 8th, and SA Venus–Uranus (natally in the 8th) had reached Pluto at 28° Leo (also suggesting the sudden death of Lennon and eliminating any hope of a Lennon–McCartney reunion).

124

4.18 • Fairytale Princess

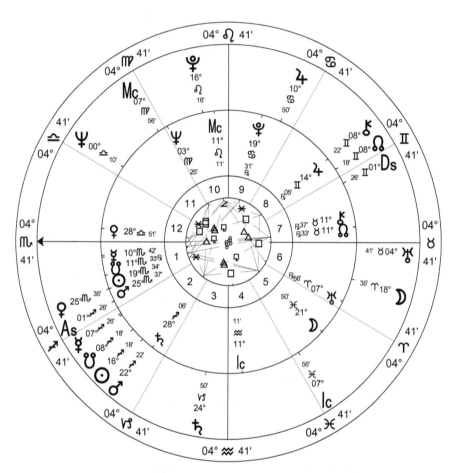

Inner Wheel (natal chart): 12 November 1929 at 05:31 EST
in Philadelphia, Pennsylvania, USA (39N57, 75W10).

Outer Wheel: Solar Arc directions to 19 April 1956.

Data Source: Birth certificate, as obtained by Bob Garner; copy on file.

The ice-blonde, coolly elegant Hollywood star **Grace Kelly** met Prince Rainier of Monaco on 6 May 1955. They married on **19 April 1956** when a series of apt Solar Arc directions occurred. Here are a few, with quick one-line suggested interpretations.

- SA Venus (ruler of the Descendant, natally in Libra conjunct a Scorpio Ascendant) conjuncts natal Mars in Scorpio – the powerful marriage union of Hollywood royalty to the Royal House of Grimaldi.

- SA Uranus (natally in the 6th) conjuncts the natal Descendant in Taurus – Grace's relocation to Monaco and the abrupt end of her film career.

- SA MC in Virgo quincunxes natal Uranus in the 6th in Aries – the sudden change in her daily life and routine; a new role in service to Monaco.

- SA Neptune travelling through the 11th House and entering the sign of Libra (two months before the marriage) – the 'fairytale princess' and a marriage of social functions; the sacrifice of acting ambitions for the partnership. (Note natal Moon in Pisces in the 5th square Saturn.)

- SA Jupiter sits at almost 11° Cancer, which is the degree of her Descendant when relocated to Monte Carlo, Monaco.

The transits/directions occurring at the start of any enterprise will be descriptive of that enterprise and its outcome. It is said that Grace later felt trapped (Uranus) in a marriage of convention and endless, boring social events, and that she longed to return to acting (Neptune). The marriage also ended abruptly with Grace's car crash.

The directions at the time of her death (apparently losing control of her car while having a stroke) are very descriptive: Solar Arc Ascendant just past Saturn in Sagittarius in the 2nd, and directed Mars in the 3rd opposing Pluto (both rulers of her Ascendant). In the last year or so of her husband's life (2004–5), while his health was declining rapidly, Grace's chart was very active: SA Descendant conjunct her natal Pluto, Mars conjunct natal IC, and Neptune conjunct Sun.

4.19 • Tackling the Bullies

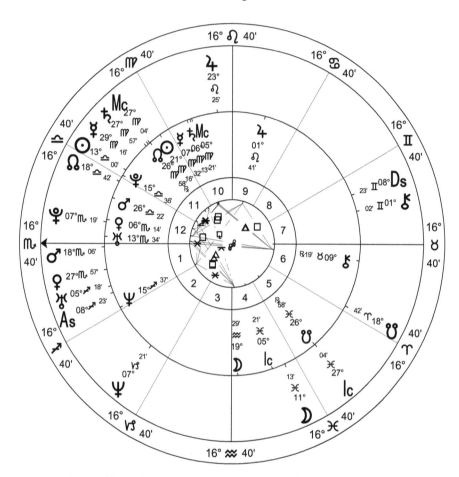

Inner Wheel (natal chart): 14 September 1978 at 12:00 BST
in Northampton, England (52N14, 0W54).

Outer Wheel: Solar Arc directions to 14 November 2000.

Data Source: Hospital record ('12 o'clock midday'), as quoted in
Cohen's autobiography *Carry Me Home*; copy on file.

It's rare for a rugby player to take a stand against homophobia and bullying, but former England rugby union star player **Ben Cohen** did just that by setting up The Ben Cohen StandUp Foundation in May 2011 (as Solar Arc Jupiter was approaching his MC). His chart – with Mercury–Saturn conjunct the MC in Virgo, and Moon in Aquarius square Uranus – reflects a need to speak up against prejudice, discrimination and intolerance. With an elevated Mercury–Saturn, Cohen has also been working to make rugby more accessible to hard-of-hearing players (Cohen is clinically deaf and has suffered from tinnitus since childhood, too).

Back in October 2000, Cohen's family life had been changed irrevocably by bullying. His father was severely beaten when coming to another man's aid in a nightclub. He died a month later, on **14 November 2000**, from a blood clot brought about by his injuries. Ben's chart had Solar Arc Uranus square the MC–IC axis (reflective of the sudden change to his home life and the new course his life would soon go on) and TR Pluto in Sagittarius was square SA Moon at 11° Pisces (Pisces can feel victimized or disenfranchised, and Pluto can move from the powerless to the powerful).

In an interview with *The Mirror* in 2014, Ben spoke of how important this time was for him. 'My father died because he stood up to bullies … Every single thing that has happened to me since is down to that … From that point on I was determined to become the best winger in the world and to win the World Cup. I was, if you like, a man on a mission, driven by anger and emotion … This year we want to use the day to remind people why it's so important to stand up to bullying and share their stories to inspire other people to stand up.'

Charismatic Cohen – a 6'2" powerhouse – began his career in 1996, won the Rugby World Cup as part of the England national team in 2003 and retired in May 2011, having scored 31 tries in 57 Tests. He was married to his childhood sweetheart from 2003 to March 2016, but Cohen fell in love with his *Strictly Come Dancing* partner following his autumn 2013 stint on the TV dance show (he was eliminated in week 9 as TR Saturn crossed his Ascendant). They had a daughter together on 24 June 2016.

His good looks and pro-gay stance have made him a gay icon, and he was inducted into the National Gay and Lesbian Sports Hall of Fame in August 2013.

4.20 • A Bizarre Spectre

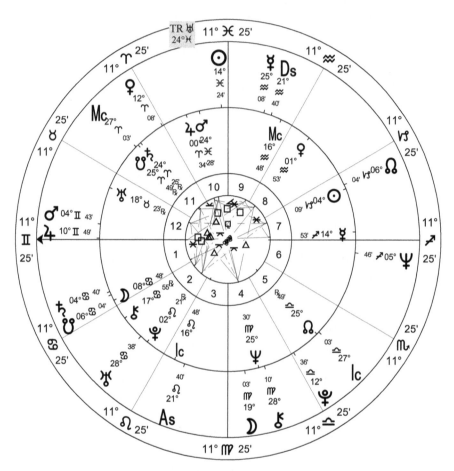

Inner Wheel (natal chart): 26 December 1939 at 14:55 EST
in Prospect Hospital, Bronx, New York, USA (40N51, 73W54).

Outer Wheel: Solar Arc directions to 13 April 2009.

Data Source: Hospital birth certificate, as quoted by Sy Scholfield; copy on file.

The legal trials and tribulations resulting from the behaviour of reclusive music producer and influential auteur **Phil Spector** have, to a large extent, overshadowed his creative achievements, which include his pioneering 'Wall of Sound' production technique and his creation of a myriad of 60s pop classics with orchestral flair for artists such as The Righteous Brothers and Tina Turner (whose Descendant conjuncts Spector's MC).

Professionally, Spector was known to be temperamental and quirky, while privately he was an obsessive, paranoid control freak, exerting dominion over every aspect of his girl group, The Ronettes – particularly the daily life of his wife, 'bad girl' Ronnie Bennett. According to her autobiography, *Be My Baby*, she was imprisoned and mentally abused by Spector, who was fearful of her potential infidelity and autonomy. Spector also had a fondness for Russian roulette, waving loaded guns in people's faces, and got off on other intimidating behaviour (in her book, Ronnie cites the glass coffin in the basement prepared for her if she ever decided to leave him).

Ronnie did escape in 1972 and Spector had a near fatal car crash on 31 March 1974 (SA Mars at 29° Aries sesquiquadrate Mercury), which forced the eremitic producer into further hiding (SA Saturn at 29° Taurus in the 12th). Some years later, his controlling behaviour reached a crescendo. Spector murdered actress Lana Clarkson at his home on 3 February 2003. Indicted on 20 November 2003 and ordered to stand trial in September 2004, the legal soap opera went on for years, often proving shocking, salacious and bizarre. It detracted from the horrific crime committed and shifted focus away from the actress that Spector had killed in cold blood.

The first attempt to convict (25 April 2007, as SA North Node conjunct his 7th House Sun) ended in a mis-trial on 26 September 2007, while the second resulted in a conviction of second-degree murder on **13 April 2009**. This second trial – some six years after the murder – occurred when Solar Arc Saturn opposed natal Sun (time to pay the price of his actions) and both were squared by a non-negotiable transit from Pluto. From evidence at the trial, it seems Spector suffered from delusions of persecution: note the distortion of Jupiter conjunct Mars in Pisces, which is closely opposite Neptune. This tight opposition was triggered when he was found guilty: transiting Mars and Uranus in the sky conjunct his natal Mars. Spector is serving a prison sentence of 19 years to life.

4.21 • Only in America

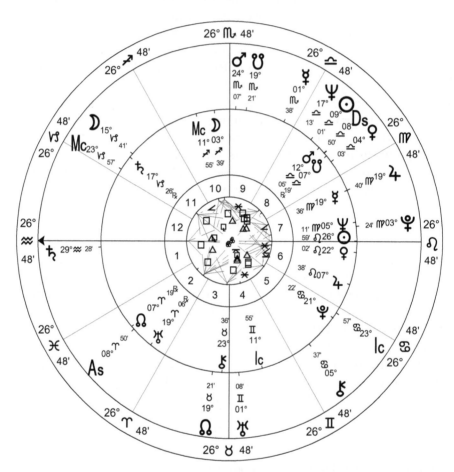

Inner Wheel (natal chart): 20 August 1931 at 19:15 EST
in Cleveland, Ohio, USA (41N30, 81W42).

Outer Wheel: Solar Arc directions to 30 October 1974.

Data Source: Birth certificate, as obtained by Frank Clifford; copy on file.

Additional Data: James Earl Jones, 17 January 1931 at 06:05 CST in
Arkabutla, Mississippi, USA (34N42, 90W07). Data from his autobiography,
Voices and Silences; copy on file.

Flamboyance and the talent for publicity and self-promotion (getting one's name 'out there') are linked to Jupiter and the 9th House (and, to a lesser extent, the sign of Leo), and gaining an audience/following is shown by the 5th House and its ruler.

Larger-than-life boxing promoter **Don King** has MC ruler Jupiter in Leo trine the Jupiter-ruled Moon and MC in Sagittarius. The lunar link also speaks of his much-publicized flamboyant patriotism, as well as the huge revenue from pay-per-view fights screened into televisions in homes across the world. In King's case, he's promoting his 'other half' – his boxer – so the Descendant/7th House should be more active than the 5th. The 7th House ruler (Sun) is in Leo on the Descendant (conjunct 9th House ruler Venus).

In the early 70s, King convinced Muhammad Ali to box at a charity exhibition (on 28 August 1972, as TR Neptune conjunct King's Moon), and the pair worked together over the next few years. King was the promoter of 'The Rumble in the Jungle' (**30 October 1974**) and 'The Thrilla in Manila' (1 October 1975), two of Ali's most legendary fights.

It was the Rumble in 1974, when Solar Arc Jupiter conjunct King's Mercury in the 7th (and SA Pluto squared his Moon), that established King's reputation as a boxing promoter, deal-maker and hustler (Mercury–Jupiter) on the world stage – it remains one of the most culturally influential (Pluto) sporting events of the twentieth century. In the months that followed, TR Pluto conjunct his SA Sun, and TR Neptune crossed his natal MC.

King had a colourful early life, working scandalous Neptune square Moon–MC to interesting effect: after quitting college, he ran an illegal bookmaking operation and was later linked to two homicides. King was convicted of second degree murder (reduced to non-negligent manslaughter) for the second homicide, and served almost four years. Since then, he has been dogged by various controversies, including alleged jury tampering, tax evasion, insurance fraud, lawsuits from boxers and links to organized crime.

King allegedly coined the phrase 'Only in America' and is known for his promotion of all things American (his MC is on the USA's Sibly Ascendant, and his Ascendant is on the USA's Moon). Both Paul Winfield (22 May 1939, Sun opposite King's Moon) and James Earl Jones (Venus conjunct King's MC) have portrayed characters based on, or inspired by, the extravagant escapades of Don King.

4.22 • Passing with Honour

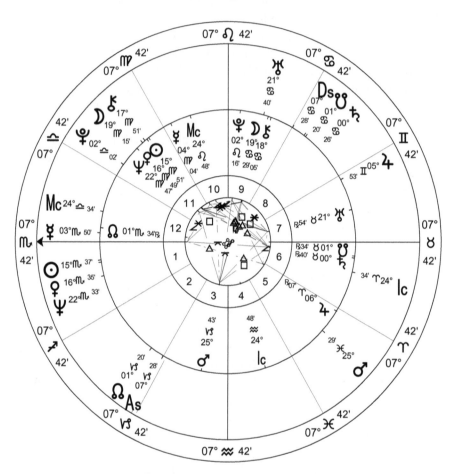

Inner Wheel (natal chart): 9 September 1939 at 11:55 BST
in Glasgow, Scotland (55N53, 4W15).

Outer Wheel: Solar Arc directions to 6 March 2000.

Data Source: Birth certificate, as quoted by Caroline Gerard.

Additional Data: Julie Walters, 22 February 1950 at 15:00 GMT in Birmingham,
England (52N30, 1W50). Data from Walters to David Fisher, quoting her mother.

Marie Stubbs drew much attention and acclaim for being the headmistress who reformed St George's Roman Catholic Secondary School in London. Prior to her arrival, St George's had suffered from poor student attendance and performance, as well as theft and violence. In addition, the faculty and student body were still in shock following the murder of the previous headmaster Philip Lawrence at the school's gates on 8 December 1995. (Lawrence, born 21 August 1947, has his Sun–Mercury–Venus on Stubbs's Leo MC.)

Marie's chart reveals a determined, no-nonsense agenda and a stance of zero tolerance: Pluto squares a Scorpio Ascendant, and Pluto and the tough–tender Cancer Moon oppose Mars in Capricorn in the 3rd. For a teacher, it's interesting that she has no planets in Air. Four planets in Virgo speak of the clean-up job she excelled in, and her Sun–Venus in Virgo philosophy is clear in her statement: 'Every child should be intrinsically valued.' Although initially branded 'relentlessly optimistic', *The Scotsman* later said she possessed 'the sort of optimism that tends to become a self-fulfilling prophecy' (5th House ruler Jupiter in Aries trine Pluto in the 9th).

Lady Stubbs had retired around her 60th birthday back in September 1999 (as a New Moon fell on her birthday/Sun, and Solar Arc Saturn stood at 29° Gemini) but some five months later was asked to take over and restructure St George's. Starting the job on **6 March 2000**, Stubbs was given three and a half terms to do the almost impossible: turn the school's fortunes around. Over those seventeen months, she would face opposition from staff (three resigned in July 2000) and belligerence or, at best, indifference from students. Yet, with charisma, energy, old-fashioned discipline, a numinous ethos and a hard-working team, she did what she set out to accomplish – and in the process demonstrated that good people can do extraordinary things when they make small but instrumental (Virgo) changes to the system. During her tenure, Solar Arc Midheaven in Libra was squaring natal Mars in tough, disciplined Capricorn in the 3rd House of schooling. A very apt direction.

A TV dramatization, *Ahead of the Class*, aired 30 January 2005 with Julie Walters as Stubbs. Walters has a natal Moon at 6° Taurus and Ascendant at 8° Leo, connecting tightly to the degrees of Stubbs' houses, and Walters' Saturn is on Stubbs's Sun–Venus conjunction. Walters, who described it as one of her favourite roles, filmed it when her SA Uranus reached the degree of Stubbs's MC at 24° Leo.

134

4.23 • Roy Orbison's Triple Tragedies

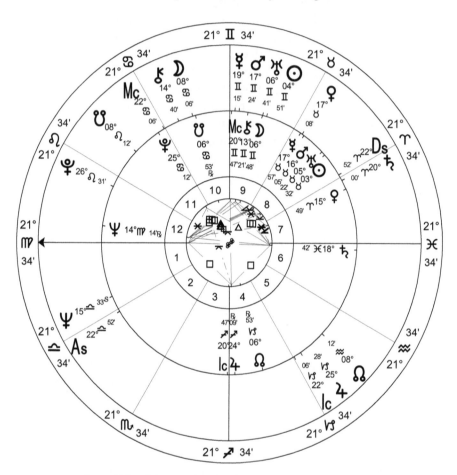

Inner Wheel (natal chart): 23 April 1936 at 15:50 CST
in Vernon, Texas, USA (34N09, 99W16).

Outer Wheel: Solar Arc directions to 16 September 1968.

Data Source: Handwritten note from birth registry to Ed Steinbrecher; copy on
file. (Orbison's family website, www.royorbison.com, states a time of 15:30.)

With Neptune rising and chart ruler Mercury in Taurus, **Roy Orbison** possessed a mysteriously soft and vulnerable voice. The Texas-born singer also had a soaring, symphonic three-octave range and is rightly lauded as one of the great male singers of the modern era.

But looking further at his birth chart, the unaspected duet of Sun–Uranus in Taurus and two further planets in the 8th speak of the shattering family losses off-stage that impacted workaholic Orbison's life in the 1960s.

The first major event was the discovery of his wife Claudette's infidelity. The **couple divorced** in **November 1964** (bi-wheel, right, is set for 1 November) – as Mars directed to Chiron in Gemini, and Saturn directed to his Venus in the 7th (and transiting Uranus squared Solar Arc Mars). But they reconciled ten months later. On 6 June 1966 (perhaps the most inauspicious of days), Claudette died in a motorcycle accident. Transiting Uranus and Pluto were conjunct at 15° Virgo and making a square to Solar Arc Mars (ruler of the 8th and placed there natally).

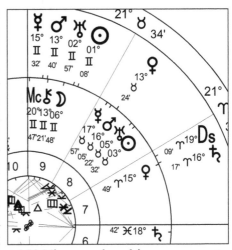

Then, two years later, on **16 September 1968**, his Tennessee house caught fire, claiming his two eldest sons. The chart for this event (opposite) shows a set of dramatic Solar Arcs that reflect the loss of his children and the house fire: SA Uranus conjunct natal Moon; SA Saturn, ruler of the 5th, approaching the 8th House; SA Jupiter in the 5th opposite Pluto. By transit, Pluto was on his Ascendant. At the same time, Orbison was experiencing SA Neptune opposite Venus – a new love emerged just a few days before the tragedy. He married Barbara six months later as the Neptune–Venus aspect became exact and SA Venus directed to join Mercury.

Interest and hits dried up in the 1970s, but the film *Blue Velvet* revived Orbison's career upon its release in September 1986. Solar Arc Sun moved over his Equal 10th House cusp and SA Moon conjunct Pluto, coinciding with the resurrection of his career.

4.24 • Jerry Springer is Elected to the Cincinnati City Council

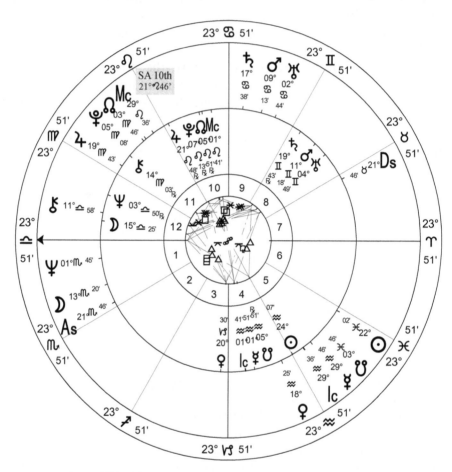

Inner Wheel (natal chart): 13 February 1944 at 23:45 GWT
in Highgate, London, England (51N34, 0W10).

Outer Wheel: Solar Arc directions to 1 December 1971.

Data Source: From him to Frank Clifford.

Jerry Springer is best known as the host/ringmaster of *The Jerry Springer Show*, the violent, confrontational and infamous 'talk show', which has been on air from 30 September 1991 to the present day. But he has also had a varied career as a liberal politician, mayor and news anchor.

Springer was born in wartime London and some of his relatives were murdered in the Holocaust. In January 1949, when TR Neptune reached his Moon and SA MC approached Pluto, Jerry and his family moved to Queens, New York, to start a new life.

Springer went to law school to please his parents but politics beckoned. He idolized Democratic hopeful Robert Kennedy (Springer's Venus is on Kennedy's Venus–MC–Jupiter conjunction) and went into a deep depression when his hero was murdered on 5 June 1968 (as TR Neptune squared Springer's Sun and TR Saturn conjunct his Descendant).

On 25 November 1969, Springer announced his candidacy for the Democratic nomination for Congress. Called up for six-month service three days later (as SA Saturn squared 10th House ruler Moon), nevertheless he returned to win the nomination but lost the race for Congress on 3 November 1970.

Springer then announced his intention to run for city council in Cincinnati and won on **1 December 1971** (as the SA 10th cusp conjunct Jupiter – i.e. SA Ascendant square to Jupiter – and SA MC reached fixed star Regulus at 29° Leo), but almost immediately began antagonizing people with his anti-war stance (Mars–Uranus in Gemini). He was re-elected, however, two years later, becoming Cincinnati's popular public crusader best known for staging outrageous stunts to publicize his political causes (his natal MC ruler Sun opposes Jupiter in Leo). Springer's personal charm (the Libra Moon and Ascendant) won much public empathy and support, even though he has admitted to always feeling the outsider (Aquarius).

A month after his Saturn Return, Springer married (16 June 1973) and the couple's disabled daughter was born in July 1976. In April 1974, facing his first brush with infamy, he was threatened with exposure for paying prostitutes. Shattered by the revelations, he resigned in late May and resumed his job as a lawyer (TR Uranus conjunct Ascendant, SA Ascendant square Sun in the 5th). His indiscretion became part of local folklore when he re-campaigned for city council in late 1975 and won.

4.25 • Jerry Springer's Infamous Talk Show Airs

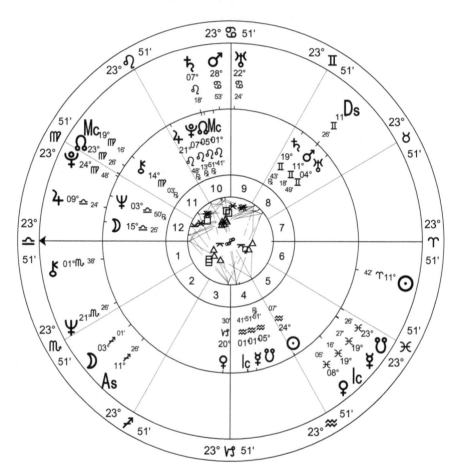

Inner Wheel (natal chart): 13 February 1944 at 23:45 GWT
in Highgate, London, England (51N34, 0W10).

Outer Wheel: Solar Arc directions to 30 September 1991.

Data Source: From him to Frank Clifford.

Additional Data: David Soul, 28 August 1943 at 02:55 CWT in
Chicago, Illinois, USA (41N52, 87W39). Data from birth certificate,
as obtained by Tom and Thelma Wilson; copy on file.

Jerry Springer – by now considered the Comeback Kid – was elected Cincinnati's youngest ever mayor in 1977 (as Saturn directed to his 10th House cusp, and SA Venus conjunct his Sun).

Someone with natal Pluto on the MC can be adept at career sabotage but is nevertheless a master of reinvention and resurrection. In December 1981, Jerry Springer resigned his position as Mayor to run in the primary for Governor of Ohio but, losing out, he moved into TV as a political news commentator, making his debut on 2 November 1982. By 1987, he had been voted best anchor in Cincinnati and picked up numerous Emmy Awards.

On **30 September 1991** (as his SA Descendant conjunct Mars in Gemini in the 8th – a portent of his infamous show if there ever was one – and SA Saturn conjunct Pluto in the 10th), *Springer*, his own talk show, aired – initially without controversy. But by 1994 (the year Jupiter entered Scorpio, and his SA Mars moved to the MC), the show had a new angle, targeting teenage viewers with its Friday night fraternity party stance (natal Jupiter in Leo opposite Sun in Aquarius).

Soon, Jerry Springer was being heralded as the undisputed King of TV Sleaze, and the host soon became adept at justifying the show and its ability to find novel ways of inciting vicious violence between guests. Over the show's 26 seasons (to date), viewers, sponsors and regulators have often objected to its violence, nudity and use of profanity and have questioned the authenticity of the show's bizarre guests.

In May 1998 (following SA Jupiter over his 12th House Moon and SA Venus in the 5th opposite Chiron), a newspaper reported his alleged dalliance with a porn actress and her stepmother, casting Springer once again in the role of adulterer. In early 2003, he spoke of running for Senate but his plans soon dissipated.

A provocative stage show, *Jerry Springer: The Opera*, was first performed in London in April 2003. David Soul later took on the role of Springer (his natal Moon is on Jerry's MC–Pluto and both share Jupiter in Leo and a Mars–Uranus conjunction in Gemini). Soul joined on 12 July 2004 (his SA Mars was on Springer's Leo MC) and appeared in a BBC transmission of the show on 8 January 2005, which caused a religious furore with 55,000 complaints and accusations of blasphemy (Soul's SA 10th was conjunct natal Saturn, TR Uranus opposed his Sun, and TR Saturn was on his Ascendant).

4.26 • Duffy's Recognition

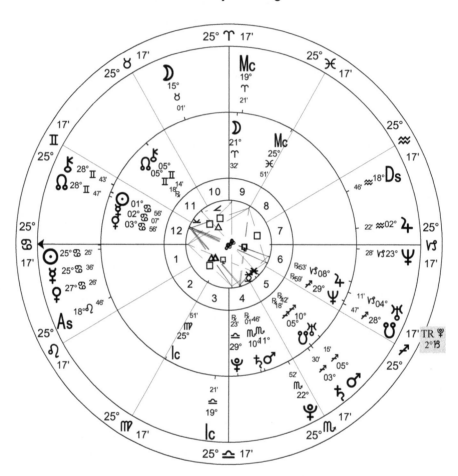

Inner Wheel (natal chart): 23 June 1984 at 06:55 GDT
in Bangor, Wales (53N13, 4W08).

Outer Wheel: Solar Arc directions to 8 February 2009.

Data Source: Birth certificate (a twin), obtained by Frank Clifford; copy on file.

Additional Data: Whoopi Goldberg, 13 November 1955 at 12:48 EST in
New York, New York, USA (40N43, 74W00). Data from her birth certificate, read
by Ron Holder of Goldberg's office to Richard Nolle by telephone.

The Welsh singer **Duffy** scored the UK's biggest album of 2008 with her debut *Rockferry*, which went on to sell more than nine million copies worldwide. Her Neptune-soaked chart speaks of an ability to infiltrate the music market (Sun–Mercury–Venus opposes Neptune, T-square the MC in Pisces), but as is often the case with Pisces/Neptune, acclaim is rejected for a calling that feels more authentic.

Duffy's parents divorced when she was ten and she moved town with her mother and sisters. With Mars–Saturn in Scorpio and Pluto all positioned in the 4th House, there was drama at age 13 (as Solar Arc Pluto conjunct Mars) when she and her twin sister were placed briefly into a police safe house when Duffy's step-father's ex-wife paid someone to murder her former husband. With Saturn retrograde, Duffy went to work young (at a seafood restaurant – Pisces MC!) at age 13. She planned to become a writer, although the family wanted her to train as a nurse (Cancer planets, Virgo IC). When, at 15, the wayward teen (who admits she was always looking for trouble) ran away to stay with her father, it created tension and her mother and sisters didn't speak to her for a year.

Duffy was first inspired by the soul music in *Sister Act* (the film's star Whoopi Goldberg has Venus–MC conjunct Duffy's Uranus in the 5th) but her first taste of fame – she was runner-up in a Welsh version of *Idol* called *Wawffactor* (which aired from late 2003 to early 2004) – resulted in 'the unhappiest time in my life'. An EP was released in 2004 and Duffy was discovered by a major record label in August that year (as transiting Saturn honed in on her Ascendant). She spent the next four years making her debut album and, when released in March 2008, she emerged a star – the year's brightest. A slew of accolades from the industry followed, including Brit Awards and a Grammy in **February 2009** (SA Sun and Mercury moved to the Ascendant and trined the MC – prominence for the performer/songwriter). But at the time, transiting Pluto in the 6th opposed her personal planets in Cancer in the 12th and she admitted that the media intrusion had brought her very close to a nervous breakdown.

After a second album flopped commercially, Duffy announced a sabbatical in early 2011 to focus on her relationship and family (as SA MC reached her Moon in Aries) but the relationship dissolved mid year (as SA Neptune reached the Descendant). Rather than deliver a third album, she emerged a few years later as an actress and then stepped back into the music business with little fanfare.

4.27 • Alex Haley's Roots

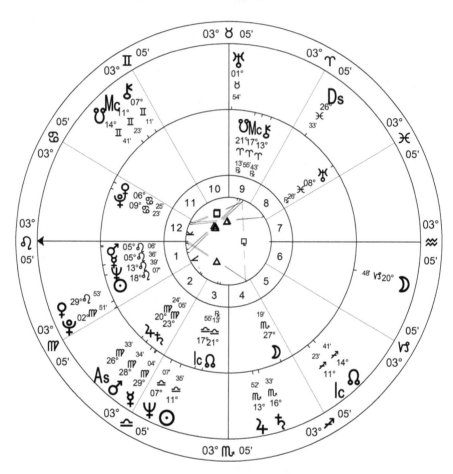

Inner Wheel (natal chart): 11 August 1921 at 04:55 EDT
in Ithaca, New York, USA (42N26, 76W30).

Outer Wheel: Solar Arc directions to 17 August 1976.

Data Source: Birth certificate, as quoted in *Contemporary American Horoscopes* by Janice Mackey and Jessica Saunders (Astrolabe, 1990).

Alex Haley's *Roots* – the Pulitzer Prize-winning book and Emmy-awarded mini-series – was the phenomenon of the mid 1970s. Translated into 37 languages and spending 46 weeks on *The New York Times* bestsellers' list, this novel had a profound impact on America and the world. In total, Haley spent twelve years (one Jupiter cycle) obsessed with discovering his roots, and lecturing and researching across America. (Eventually, he believed he had traced his ancestors back to a village, Juffure, in Gambia.)

Before writing *Roots*, Alex Haley had garnered a measure of literary recognition as a pioneering African-American writer: his Midheaven is in Aries, and its ruler, Mars, conjoins Mercury in Leo. Hugh Hefner was looking to launch the *Playboy* interview; Haley stepped into the ring by interviewing pugnacious musical genius Miles Davis, and delivered the first in the series. It was published in September 1962, as Solar Arc Uranus directed over Haley's Aries MC. This gave Alex Haley a level of renown that led to some major interview coups and to his becoming co-writer of 1965's *The Autobiography of Malcolm X* (based on more than 50 interviews with the minister).

Although excerpts from *Roots* first appeared in the *Reader's Digest* in May and June 1974, the novel wouldn't be completed for another two years. By early 1976, Haley was under extreme pressure to complete this enormous task: publishers were ready, TV producers were waiting for the script and he was flat broke. However, with a New Moon in Taurus in late April 1976 conjunct Jupiter, which was transiting his 10th House, there were the makings and the promise of a truly epic summer ahead.

As the manuscript was sent to the printers (and filming of the mini-series had already started), transiting Saturn left Haley's 12th House and crossed over his conjunction of the Ascendant, Mars and Mercury in Leo. (Saturn's transits so often coincide with times when the blood, sweat and tears start to pay off.) On the day of publication (**17 August 1976**), transiting Mercury had reached Haley's Jupiter, a 'minor' transit but an auspicious omen of what was about to happen to Haley and to America. Haley's SA Venus was on Regulus at 29° Leo, and SA Uranus was fast approaching his (Equal) 10th House. His life was about to undergo some irrevocable change.

When *Roots* was published in August 1976, it was just weeks after the nationalistic fervour of the United States' bicentenary. This

4.28 • Alex Haley's Hoax

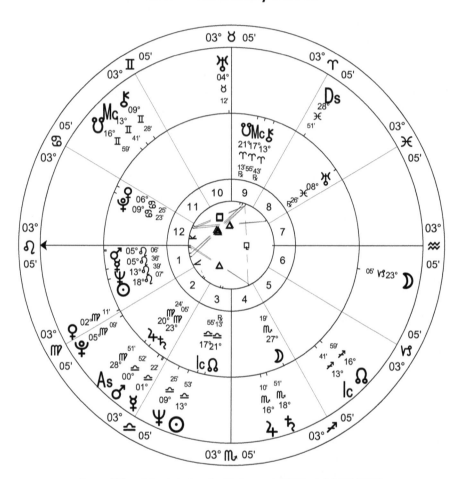

Inner Wheel (natal chart): 11 August 1921 at 04:55 EDT
in Ithaca, New York, USA (42N26, 76W30).

Outer Wheel: Solar Arc directions to 14 December 1978.

The text opposite is an excerpt from an article I co-wrote with Samuel Reynolds
for the February–March 2015 issue of *The Mountain Astrologer*.

timing was astrologically apt, too: the US Sibly chart's Ascendant had Solar Arc directed to 0° Cancer for the first time in the country's history. Not only was it a summer to celebrate one's past, it was also an occasion to face with honesty the foundations on which America was built. In *Roots*, readers and viewers were given mental and emotional images that no history book could provide. It gave much of America a chance to begin to understand slavery and reconcile feelings linked to race and racism. African-Americans were offered an ancestral identity (Cancer), while White America could start confronting one of the most shameful aspects of its past.

But **Alex Haley** was about to encounter some shaming of his own. Haley had quickly become a cultural hero, his story the stuff of legend (Sun–Neptune in Leo). But soon after the publication of *Roots*, Haley was sued for plagiarism. The first lawsuit was thrown out of court, but the second led to a notorious trial that did much to damage Haley's reputation as a researcher and biographer.

As a sign, Leo's great fear is of being 'found out' – of others discovering that he is not the great immortal he has been written up to be. Leo loses dignity and credibility when he makes false claims to bolster his ego, when he pretends to be something he isn't – in short, when it is discovered that he or his work is a fake.

It was established irrefutably that many sections of *Roots* had been lifted from *The African*, a 1967 book by (white) writer Harold Courlander. On **14 December 1978**, in the sixth week of trial and just before the summation, Haley settled the case for a reputed $650,000. Later, the judge asserted that Haley had perpetrated a hoax on the public.

At the time of the case and settlement, the major directions and transits involved Saturn (a time of reckoning), the MC (reputation) and the Sun (mission/purpose): SA Saturn had squared Haley's Sun in Leo, SA Sun was opposite Chiron (natally placed on the MC), TR Saturn was square SA MC, TR Uranus was square natal Sun (and conjunct SA Saturn), and TR Pluto was on the IC.

The judgment did little to dent Haley's public popularity and the importance of his work to the American people, who were reluctant to accept a truth that deviated from Haley's family legend. Haley defended his actions, claiming that the book was 'faction', that he had purposefully presented fact in a fictionalized format because 'Blacks long have needed a hypothetical Eden like whites have'.

4.29 • The Capitalist Guru

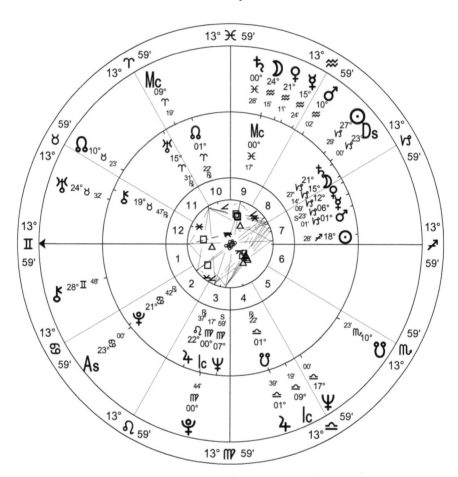

Inner Wheel (natal chart): 11 December 1931 at 17:13 IST
in Bhopal, India (23N15, 77E23).

Outer Wheel: Solar Arc directions to 1 April 1970.

Data Source: Ed Steinbrecher quotes a letter from Osho's ashram
(birth time from his mother's memory).

Additional Data: Ma Anand Sheela, 28 December 1949 in Vadodara (formerly
Baroda), India (22N19, 73E12). Data from online sources.

Bhagwan Shree Rajneesh was a charismatic guru (Sun in Sagittarius in the 7th trine Jupiter in Leo in the 3rd) who offered a blend of New Age philosophies and capitalism to his followers in India. Back on 21 March 1953, he had become spiritually enlightened (as SA MC trined Pluto, transiting Uranus opposed natal Moon, and TR Pluto conjoined Jupiter). Many years later, in 1968, as his SA Ascendant–Descendant axis aligned with his powerful Pluto–Saturn opposition, he scandalized Hindu leaders by calling for freer acceptance of sex (earning him the 'sex guru' moniker). In **spring 1970** (as SA Saturn and Pluto connected to his MC–IC axis), he introduced his influential Dynamic Meditation method (Gemini–Sagittarius, Uranus) to his followers and that September initiated his first group of disciples. Four years later he established an ashram in Pune (then Poona, near his Jupiter–IC line).

With a playful, irreverent style and hypnotic oratory, Rajneesh attacked traditional religious concepts and promoted the shedding of inhibitions (note the planets in Capricorn squared by dissident, anti-establishment Uranus). Whether he was quoting the Bible, Plato or *Playboy*, whether he was promoting a minimalist lifestyle or indulging in displays of conspicuous consumption (driving one of his 93 Rolls-Royces), Rajneesh revelled in paradox (Gemini).

Amid tensions in Pune, he relocated to Oregon on 29 August 1981 to build a Shangri-La in 65,000 acres of arid land (near his Jupiter–MC line, as SA MC in Aries squared Saturn–Pluto, and TR Pluto crossed his SA IC). A series of legal battles over land use with locals escalated into threats and murder plots, culminating in the salmonella poisoning of 751 Oregonians in September 1984 by the ashram in an attempt to gain a political foothold. The aggressive recruitment of 3700 homeless people that same month served a similar political purpose. Rajneesh, who had been publicly silent since 1981, began speaking again on 30 October 1984 (as SA Mercury reached his MC) to address dissent. His trusted secretary, Sheela (infamous for her insult-laced rhetoric aimed at locals and the press – natal Sun–Mars–Uranus T-square), fled on 13 September 1985 (TR Uranus on his Descendant). Rajneesh feigned ignorance of the acts committed in his name and denounced Sheela as a ruthless despot. On 28 October 1985, he was arrested and later deported. Rajneesh returned to Pune and in February 1989 changed his name to Osho, at the time when Solar Arc Uranus reached his Ascendant.

4.30 • Whose Line is it Anyway?

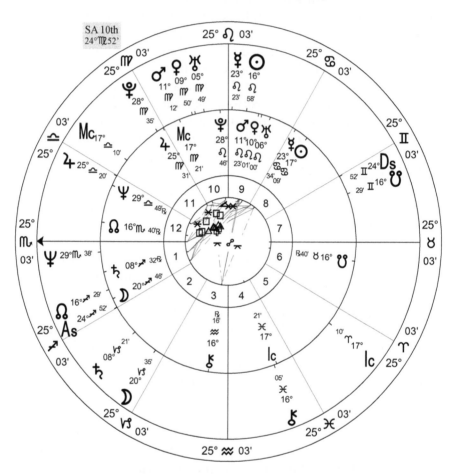

Inner Wheel (natal chart): 9 July 1957 at 17:05 GDT
in Parsons Green, London, England (51N28, 0W12).

Outer Wheel: Solar Arc directions to 23 September 1988.

Data Source: From Merton's autobiography, *Only When I Laugh* (Ebury, 2014),
quoted by Sy Scholfield.

A strong Uranus is one of the key signatures in a comedian's chart, and the Ascendant often describes the comedic outlook. **Paul Merton** has Uranus conjunct Venus and chart ruler Mars but the public, however, tends to see his Scorpio Ascendant and Saturn in the 1st: the deadpan manner, the sardonic delivery and the surly, taciturn persona that suggests fools will not be entertained.

Merton worked for the civil service but, following TR Neptune across his Moon, he knew he needed to focus on comedy full-time. He quit his job on 29 February 1980 and signed on for unemployment benefit (TR Uranus was on his Ascendant). It took him two years to build up the confidence to perform, but he was a hit when he finally went on stage in April 1982 at the Comedy Store in Soho. In August 1987 (as TR Uranus caught up to his SA Ascendant – a Shadow Transit), he put on a show at the Edinburgh Festival, but broke his leg after the first night and was out of work for months.

On **23 September 1988**, the UK version of the improvisational comedy series *Whose Line is it Anyway?* debuted and Merton was in the original line-up. It proved to be his big break. Aptly, his SA Equal 10th House was close to Jupiter, the SA Sun in Leo was square to the Nodes (often a time of exposure, accomplishment or vocational fulfilment), and his SA MC squared natal Sun (ditto). The squares suggest the hard work, energy and striving needed to make these ambitions a reality. The show aired just after a Solar Eclipse at 18° Virgo (close to his MC). While working on *Whose Line ...*, Merton started with another show that would make him more famous and showcase his merciless wit and gift for satire: *Have I Got News for You*. It first aired on 28 September 1990. Merton's SA MC-ruler Mercury moved into his 10th House.

Merton has lived through some harrowing experiences. Back in January 1990, anti-malarial medication he took while on holiday in Kenya (on his Neptune–MC line) resulted in him being committed to a psychiatric ward for six weeks. Merton's marriage to comedy actress Caroline Quentin effectively ended when they separated on 14 April 1997 (following Merton's Uranus half-return and TR Neptune on SA Moon). He remarried but his new wife was diagnosed with breast cancer in February 2002 (his SA MC at 0° Scorpio on Neptune, TR Pluto square MC). And sadly, on 23 September 2003, as TR Neptune opposed Venus–Mars and TR Pluto squared the MC again, Merton was widowed.

4.31 • The Voice of Country

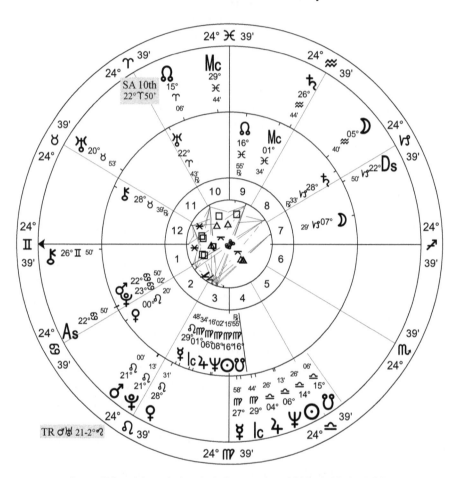

Inner Wheel (natal chart): 8 September 1932 at 23:15 EST
in Winchester, Virginia, USA (39N11, 78W10).

Outer Wheel: Solar Arc directions to 14 June 1961.

Data Source: From hospital records, as read out to Frank Clifford by staff at
Winchester Memorial Hospital in 1995.
(Cline's birth certificate, obtained by Stephen Pryzbylowski, states 23:05.)

It took a woman with **Patsy Cline's** swagger, husky alto and an aching hiccup in her voice to break through the male-dominated world of country music and tread the boards of the Grand Ole Opry. The dignified beauty of her voice on 'Crazy', 'Sweet Dreams' and 'I Fall to Pieces' was matched only by her regal stage presence and confidence (Venus and Mercury bookend the sign of Leo).

After seven years of career delays due to a restrictive contract, money worries and the birth of her baby, Cline's career finally gathered momentum in 1961. But as she was hitting the big time, her potent T-square involving Mars–Pluto, Saturn and Uranus was triggered, and two accidents befell her.

The first of Patsy's accidents was a car crash at 16:43 on **14 June 1961** in Madison, Tennessee, that almost killed her. She was thrown with violent force through the windshield, leaving her with a jagged cut across her forehead and a dislocated hip. It was during her SA 10th conjunct Uranus and her exact Saturn Return (coinciding with her career moving up a gear after seven years – a Saturn square – of struggle). SA Ascendant was at 22° Cancer (conjunct the tight natal Mars–Pluto conjunction) and, to add to the potency of this aspect, TR Mars–Uranus were conjunct in the sky at the degree of her SA Mars–Pluto at 21° Leo. Transiting Jupiter was conjunct her SA Moon in the 8th, and SA MC was at the final degree of Pisces.

Patsy never felt she would live to see thirty. She did, but for only six months. On 5 March 1963 at around 18:20 just outside Camden, Tennessee, she was involved in a fatal plane crash (Mars–Pluto had directed to sesquiquadrate her Moon). Her early death resulted in a legacy of a few dozen timeless songs and an enduring mystique surrounding Cline herself.

Discussing and dissecting the astrology of accidents can be troublesome. Firstly, we can scare clients unnecessarily and even create a self-fulfilling prophecy (I'm more inclined, for instance during a Mars–Uranus time, to discourage clients from doing physically risky activities or evoking the planetary energies in a *physical* manner). Secondly, there's no 'definitive' aspect, transit or direction that would foretell an accident, but in hindsight the provocative symbolism is often very clearly present in the horoscope.

4.32 • The Man of Steel

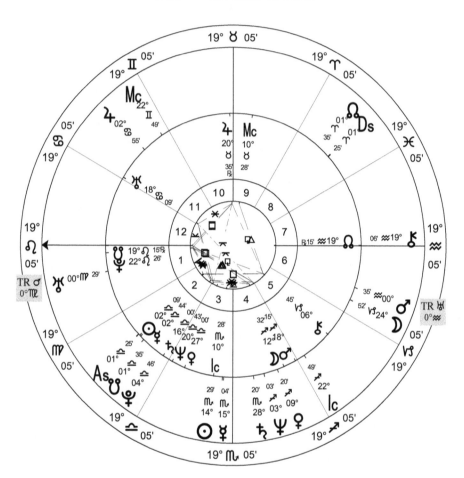

Inner Wheel (natal chart): 25 September 1952 at 03:12 EDT
in Manhattan, New York, USA (40N46, 73W59).

Outer Wheel: Solar Arc directions to 27 May 1995.

Data Source: Letter from Reeve to Linda Clark.
(Reeve gave 03:14 to Penny Thornton.)

It's rare that a celebrity death leaves me very emotional, but **Christopher Reeve's** passing on 10 October 2004 – almost nine and a half years (a half nodal cycle) after his horse-riding accident – saddened me greatly. The accident – during an equestrian competition on **27 May 1995** at 15:05 in Culpeper, Virginia – had left Reeve a quadriplegic and he was told he'd be confined to a wheelchair and on a permanent portable ventilator for the rest of his life.

Yet he refused to give up: he began to raise awareness and funds for those with spinal injuries, wrote two books, acted and directed in films, and made a pledge to breathe unassisted again. I truly believed he could. With Jupiter elevated and square to Pluto rising in Leo, this was a man who could move mountains and achieve the near impossible. But it wasn't to be. Not even for Superman.

Reeve's natal Moon–Mars in Sagittarius suggests his love of competitive horsemanship. But the tight natal quincunx from Mars to Uranus warns of the *possibility* of a sudden accident when triggered. At the time of the accident, Solar Arc Mars had reached 0° of the Air sign Aquarius and Uranus had reached 0° Virgo, starting a very new script in his life. By transit, Mars was at 0° Virgo on SA Uranus, while transiting Uranus was at 0° Aquarius on SA Mars – a remarkable repetition of planetary aspects and Shadow Transits.

In addition, Chiron, associated with horses and motorcycles, had directed to the Descendant, adding to the list of significators suggesting the catastrophic accident and his future reliance on others. Another link to horses, Jupiter, ruler of the 5th House and dispositor of Mars, had directed to square natal Mercury (Jupiter is linked to trips and slips).

When Reeve died in 2004, doctors believed it was from a reaction to an antibiotic given for an infected pressure ulcer. TR Jupiter had crossed over his Sun–Mercury conjunction in Libra, and SA Neptune was conjunct his Moon (perhaps suggesting a greater vulnerability to infections and medication).

Tragically, his widow Dana was diagnosed with lung cancer on 9 August 2005 and died on 6 March 2006. As an example of how birth charts continue to be activated after our deaths, Christopher's SA Pluto was on his Saturn (a classic signature for the irrevocable removal of an anchor/fixture), SA Chiron in the 7th had moved into Pisces, TR Neptune was conjunct his Descendant, and TR Uranus in the 7th was opposite SA Uranus (a Shadow Uranus Half Return).

4.33 • Jacqueline Kennedy Dies

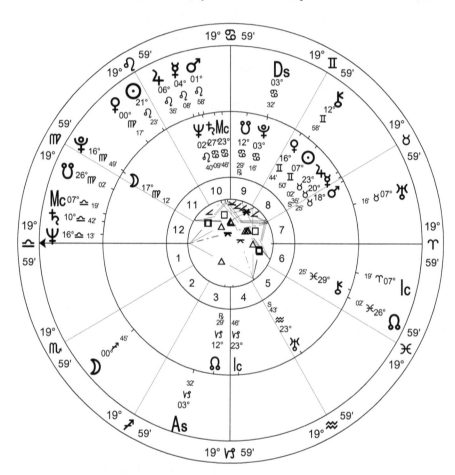

Inner Wheel (natal chart): 29 May 1917 at 15:00 EST
in Brookline, Massachusetts, USA (42N20, 71W07).

Outer Wheel: Solar Arc directions to 19 May 1994.

Data Source: From Kennedy's mother, as quoted by Garth Allen
in *American Astrology* (May 1960).

As we've just seen, horoscopes 'live on' – they are triggered by transits and directions long after we have died. In the bi-wheel opposite, we have the natal chart of **President John F Kennedy** along with directions to the date his wife, Jacqueline, died. Although Jackie married again, it is not surprising that JFK's chart would register her death – some thirty years after his own.

In the directions for Jackie's death on **19 May 1994**, Pluto is very active: JFK's SA Descendant has reached his natal Pluto, and SA Pluto is within orb of conjoining his Moon. The closest Solar Arc aspect is a square from Pluto to Venus, another indication of the loss he *would* have suffered had he been alive. SA Mars (ruler of his Descendant) is also eight months away from exactly conjoining his Neptune. (This brings us to an interesting conclusion: to get a clearer idea of our own 'fate', we could check out the charts of those who are/were closest to us.)

In the light of Bill Clinton's Solar Arcs to his 10th and MC (see pages 96–9), Kennedy's chart offers an interesting comparison. At the time he was sworn in as President (20 January 1961), the Sun was conjunct Kennedy's 10th House (TR Jupiter was opposite both) and SA Mars had entered patriotic Cancer (in his inaugural address Kennedy famously said, 'Ask not what your country can do for you; ask what you can do for your country.') Soon after, the Moon reached the final degree of Libra, triggering further diplomatic crises with Russia and a failed military invasion in the Bay of Pigs.

On **22 November 1963** (bi-wheel, right), **Kennedy was assassinated in Dallas**. A birth time of five minutes earlier would put SA Sun on the MC (reflecting the tragic but most defining image of Kennedy), while SA Mars was conjunct his Pluto (and SA Pluto approaching a square to Mars), and SA Neptune was conjunct MC ruler Moon (the idealized 'Camelot', as his presidency would soon become known).

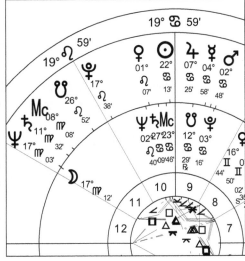

4.34 • Pamela Anderson's Summer of Exposure

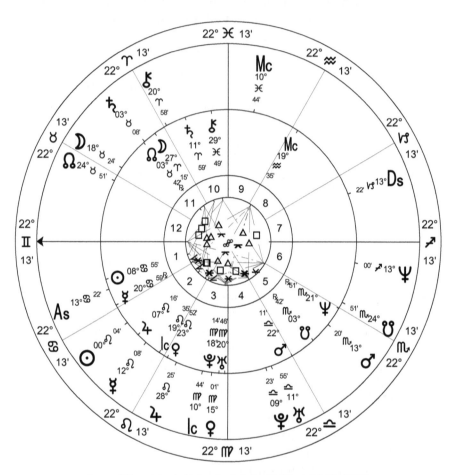

Inner Wheel (natal chart): 1 July 1967 at 04:08 PDT
in Ladysmith, Canada (48N58, 123W49).

Outer Wheel: Solar Arc directions to 1 September 1989.

Data Source: Birth announcement in *The Ladysmith-Chemainus Chronicle*;
copy on file.

Pin-up model and actress **Pamela Anderson** was discovered in the summer of 1989 while at a football match (the exact date is unknown but the football season began mid July). Suddenly the stadium cameras zoomed in on Anderson, who was wearing a tight T-shirt with the logo of a beer company on it. The young blonde model was cheered and then brought down to the field to receive the crowd's further ovation! Following another similar event, the beer company had the sense to hire her and this led to her first cover shoot for *Playboy* magazine (the October 1989 issue, with TR Jupiter on her Sun). The outer wheel has been set for **1 September 1989**.

With the natal Sun in Cancer, Pamela Anderson epitomizes the modern girl-next-door, the Barbie doll with huge breast implants – modern-day weapons of mass *distraction*. What is telling about her Solar Arc positions for 1989 is that her Sun was moving into Leo that summer, just after her discovery and at the exact time she was being photographed for her first *Playboy* cover. This brought her notice and publicity, demonstrated in the most blatant of Leonine imagery: the centrefold.

By ingressing into the sign of Leo, the Sun became prominent and was in immediate 'dialogue' with two planets in that sign: Jupiter and Venus (together, they could be said to symbolize her mass popularity as a pneumatic sex symbol). The directed Moon in Taurus was trine Pluto, suggestive of her 'baring all' (Pluto), her mass appeal (Pluto) and some major financial opportunities (the Moon rules the 2nd, and the trine is between Earth signs).

Uranus–MC aspects are often seen in the charts of those whose reputations change overnight and are in the right place at the right time (or perhaps in the wrong place at the wrong time). Anderson has Uranus co-ruling the MC and in quincunx to it. With a natal quincunx, the plot changes – whether we like it or not.

Neptune–MC aspects can suggest a lack of awareness of how we're perceived by others in our social or professional lives, and can also give us a reputation for being glamorous, photogenic, sleazy or otherworldly. Anderson has Neptune square her Aquarian MC and square her Venus in Leo, which describes her image as a big-haired glamourpuss as well as her dual career pursuits: aside from her modelling/acting, she is a vegan and an activist for PETA (People for the Ethical Treatment of Animals), an organization that fights to alleviate animal suffering.

4.35 • Sun, Sand and Stardom

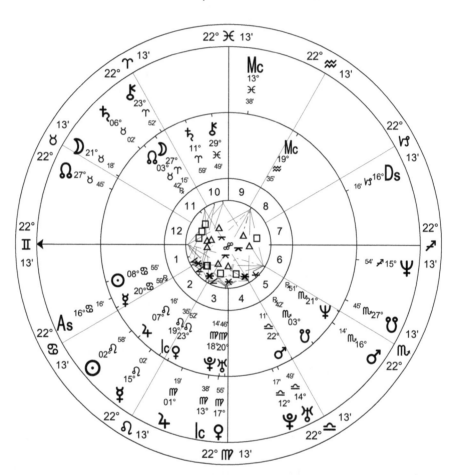

Inner Wheel (natal chart): 1 July 1967 at 04:08 PDT
in Ladysmith, Canada (48N58, 123W49).

Outer Wheel: Solar Arc directions to 14 September 1992.

Data Source: Birth announcement in *The Ladysmith-Chemainus Chronicle*;
copy on file.

Pamela Anderson's Moon directed to oppose Neptune three years later – the time she joined the cast of *Baywatch*. Aptly for Moon–Neptune, it was a TV show about the idealized life of glamorous Californian lifeguards on a beach. Her first episode aired on **14 September 1992** (as TR Pluto squared her MC) and it would make her a global sensation (Neptune's job is to mass-market, disseminate and sell to everyone). At the same time, SA Venus (natally in Leo) conjunct Pluto to suggest the huge impact she was about to make as a sex symbol, as well as some of the new resources (power, money) coming her way.

At its peak in 1993, *Baywatch* was baptised as 'the most watched TV show in the world' with 1.1 billion viewers across 148 countries (and 44 languages). Note Anderson's natal Moon is opposite Mars and is in dynamic, adventurous Aries, a sign well-suited to running (albeit in slow motion) in a red bikini to rescue swimmers in distress!

Pamela married Mötley Crüe drummer Tommy Lee on 19 February 1995 (four days after they had started dating), just as SA Venus was coming to a half-degree conjunction with Uranus. It was to prove a tumultuous, Venus–Uranus match-up in many ways.

In October 1995, a private recording of the couple having sex on their honeymoon was stolen from their home. Attempts to block it being sold or shared online (the Internet is too Neptunian) were in vain. The couple capitulated, signing a deal on 25 November 1997 to profit from the film; it was the first celebrity sex tape to go viral.

On **20 May 1998** (chart on right, as SA Mars conjunct Neptune and TR Saturn on her Moon) Tommy **was sentenced to six months** (serving four) **for spousal abuse**. The marriage dissolved soon after but the couple attempted to reconcile later that year and again in 2008. By 1999 (as SA Neptune, natally square to Venus, inched its way towards her Descendant), the video and the on-off marriage ensured that Pamela was tabloid fodder on a daily basis.

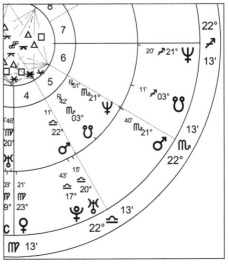

4.36 • Death was Only the Beginning

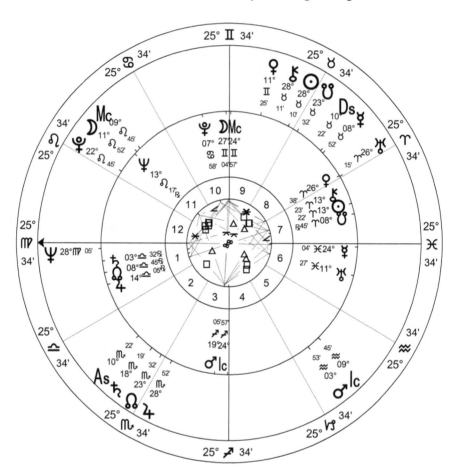

Inner Wheel (natal chart): 3 April 1922 at 16:30 CST
in Cincinnati, Ohio, USA (39N10, 84W27).

Outer Wheel: Solar Arc directions to 20 April 1968.

Data Source: Birth certificate, obtained by Frank Clifford; copy on file.

Actress and animal rights campaigner **Doris Day** suffered a great shock when her husband–manager, Marty Melcher, died suddenly on **20 April 1968**. Appropriately, by Solar Arc, she was receiving a Venus–Uranus double whammy: SA Venus had moved to 11° Gemini (square natal Uranus), and SA Uranus had reached 26° Aries, conjunct natal Venus in the 8th House. By transit, Uranus was on her Ascendant.

But this was just the start of a series of shocks and crises that left her in a near-catatonic state (Uranus). Both Solar Arcs are linked to Venus and to the 8th House and soon after her bereavement, in July 1968, Day discovered enormous debts of some $450,000. SA Jupiter was now at the crisis degree of the crisis sign, 29° Scorpio. Day's husband had left her penniless and her attorney, Jerry Rosenthal, had ripped her off. Both men had squandered current holdings and borrowed against future earnings (Jupiter), including an album she had yet to record and a TV show and specials she had no idea she'd been committed to filming.

After firing Rosenthal, she filed suit against him in February 1969, as SA Sun–Chiron entered the final degree of Taurus in her 9th House. As might be expected with Taurus, it was a long, slow battle that would include a complex, 99-day trial in March 1974 and culminate on 18 September in a judgment of $22.8 million in her favour (then, the largest civil award in California history). Rosenthal declared bankruptcy and Day eventually settled with his insurers for $6 million, although he continued to counter-sue into the late 1980s.

Natally, Jupiter opposes the Sun from the 1st in Libra to the 7th in Aries, indicating the influence (Sun–Jupiter) that both men had on her life and how she had elevated them (Jupiter) and allowed them to (mis)manage the bulk of her fortune and her professional decisions. (Back on 3 April 1951, transiting Jupiter was conjunct her Descendant in Pisces when she had married Melcher, and Jupiter is also reflected in their shared devotion to Christian Science, a faith she left soon after his death. Interestingly, Melcher died from complications linked to an enlarged heart: Sun–Jupiter.)

Day's victimization and exploitation by her husband and her advisor are also reflected by Mercury in Pisces on the Descendant, the Sun in the 7th House ruling the 12th, the all-important Jupiter ruling the IC/4th and the Descendant, plus Sun–Chiron in naïve Aries in the 7th (relationships) squaring Pluto in the 10th (career).

4.37 • A Long Fight for Justice

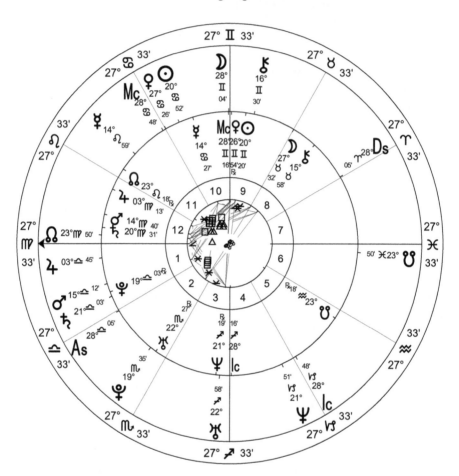

Inner Wheel (natal chart): 11 June 1980 at 13:16 AEST
in Mount Isa, Queensland, Australia (20S44, 139E30).

Outer Wheel: Solar Arc directions to 12 June 2012.

Data Source: Hospital baby card, as obtained by Sy Scholfield; copy on file.

Just after 8 p.m. on 17 August 1980, while camping with her husband Michael and three children at Ayers Rock in the Outback, Lindy Chamberlain noticed a dingo emerging from her tent shaking an object in its mouth. Rushing to check on her nine-week-old daughter **Azaria Chamberlain**, whom she had left sleeping inside the tent, Lindy soon realized the dingo had run off with the infant and shouted, 'The dingo's got my baby.' Azaria was never found, but it was the start of Australia's most notorious trial-by-media and one of the most contentious events in the country's history.

From the start, everyone had an emphatic viewpoint, and opinions on what really happened polarized the nation for years. But, looking back, this is really the story of a couple's 32-year fight for the truth and to establish legal vindication of what happened that night.

As the press and public lined up to condemn the couple, there were wild rumours about their religion (Michael was a Seventh-Day Adventist minister), nonsense about the name 'Azaria' meaning 'sacrifice in the wilderness', and vicious speculation that the child had been killed because she was disabled. The first inquest in February 1981 found a dingo liable, but the police refused to accept the finding and Lindy was arrested for murder twelve months later. The trial began on 13 September 1982. The evidence was circumstantial: the prosecution had no motive, confession, weapon, body or witness, yet a jury came back with a guilty verdict. Lindy, now the most hated woman in Australia and eight months pregnant, was sentenced to life imprisonment and hard labour.

Over three years later, in early February 1986, a piece of evidence crucial to the trial – Azaria's missing matinee jacket – was unearthed 200 metres away from the campsite. Lindy was freed and the couple pardoned, but they pushed for their convictions to be overturned and for a cause of death to be established legally.

Azaria's chart has the Sun in Gemini in a mutable T-square with Saturn and Neptune (suggesting the false reporting as well as the failure of the authorities). Her natal Moon in Taurus on the cusp of the Equal 9th (opposite Uranus) is reflective of her mother's stubborn determination to establish the truth in a court of law. When that Moon directed to the MC in Gemini (almost 32 years after the tragedy, and during Azaria's Shadow Saturn Return), a fourth inquest on **12 June 2012** ordered that the baby's death certificate be changed to confirm that she was in fact killed by a dingo.

4.38 • Madonna Signs Her First Record Deal

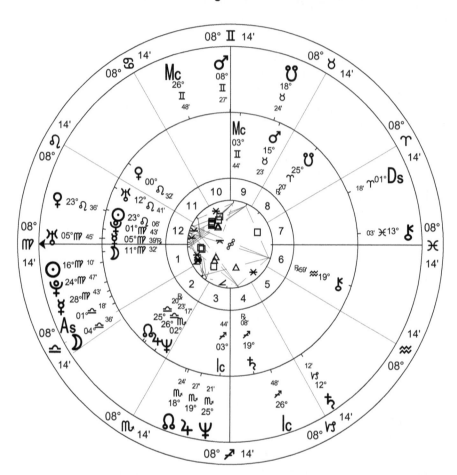

Inner Wheel (natal chart): 16 August 1958 at 07:05 EST
in Bay City, Michigan, USA (43N36, 83W53).

Outer Wheel: Solar Arc directions to 1 July 1982.

Data Source: Tashi Grady quotes Madonna's father
(who called the hospital to look up the records).

There are music icons and then there's **Madonna**. As a performer and public figure, she redefined the image of the modern female pop star as self-determining, sexually aggressive, wildly independent and always in the driver's seat. She was also a self-possessed fashion icon to millions of teens (Venus in Leo square Jupiter–Neptune).

With a dominant Pluto, she shaped her generation, provoked outrage and censorship (Mars square Uranus) and succeeded through her sheer force of personality and willpower (Sun in Leo conjunct Pluto) and a work ethic second to none, always determined to stay in control of every aspect of her brand (Pluto and the Virgo emphasis). She did, after all, say from the start that she wanted to rule the world, and as the mother of reinvention (Sun–Pluto–Mercury–Moon), Madonna has continued to influence the music business long after singers from her original era have retired, faded into the background or died.

Once a celebrity attains a level of fame and acclaim, it's often difficult astrologically to differentiate one success from another, particularly if we're not privy to their personal opinions about their achievements and what means the most. But the early breakthroughs and achievements – the ones that change a performer's life – are often very clearly shown in transits or directions to their natal chart. And so we return to 1982, when a highly ambitious 23-year-old pushed her way onto the music scene, secured a record deal (**mid 1982**, see bi-wheel) and released her first single, 'Everybody' (October 1982).

In the bi-wheel, we can see that Venus was conjunct her Sun in Leo at the start of 1982 (when she was preparing her demo). By mid 1982, SA Mars had moved into her 10th House (it was on her MC four years earlier when she had made a break from her family in Michigan and arrived in New York hungry for stardom). With Mars in Gemini on the 10th at the start of her recording career, it suggests the hyphenate she would soon become known as: singer–songwriter–dancer. By Solar Arc, Uranus was on her Mercury (the Ascendant and MC ruler), again reflecting the provocative persona and reputation of defiance that would soon define her.

It would take just over two years (as SA Uranus crossed her Ascendant) before Madonna was to become the global music phenomenon of the age. At the same time, she married actor Sean Penn. It was a tempestuous union (Uranus) and was off-on-off again as SA Uranus crossed over her Moon.

4.39 • Goodbye Hubby, Hello Freedom

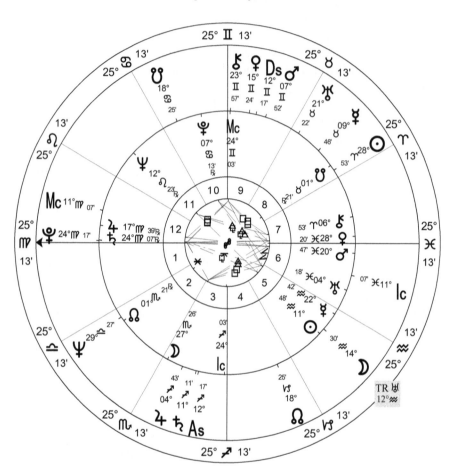

Inner Wheel (natal chart): 31 January 1921 at 21:00 PST
in Seattle, Washington, USA (47N36, 122W20).

Outer Wheel: Solar Arc directions to 19 May 1998.

Data Source: Birth certificate; copy on file.
(Channing gives 20:30 in her 2002 autobiography, *Just Lucky I Guess*.)

On **19 May 1998**, **Carol Channing** suddenly filed for divorce from her controlling husband–manager, Charles Lowe. It baffled many, as it came 42 years into their marriage and some months after Lowe's debilitating stroke.

They had married back in 1956 (Channing's third trip down the aisle) when her SA Saturn reached 29° Libra. Theirs was a show-must-go-on partnership of Saturnian dedication, discipline and workaholic drive – the two were seemingly inseparable and secure.

Fast forward to 1998 again and transiting Uranus was conjunct her Sun in Aquarius (natally in the 5th House opposite Neptune), coinciding with Lowe's sudden stroke and her break (Uranus) from her husband (Sun) – a man she claimed had always controlled and victimized her (Neptune). Solar Arc Pluto was now at 24° Virgo in Channing's chart, conjunct controlling Saturn and square her Midheaven (MC), and SA Chiron was minutes from her MC.

Lowe was certainly Channing's 'rock' for many years: supporting her, handling her business and engineering her greatest stage triumphs. In her natal chart, we find Saturn in Virgo opposite Venus–Mars in Pisces straddling the Ascendant–Descendant axis, and the Sun opposite Neptune. The Moon in controlling Scorpio is in square to both Mercury in independent Aquarius and explosive Uranus.

At the time of their split, Neptune had moved to the final degree of Libra in her 2nd House (where SA Saturn had been when they married 42 years earlier). It was a messy, bewildering dissolution of a long-term personal and professional partnership. After years of quiet obedience, newly independent Channing went on a rampage (as SA Sun travelled through the final degree of Aries). There were claims that Lowe was impotent, gay and had only had sex with her twice (both occasions on their honeymoon). He had allegedly left her close to bankruptcy and sold off her prized possessions. In her petition, Channing asserted that he was 'spending [my] money like a drunken sailor' (SA Neptune at 29° Libra in the 2nd).

Lowe died in September 1999 before the divorce was finalized and Channing did an about-face, never again discussing in public their marriage or split. In early 2003, Channing reconnected with old flame Harry Kullijian, after 70 years apart. They married on 10 May 2003, but sadly he died on 26 December 2011, when Channing's SA Sun in Taurus had reached a square to natal Neptune, SA MC was on Saturn, and SA Saturn was conjunct the IC.

4.40 • Upside Down

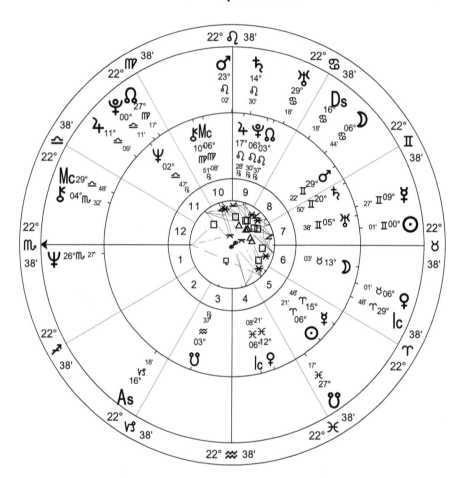

Inner Wheel (natal chart): 26 March 1944 at 23:46 EWT
in Detroit, Michigan, USA (42N20, 83W03).

Outer Wheel: Solar Arc directions to 24 April 1999.

Data Source: Birth certificate, as quoted in *Contemporary American Horoscopes* by Janice Mackey and Jessica Saunders (Astrolabe, 1990).

It was **24 April 1999**, a day that pop pioneer **Diana Ross** later described as the worst of her life: live on Norwegian TV, her husband of 14 years, Arne Naess, announced the end of their marriage – and shortly afterwards took up with another woman.

Just two weeks earlier, Ross's Solar Arc Sun had left the safety of Taurus (the sign of her Moon and Descendant) and entered Gemini for a 30-year stretch. In Ross's chart, the mutable sign of Gemini is occupied by unpredictable, unstable Uranus (in the 7th) as well as Mars and Saturn. This suggests somewhat uncomfortable ground for the singer, who has a fixed Moon and Ascendant.

At the time of her husband's announcement, she was having some major Solar Arcs. Her SA Venus was square natal Pluto, and SA Pluto had entered the first degree of Libra. In addition, Ross's SA MC had reached the final degree of Libra – the last attempt at (and end of) relationship mediation and the end of the public's perception of a fairy tale marriage (natally, Neptune is in Libra).

Deeply affected by Naess's betrayal and his refusal to discuss their problems (natal Mars in Gemini in the 8th, Saturn in Gemini in the 7th), Ross had what she characterized as 'almost an emotional breakdown'. She was also going through a devastating menopause. Fittingly, SA Uranus was at 29° Cancer in her 9th House, which also suggests the shattering end to their bi-continental marriage.

Later that year, on 21 September 1999, she was arrested for manhandling a security officer at Heathrow Airport: SA Sun remained at 0° Gemini, but the MC had plunged into Scorpio. The woman with the legendary work ethic and drive was unravelling – losing control of her carefully crafted reputation and direction (natal MC in Virgo). The next few years were to see Ross enter rehab (21 May 2002), find herself under arrest for drunk driving (30 December 2002, serving time in February 2004) and be forced to deal with the accidental death of Naess, father of her two teenage sons, while he was mountain-climbing. The fatal tragedy occurred on 13 January 2004, when her Solar Arc Ascendant in Capricorn made a sesquiquadrate to Uranus in the 7th.

The year 1999 was not without some successes, however: Ross had a new album in the stores, there were optimistic plans to reunite with the Supremes and go on tour, and she was heralded as the most successful female singer of all time. Mars (directing through Leo) had just moved into the 10th House.

4.41 • Cassius Clay becomes Muhammad Ali

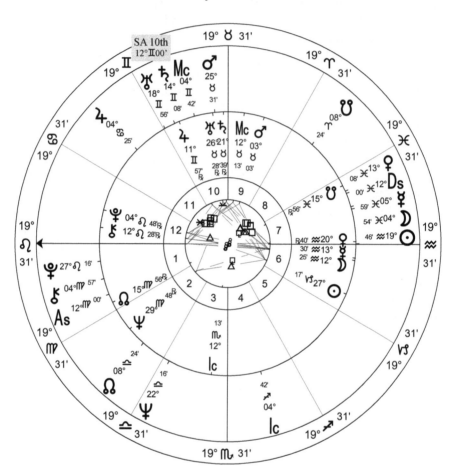

Inner Wheel (natal chart): 17 January 1942 at 18:35 CST
in Louisville, Kentucky, USA (38N15, 85W46).

Outer Wheel: Solar Arc directions to 6 March 1964.

Data Source: Birth certificate, obtained by Ed Steinbrecher; copy on file.

In early 1964, Cassius Clay began meeting with the controversial, charismatic leader Malcolm X. It's not known precisely when Clay first embraced the Muslim faith but on the night of **6 March 1964**, Clay was renamed **Muhammad Ali** and officially became a member of the Nation of Islam. The move generated its own outrage with Ali once stating, 'We who follow the teachings of Elijah Muhammad don't want to be forced to integrate. Integration is wrong. We don't want to live with the white man; that's all.'

At this time, the Sun (ruling his Leo Ascendant) directed over the Descendant in Aquarius. This is indicative of Ali renaming himself and changing his identity – Sun to the ASC–DSC axis – and embracing a new 'father' (Sun) and community (Aquarius). Malcolm X's widow, Betty Shabazz, said, '[Malcolm] felt his job was to get this young man [Ali] to believe in himself and stand squarely on both feet with his shoulders back.' His daughter, Attallah Shabazz, said, '[Ali] underwent a social and political awakening... [and joined] a family of supporters.'

On 25 February 1964, a week before the official conversion, the motor-mouth braggart dethroned the World Heavyweight Champion Sonny Liston and declared cockily, 'I am the greatest!' (Jupiter). Ali's Equal 10th House cusp (not his MC)* had directed to an exact conjunction with Jupiter in Gemini in the 10th (i.e. the SA Ascendant – 90° to the Equal 10th cusp – squared Jupiter, see shaded area, opposite). Soon after his victory and conversion, commentators were wondering whether Ali's chief role was as a Heavyweight Champion or a religious crusader (Jupiter).

In early 1971, the MC directed to that same Jupiter in Gemini in the 10th, some seven years after the 10th cusp had done so (note that his MC and 10th House cusps are seven degrees apart). Ali suffered his first-ever professional loss (to Joe Frazier, 8 March 1971) in 'The Fight of the Century', one of the most famous and publicized (Jupiter) matches of all time. Muhammad Ali had been away from the ring for a number of years because of his stance against the Vietnam War. It was headlined as an anti-establishment (Ali) vs. conservative/pro-Vietnam (Frazier) match and, although he lost, Ali had secured the respect of the American public.

More importantly, this SA MC conjunct Jupiter reflected an important moral victory for Ali while this aspect was still in orb three months later. Ali had declared himself a conscientious

4.42 • Ali's Convictions

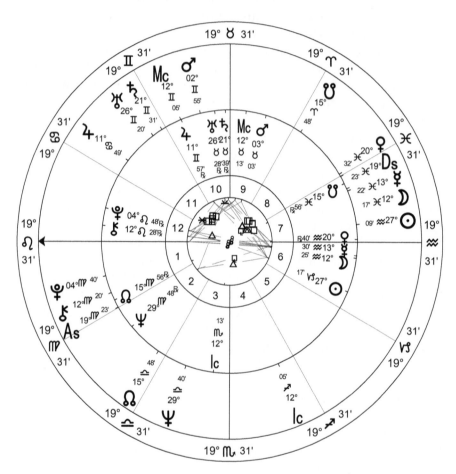

Inner Wheel (natal chart): 17 January 1942 at 18:35 CST
in Louisville, Kentucky, USA (38N15, 85W46).

Outer Wheel: Solar Arc directions to 28 June 1971.

Data Source: Birth certificate, obtained by Ed Steinbrecher; copy on file.

objector and been arrested and stripped of his title in April 1967. He was found guilty by jury of draft evasion, but in the four years of appeals that followed, support for Ali and condemnation of the Vietnam War had grown.

Finally, on **28 June 1971** – with directed MC to Jupiter – the Supreme Court reversed his conviction (incidentally, natal Jupiter is retrograde, suggesting a second chance, victory or new faith later in life). Natally, with the MC in Taurus (and Mars nearby), Ali was known for his steadfastness in the face of opposition and bigotry. When that MC reached Jupiter, it wasn't a professional victory as it had been in 1964, when the 10th House cusp (career) conjunct Jupiter. It was linked to a defining event that shaped his reputation (MC) as a man who stuck stubbornly to his principles (Taurus) and beliefs (Jupiter).

* One of the reasons I use Equal houses is to give importance to the 10th and 4th House cusps (the nonagesimal and nadir, respectively) when using directions (or transits, for that matter). So often, the 10th and 4th House cusps speak of actual work (10th) and home matters (4th). The 10th House is the job, the career. The MC and IC speak of our reputation and roots, and the actualization in society (MC) of deep-rooted principles embedded in childhood (IC).

Most charts (unless births are near the Equator or the Ascendant is around Pisces/Aries or Virgo/Libra) have a 10th House cusp and MC that are some distance away from each other. A direction to or from the 10th House cusp degree is a new chapter in our life path or our work. A direction to or from the MC degree speaks more of a fundamental change in our reputation and how we impact our outer environment (and how it impacts us).

174

4.43 • Disgraced Champion

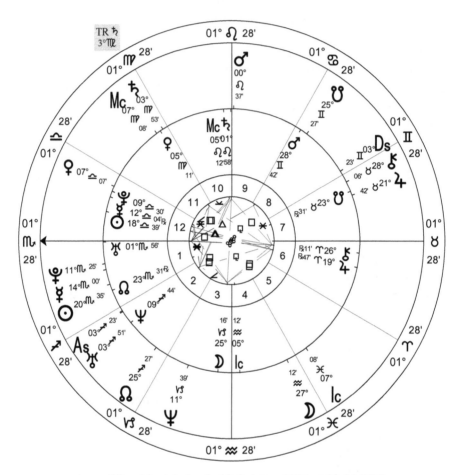

Inner Wheel (natal chart): 12 October 1975 at 08:01 PDT
in Los Angeles, California, USA (34N03, 118W15).

Outer Wheel: Solar Arc directions to 5 October 2007.

Data Source: Birth certificate, as quoted by Pat Taglilatelo.

Additional Data: Florence Griffith-Joyner, 21 December 1959 at 00:11 PST
in Los Angeles, California, USA (34N03, 118W15). Data from birth certificate;
copy on file.

With Saturn on the MC in Leo, athlete and Olympic champion **Marion Jones** was held up as a shining example of blue ribbon (and gold medal) achievement. But Saturn holds us accountable (particularly when strong in the horoscope). If we aren't stringent and ethical (Saturn), we invite Saturn into our lives in the guise of a judge or police officer, for instance, to impose Saturn *upon us*.

Saturn–MC conjunctions (natally or by transit) are sometimes 'fall from grace' aspects, and a tight square from Uranus suggests a possible reversal of Jones's standing. And with a Leo MC, the impact of a male Svengali on her life is likely. (There are a number of other signs in the chart that act as significators for her life events, and remarkably, two of her partners have been involved in drug scandals – note the Descendant ruler Venus is square to Neptune.)

Here's a chronology of events during her Saturn Return (at the MC) and the resultant Shadow Transits:

- February 2006: After being accused of taking steroids, Jones wins/settles a defamation lawsuit, but the International Olympic Committee says it will investigate further – TR Saturn Return and TR Saturn conjunct MC.

- 5 October 2007: Jones retires, admitting steroid use and lying in a federal investigation – TR Saturn conjunct SA Saturn (Shadow Saturn Return).

- December 2007 to January 2008: Jones is formally stripped of her Olympic medals in December and banned from competing; in January, she is sentenced to six months in prison – TR Saturn conjunct SA MC.

- 7 March 2008: She reports to the prison – Shadow Saturn Return again.

I find it interesting that, at the time of her confession and public condemnation (**5 October 2007**), Marion's Solar Arc MC was closely conjunct Florence Griffith-Joyner's natal 12th House Moon–Pluto conjunction at 6° and 7° Virgo. Flo Jo's extraordinary (and much debated) 1988 Olympic gold medals and world records had been the inspiration for a teenage Marion Jones.

4.44 • The End of the Acid Reign

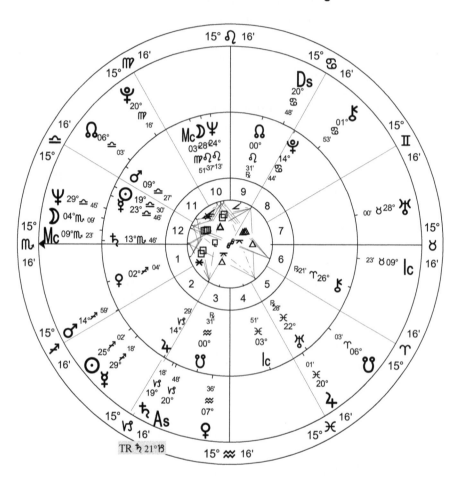

Inner Wheel (natal chart): 13 October 1925 at 09:00 GMT
in Grantham, England (52N55, 0W39).

Outer Wheel: Solar Arc directions to 22 November 1990.

Data Source: Charles Harvey quotes Thatcher via her private secretary.

The chart of former UK Prime Minister **Margaret Thatcher**, with natal Saturn conjunct her Scorpio Ascendant, depicts a controlled, humourless Iron Lady who was famously 'not for turning'. As PM, she was an unyielding conservative with a strong work ethic, and her agenda was to restore balance (Libra) and old-fashioned values to her country – returning it to its glory days as a middle-class and prosperous Victorian nation (Moon conjunct nostalgic Neptune on a Virgo MC). Her planets in Libra can be read in this comment: 'The codes of right and wrong lie at the bottom of every decision ... They account for her inflexibility ... and for the lack of imagination or real interest in debate.' (Penny Junor, *Margaret Thatcher: Wife, Mother, Politician*, Sidgwick & Jackson, 1983.)

Saturn transits/directions are often pivotal times in a politician's career. During Thatcher's second Saturn Return and the planet's passage over her Ascendant (January–April and September–October 1984), she faced two of her sternest tests while in office. There was the year-long (from March 1984) coal miners' strike, followed by a narrow escape from an assassination attempt by the IRA terrorists (at 02:54 on 12 October 1984 in Brighton, England). Thatcher's unwavering focus led to a third election win in 1987.

Thatcher's chart shows immense power, control, discipline and an uncompromising stance: Saturn rises in Scorpio, while the bossy 'Attila the Hen' Moon is in Leo, and both the Sun and Mars square a tight Jupiter–Pluto opposition, forming a cardinal T-square. The latter suggests themes such as deep exploration (e.g. coal mining, as does Saturn in Scorpio), religious extremism/attacks and titanic power struggles – all of which she endured during her time in office.

In October and November 1990, while experiencing her Shadow Saturn Return, she was vulnerable again but no longer indestructible. Transiting Saturn had reached SA Saturn and SA Ascendant, now both in Capricorn. (By then, SA Saturn–Ascendant had directed just over 65°, so the transit had taken more than six years to finally catch up.) On **22 November 1990** Thatcher resigned over conflicts with key members of her Cabinet concerning European integration and a single currency, as well as the greatly unpopular poll tax. A leadership challenge and lack of support from her Cabinet (Capricorn) had been the deciding factors in her resignation. (SA Saturn was also square to the Sun in Libra, and SA Mars was quincunx Pluto at this time, too.)

4.45 • Feed the World

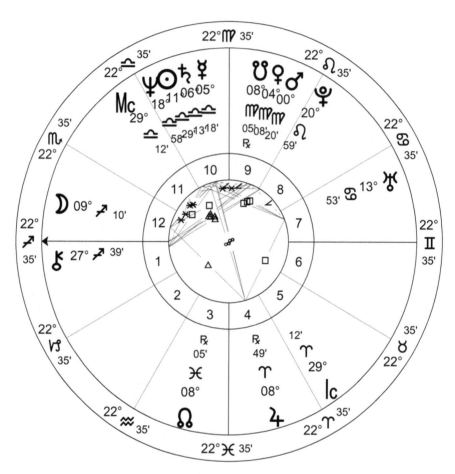

Wheel (natal chart): 5 October 1951 at 14:20 GDT
in Dublin, Ireland (53N20, 6W15).

Data Source: Jo Logan quotes Geldof's letter.

Additional Data: Midge Ure, 10 October 1953 at 08:30 GMT in
Glasgow, Scotland (55N53, 4W15). Data from his birth certificate,
as quoted by Paul Wright.

In late 1984, **Bob Geldof**, the front man for rock band The Boomtown Rats, became immersed in raising money for famine relief in Africa. His Sun in Libra is straddled by Mercury, Saturn and Neptune, describing a musician who realized a higher calling. Neptune is linked to charity and compassion for the human condition, while Mercury–Saturn in Libra suggests an authoritative spokesman for justice and the restoration of equal rights.

On 23 October 1984 at 12:25 GMT, London, the BBC aired a seven-minute, dispassionate report on the 40,000 starving refugees who had congregated in the area of Korem, a town in war-torn Ethiopia. Even though the TV segment made no mention of the famine's being man-made (the Ethiopian government was involved in a brutal civil war and was dropping bombs to disrupt food supply chains), *The Guardian* would later call it 'a watershed moment in crisis reporting'. The TV segment (broadcast on 425 stations worldwide) showed a famine of biblical proportions, a 'hell on earth' where a life was being claimed every twenty minutes.

Watching a repeat showing that evening was Geldof. (His own North Node in Pisces rises through Korem in Ethiopia, and is natally conjunct goddess of agriculture Ceres, over which his progressed Moon crossed in December 1984.) Tortured by what he saw, Geldof and his pal Midge Ure (who shares Geldof's Sun–Neptune in Libra square Uranus, and Venus–Mars in Virgo) mobilized many of the biggest names in UK music on 25 November in the hope of raising £72,000. The result was a collaborative effort called Band Aid, whose charity single, 'Do They Know It's Christmas?', went on to earn £8 million for famine relief, and reconnect rock stars with their conscience. Then followed Live Aid, a 58-band, 16-hour marathon 'global jukebox' concert from both London and Philadelphia, which began at 12:01 p.m. in Wembley, north London, on 13 July 1985 and was watched by more than one billion viewers.

Band Aid and Live Aid made Bob Geldof – the irascible, foul-mouthed, fading pop star – an unlikely hero. Yet, deeply embedded in Geldof's T-square of Sun–Mercury–Saturn opposite Jupiter and both square Uranus in Cancer – along with his Sagittarius Moon and Ascendant – are the fundamental issues of right and wrong, waking people up to the 'truth', building bridges between opposing factions, selling an idea for others to believe in, and taking huge leaps of faith into the unknown.

4.46 • The Long Walk to Justice

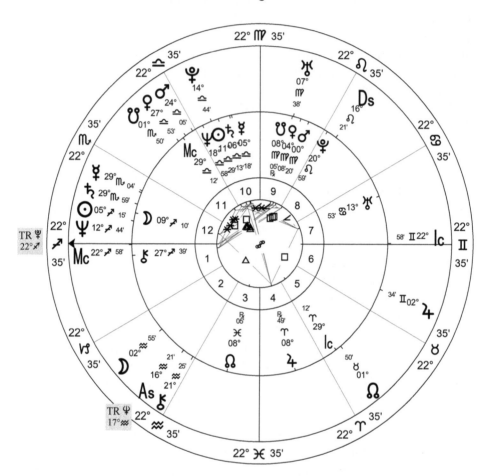

Inner Wheel (natal chart): 5 October 1951 at 14:20 GDT
in Dublin, Ireland (53N20, 6W15).

Outer Wheel: Solar Arc directions to 6 July 2005.

Data Source: Jo Logan quotes Geldof's letter.

'Saint Bob' became a people's champion, and the public entrusted him with their cash donations wherever he went. In late 1984, TR Pluto crossed over his MC. His awareness of famine (Pluto) profoundly changed his direction, reputation and world perspective (MC). Whether **Bob Geldof's** MC is in late Libra or early Scorpio, either ruler (Venus or Mars) is in Virgo, a sign related to health, (mal)nutrition and victims (the small and overlooked). In *The Book of World Horoscopes* by Nicholas Campion, a chart for Ethiopia's revolution – 12 September 1974, 06:15 GDT, Addis Ababa, 09N02, 38E42 – gives a set of astonishing inter-aspects with Geldof's natal chart: Venus at 4° Virgo (exactly conjunct Geldof's Venus), Neptune conjunct Geldof's Moon (feeding the helpless) and Mercury–Pluto conjunct Geldof's Mercury–Saturn in Libra. The horoscope for Ethiopia, like Geldof's, has Jupiter as the handle of a bucket-shaped chart, but in Pisces on the Descendant.

Geldof's chart handle, Jupiter in Aries, reflects a zealous, idealistic and well-intentioned crusader. But wherever there's Jupiter, there's also the temptation to believe one's own publicity or to adopt the godlike status bestowed by others. Jupiter's challenge is to embrace and maintain integrity.

Twenty years on, Geldof planned Live 8 (2 July 2005, a concert to 'Make Poverty History') and The Long Walk to Justice (**6 July 2005**), in which Geldof called for leaders to cancel debt and to make aid/trade equal for all (Mercury–Saturn in Libra). During both events, TR Pluto was at 22° Sagittarius, conjunct his Ascendant and on his SA MC – a Shadow Transit of 1984's event. The MC, once in Libra, was now in Sagittarius (the long walk to justice).

But on this occasion, the Long Walk idea was less practicable, as Geldof urged one million people to descend on Edinburgh during the G8 political summit being held in Scotland. When asked where people would stay, he responded that they should knock on the doors of strangers, who ought to accommodate them. At the time, he was accused of compromising the cause and supporting political agendas, and was criticized as an egotistical figure who set himself up as a messiah (Jupiter/Sagittarius).

Interestingly, at the same time, Geldof had another Shadow Transit: TR Neptune on his SA Ascendant. The original event (when transiting Neptune hit his natal Ascendant at 22° Sagittarius in late 1981) was when his rock band hit an all-time low in popularity.

4.47 • From Peter Pan to Pied Piper?

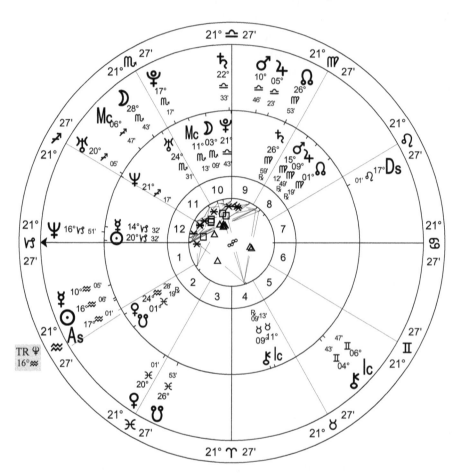

Inner Wheel (natal chart): 11 January 1980 at 07:08 PST
in Santa Monica, California, USA (34N01, 118W29).

Outer Wheel: Solar Arc directions to 1 March 2005.

Data Source: Birth certificate, obtained by Frank Clifford; copy on file.

In May 1992, teenager **Jordan Chandler** met superstar recluse Michael Jackson. Within 18 months, news of Chandler's sleepovers and his accusations of molestation were to rock Jackson's life and tarnish, in many people's eyes, the singer's reputation as a fundraiser and supporter of underprivileged children. The world wanted to know if Peter Pan had turned into an abusive Pied Piper at his Neverland home.

I don't think the natal horoscope can reveal innocence or guilt, so a more interesting question to pose, perhaps, is: can we see powerful, abusive or reclusive male figures 'written' in Jordan's script? And what of unusual friendships? Well, consider the Sun on the Ascendant in Capricorn closely square Pluto, Mars–Jupiter in the 8th, and Venus in Aquarius tightly square Uranus in Scorpio.

Chandler began his sleepovers at Neverland in March 1993. The scandal erupted from 20 and 22 August 1993, and an out-of-court settlement was reached between Jackson and the Chandler family on 25 January 1994 for $15 million. During this period, TR Neptune and Uranus travelled over the teenager's natal Sun–Ascendant (natally square Pluto in Libra) – depicting his contact and close relationship with a male superstar who introduced him to a seductive, glamorous lifestyle. It would suggest the alleged blurring and overstepping of friendship boundaries and the resulting media frenzy. The scandal brought accusations of dishonesty and extortion against Jordan and his dad (the Sun) and, during this confusing, disorientating time, the boy's contact with both his father and Jackson came to an abrupt end (TR Uranus – breaks – and Neptune – losses).

Ultimately, and regardless of the truth, Jordan's silence was bought and he went into hiding. In early 2005, there was talk of forcing Jordan to testify against his former friend when Jackson was on trial. Would he or wouldn't he show? And if he did turn up, what on earth would he say under oath? One thing I knew: there must be a Shadow Transit occurring! The chart opposite is set for **1 March 2005**. Again, Neptune was on his Sun and Ascendant, but this time it was conjunct their SA directed positions at 16-17° Aquarius. As it turned out, in Neptunian fashion, the boy wasn't called, made no comment and was alleged to have fled the country during the trial. (On 25 June 2009, Michael Jackson died suddenly. Jordan's SA Neptune was conjunct his natal Ascendant and was still in orb when his father Evan committed suicide on 5 November 2009.)

4.48 • Some Examples of the Sesquiquadrate (Sesquisquare)

Like other 'minor' aspects in the natal chart, the sesquiquadrate (also known as the sesquisquare) appears to have a *specific* function, and its nature can be seen in one or two precise storylines that are played out and repeated at various times in our lives (usually when the aspect is triggered or sparks off another area of the chart). Whereas the major aspects reveal the headlines in our life story (the key patterns, players and scripts), the minors are more akin to the important subplots we suddenly stumble upon.

The sesquiquadrate comprises the semi-square and the square ($45° + 90° = 135°$). Imagine the 'hard' aspects as an unfolding scenario, similar to the lunar cycle. At $45°$, there emerges an irritation: we're agitated because we are being asked to consider how best to work with planets that speak very different languages. But at this stage, we may vacillate or feel ambivalent as to the correct course of action. At $90°$, we are more 'in the know' but face a crisis point – an obstacle or challenge that can block our progress or motivate us to move onwards. At $135°$, we meet a disruption, a chance to take a different route. Finally at $180°$, we reach a culmination point of full realization, where the conflict (and awareness) of opposites brings about change.

Whereas the 'soft' aspects create self-perpetuating behavioural patterns and 'comfortable' situations that can trap us, all four 'hard' aspects symbolize the stages when friction erupts – but they demand awareness or activity; if we meet that demand, they offer a release of tension and an ability to move forward.

C C Zain (Elbert Benjamine) linked the sesquiquadrate to Uranus, feeling that both have abrasive, disruptive energies. Lois Rodden wrote that this aspect was prominent in the charts of adventurers, those who travel uncharted waters or blaze new trails. The aspect also appears with frequency in the charts for the moments of accidents, as well as in our own charts (by transit or direction) when accidents occur.

Rodden stated that the sesquiquadrate is present in areas that break up and are forced to reform – usually off the beaten track. In her wonderful book *Money*, she observed, 'Conditions never go entirely back to where they were before.' I've seen this aspect in the natal charts of people who started off in one direction, only to find that events steered them down an unexpected avenue. For example, a teacher whose school is threatened with closure is forced to protest and soon discovers her niche as a campaigner. Certainly, there appears to be a quantum leap ('sudden jump'), or a trigger at some stage, to a new way of life in the areas signified by the planets in sesquiquadrate.

Exploring this aspect (using orbs of no more than 2°) with clients and students always brings up some fascinating stories. One young student, with Uranus in the 2nd House tightly sesquiquadrate her Midheaven (MC) in Gemini, has been laid off from work three times; however, despite the strong resistance in the form of her heavily Earth-based chart, the final lay-off prompted her to go freelance (Uranus, Gemini).

In Solar Arc, sesquiquadrates can be triggered in two ways:

- A planet directs into a sesquiquadrate with a planet or angle. This coincides with a situation (described by the receiving planet or angle) that is disrupted to the point of no return.

- A planet in natal sesquiquadrate (to another planet or angle) directs to form a new aspect (such as a trine or square) to that planet or angle, giving the natal potential an opportunity to unfold. (Allowing for an orb of 2°, these new aspects can occur around the ages of 13–17, 43–47 and 73–77.)

In **my own horoscope** (chart overleaf), three natal sesquiquadrates (Pluto to the MC, Sun to Neptune, Jupiter to the Ascendant) were activated when I was 16. All three pairs Solar Arc directed to form a trine aspect: natal Pluto sesquiquadrate MC became SA Pluto trine natal MC, as did Neptune to the Sun, and Jupiter to the Ascendant. (The other planet/angle receiving each of these aspects would have directed around this time to quincunx [150°] the first planet.)

At the time, a consultation with an astrologer (Tad Mann) transformed (Pluto) my direction/place in the world (MC). It was a no-turning-back moment (Pluto). I was searching (Neptune) to understand myself and 'what I was all about' (Sun). I 'tuned in' (Neptune) to astrology, and it helped me to gain greater self-awareness (Sun). Astrology became a language of self-expression

(SA Jupiter in Aquarius trine my natal Ascendant in Gemini). I had started out being interested in a career in teaching (Jupiter) or behind the scenes (Pluto) in film (Neptune), but I soon saw astrology as a calling (Sun) and a way of realizing and actualizing (MC) my 'true self' (Sun). Although already fascinated by Sun sign astrology, the consultation on **17 August 1989** was an unexpected detour (sesquiquadrate), introducing me to a new life and taking me on a very different road, both personally and professionally (Sun, MC).

A client, '**Katja**', has the Moon in Cancer in the 9th House sesquiquadrate Mercury in Pisces on the cusp of the 5th. This could imply disruptive moves (sesquiquadrate) of country and home (Moon–Cancer–9th) and a nomadic existence or sporadic home life (Mercury–Pisces–4th) or sudden changes in love affairs (5th).

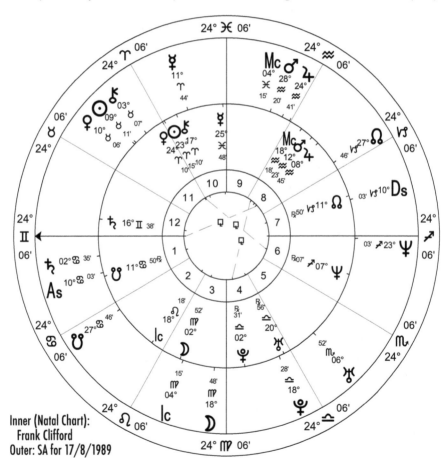

Inner (Natal Chart):
Frank Clifford
Outer: SA for 17/8/1989

Firstly, she was evacuated from Nazi Germany with her family to Norway when she was 14 months old. Not unusual in wartime, but her mother (Moon) was not accepted by the Norwegian family and a few years later they all left for Sweden.

At 17 (the bi-wheel is set for **1 August 1961**), Katja won a year's scholarship to an American high school and lived with a family in California (Moon–Cancer–9th). What the school didn't tell her was that she was an unofficial spokesperson for Sweden and was expected to give numerous speeches (Mercury) to the 2,000 undergraduates, recounting her experiences of living abroad (Moon–Cancer–9th). This terrified the shy girl but she soon became skilled in public speaking. By Solar Arc, Mercury was now sesquiquadrate natal Ascendant in Scorpio and the Equal 10th House cusp in Leo.

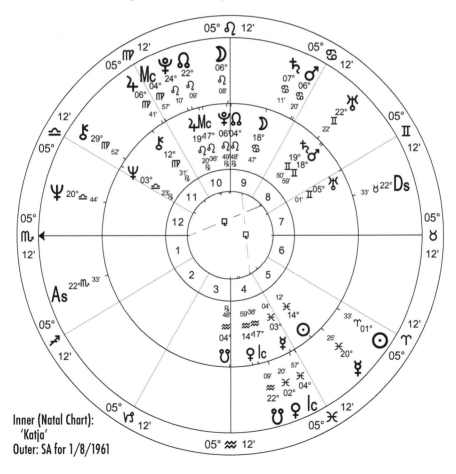

Inner (Natal Chart):
'Katja'
Outer: SA for 1/8/1961

Although dominated by a T-square of Mercury–Jupiter, Uranus and Pluto, **Brigitte Bardot's** chart has prominent sesquiquadrates:

- Uranus sesquiquadrate the Sagittarius Ascendant: from actress to activist and outspoken agitator for animal and human rights.

- Moon in Gemini on the Descendant sesquiquadrate Mercury–Jupiter in Libra: from an Aphrodite moulded by her Svengali husband to a commentator on the right to freedom of speech.

In **January 1962**, Bardot made her first public stand against animal slaughter, denouncing the methods commonly used. It was to be the first of many public appearances, some of which would result in

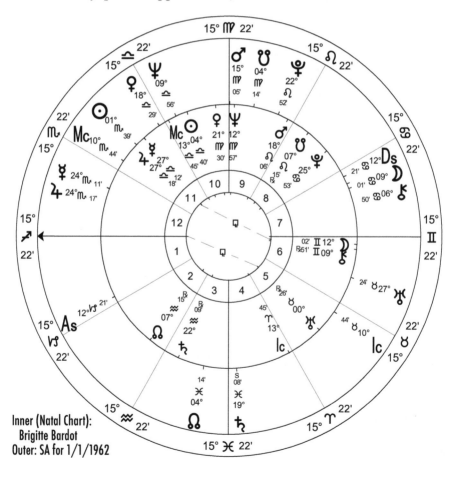

Inner (Natal Chart):
 Brigitte Bardot
Outer: SA for 1/1/1962

criminal charges. That month, all four areas of her chart with natal sesquiquadrates were being activated in a stunning series of Solar Arc directions: her SA Ascendant was now quincunx her Moon, and SA Uranus was quincunx Mercury–Jupiter. The quincunx aspect in SA suggests the emergence of an area that has been brewing or bubbling under the surface for years.

Interestingly, SA Mars had reached the Equal 10th House and was now sesquiquadrate Uranus in the birth chart, setting off the explosive natal Uranus–Ascendant sesquiquadrate. This reminds us that, when a planet that's natally in sesquiquadrate is triggered, expect some fireworks, because the aspect reveals an unstable part of the horoscope – one waiting to make drastic, irrevocable change.

Necrophiliac and cannibal **Ed Gein**, who was the 'inspiration' for characters in *Psycho*, *The Texas Chainsaw Massacre* and *The Silence of the Lambs*, had a potentially explosive natal Mars–Uranus sesquiquadrate (pictured, right). He began his full descent into madness when his beloved and domineering mother died in late December 1945. A number of Solar Arcs occurred at this time, including SA Venus in

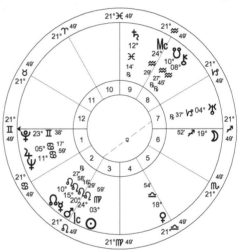

Scorpio sesquiquadrate natal Neptune in Cancer. Left alone and terrified of human contact, Gein began stealing women's bodies from graves, desecrating corpses and bringing body parts back to his home. Psychologists believe that this was, in part, due to his overwhelming desire (Venus in Scorpio) and longing (Neptune in Cancer) to have the physical presence of his deceased mother back in his life.

When Czech tennis star **Martina Navratilova** defected from the Soviet Union in September 1975, she was acting out her natal Mars in Pisces on the cusp of the 12th House sesquiquadrate Neptune in Libra in the 7th. The aspect is descriptive of the 18-year-old's secret and dramatic defection to seek asylum (i.e. refugee status –

Neptune, Pisces) in the US, fleeing from a Communist ideology she deemed unfair (Neptune in Libra) and feeling persecuted by gossip and innuendo (Pisces). Once she had defected, Martina 'ceased to exist' publicly in Czechoslovakia (very Mars–Neptune).

Her combative, independence-seeking Aries Ascendant is natally sesquiquadrate both Saturn and Pluto, also descriptive of her personal battle for freedom against a restrictive and harsh regime. Her decision to escape during the US Open (on **6 September 1975**) came when SA Mercury was sesquiquadrate to natal Mars in Pisces (and SA MC square Sun). Later, of course, Martina went on to become the greatest singles, mixed and doubles tennis player in the world, culminating on 7 July 1990 with a record ninth Wimbledon singles crown (as SA Jupiter reached her Sun).

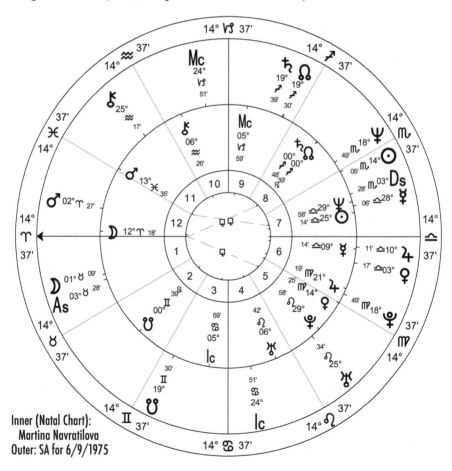

Inner (Natal Chart):
Martina Navratilova
Outer: SA for 6/9/1975

Part V

Further Examples to Research

In this section, you'll find 16 more bi-wheel examples of Solar Arcs in action. The section ends with an example of Solar Arcs through a lifetime – an 80-year listing calculated using Solar Fire software.

Enjoy exploring the birth charts, noting the Solar Arc directions and looking up the transits in your ephemeris for each, and researching the events and their meanings in the subjects' lives.

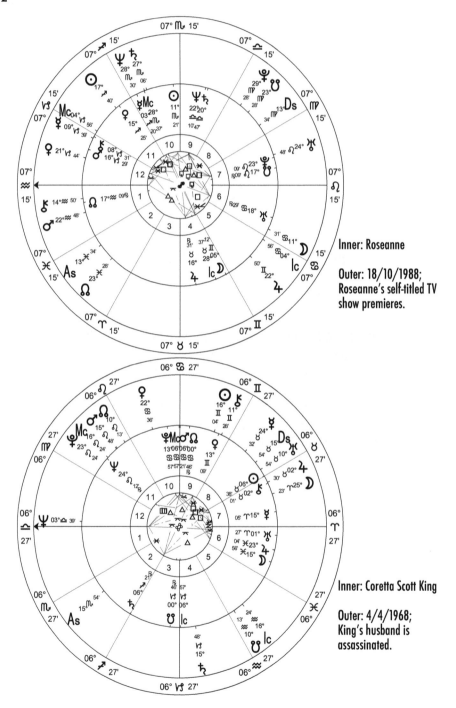

Inner: Roseanne

Outer: 18/10/1988; Roseanne's self-titled TV show premieres.

Inner: Coretta Scott King

Outer: 4/4/1968; King's husband is assassinated.

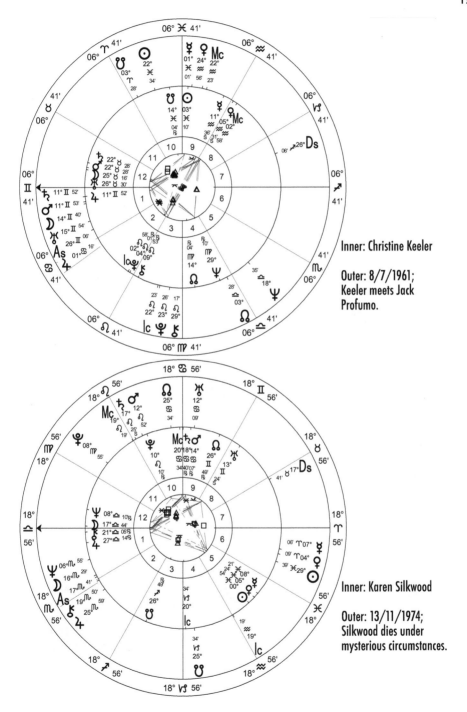

Inner: Christine Keeler

Outer: 8/7/1961;
Keeler meets Jack
Profumo.

Inner: Karen Silkwood

Outer: 13/11/1974;
Silkwood dies under
mysterious circumstances.

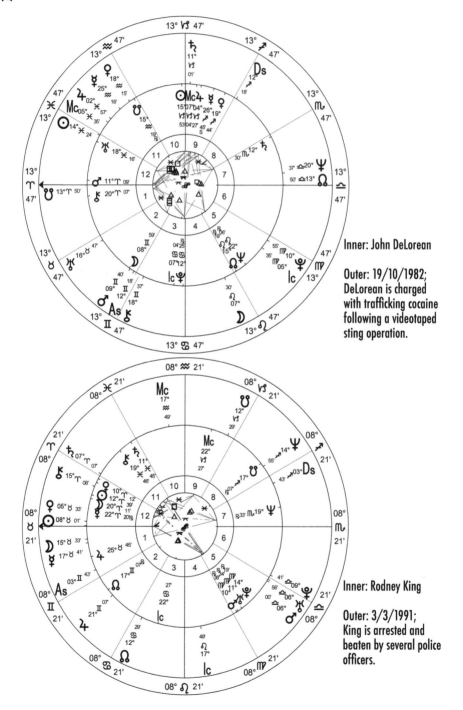

Inner: John DeLorean

Outer: 19/10/1982;
DeLorean is charged
with trafficking cocaine
following a videotaped
sting operation.

Inner: Rodney King

Outer: 3/3/1991;
King is arrested and
beaten by several police
officers.

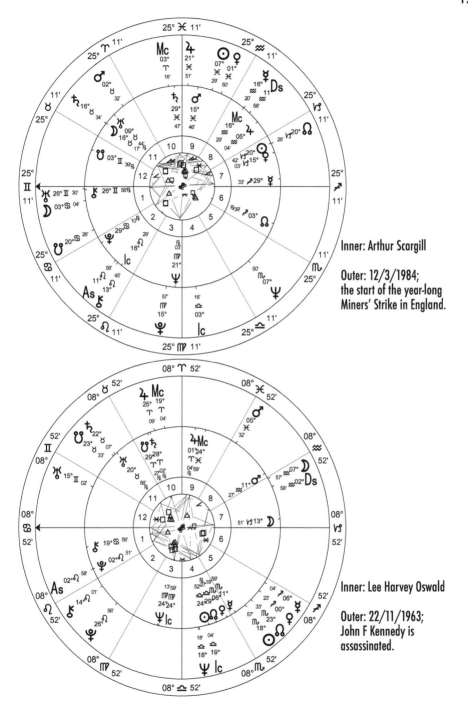

Inner: Arthur Scargill

Outer: 12/3/1984;
the start of the year-long
Miners' Strike in England.

Inner: Lee Harvey Oswald

Outer: 22/11/1963;
John F Kennedy is
assassinated.

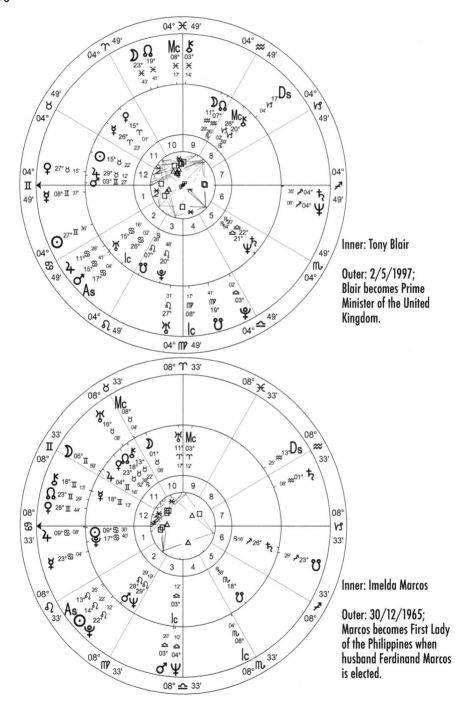

Inner: Tony Blair

Outer: 2/5/1997;
Blair becomes Prime
Minister of the United
Kingdom.

Inner: Imelda Marcos

Outer: 30/12/1965;
Marcos becomes First Lady
of the Philippines when
husband Ferdinand Marcos
is elected.

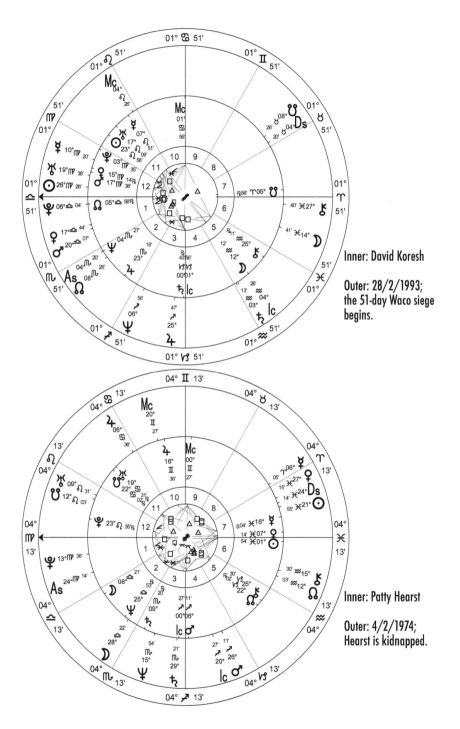

Inner: David Koresh

Outer: 28/2/1993;
the 51-day Waco siege
begins.

Inner: Patty Hearst

Outer: 4/2/1974;
Hearst is kidnapped.

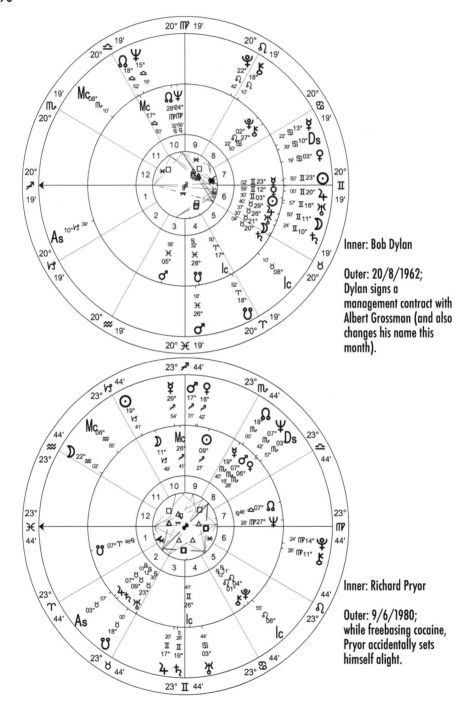

Inner: Bob Dylan

Outer: 20/8/1962;
Dylan signs a
management contract with
Albert Grossman (and also
changes his name this
month).

Inner: Richard Pryor

Outer: 9/6/1980;
while freebasing cocaine,
Pryor accidentally sets
himself alight.

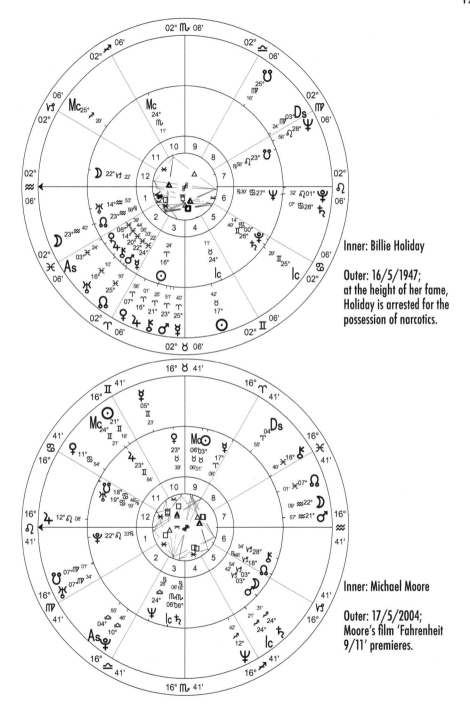

Inner: Billie Holiday

Outer: 16/5/1947;
at the height of her fame,
Holiday is arrested for the
possession of narcotics.

Inner: Michael Moore

Outer: 17/5/2004;
Moore's film 'Fahrenheit
9/11' premieres.

Donald Trump: The Worksheet

	Cardinal +	Fixed	Mutable +
Fire +		♂ASC(♀) ☽	
Earth –		MC	
Air	♃(♆)		☉(♅)
Water +	♀♇♄		

Chart Ruler
☉♐10th

Sun Dispositor
☿♋11th

Four Angles and Links
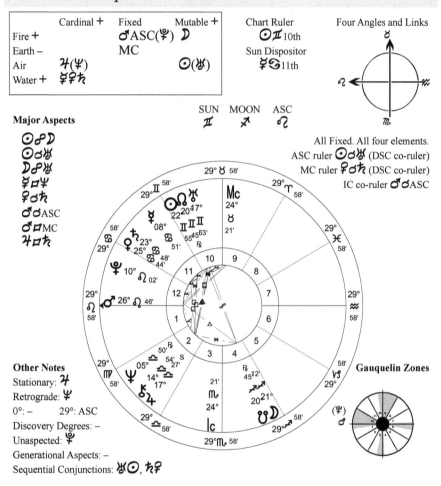

Major Aspects

☉☍☽
☉☌♅
☽☍♅
☿□♆
♀☌♄
♂☌ASC
♂⚹MC
♃□♄

SUN MOON ASC
♊   ♐   ♌

All Fixed. All four elements.
ASC ruler ☉☌♅ (DSC co-ruler)
MC ruler ♀☌♄ (DSC co-ruler)
IC co-ruler ♂☌ASC

29° ♉ 58'
29° ♊ 58'   Mc 24°
29° ♈ 58'
58' 29° II II 08° II II 55 45 63' ℞ ♉ 21' 29° ♓ 58'
69 29° ♂ 23° 25° 51' ⚷ 48' 44'
10 9
♇ 10° ♌ 02' 11 8
29° ♌ 58' ♂ 26° ♌ 46' 12 1 7 6 29° ♒ 58'
50' ℞ ♏ 54' S 27'
3 4 5
29° 05° ♍ ♆ 14° 17' 58' ♃ 21' ♏ 24' Ic R 45 12' 20 21° ☋☽ 29° 58' ♓ 58' 29°
29° ♎ 58' 29°♏ 58'

Other Notes

Stationary: ♃
Retrograde: ♆
0°: –   29°: ASC
Discovery Degrees: –
Unaspected: ♀
Generational Aspects: –
Sequential Conjunctions: ♅☉, ♄♀

Gauquelin Zones

(♀)
♂

Wheel (natal chart): 14 June 1946 at 10:54 EDT
in Jamaica, Queens, New York, USA (40N42, 73W49).

Data Source: Birth certificate and hospital record; copies on file.

The worksheet originates from the author's book
'Getting to the Heart of Your Chart' (Flare, 2017 edition).

Lifetime Solar Arcs and Key Events: Donald Trump

When looking at a Dynamic Report, you can see a lifetime of Solar Arcs and match these to corresponding life events and periods. But sometimes it's easy to lose the essence of what's happening in the natal chart. Students often get disappointed because they can't match Solar Arc directions listed to *the very day* that something happened in their lives, forgetting that there is an orb of influence and that these lists don't show planets spending a whole year at 0° or 29° (or mid degrees) of a sign. But these lifetime lists are handy when scanning a lifetime of directions and events.

For space reasons, I've included only conjunctions, oppositions and squares between the planets, North Node, Ascendant and MC. Any planet conjunct one part of an axis will show up as opposite the other. For instance, SA Jupiter conjunct the Descendant will be seen as 'Jupiter (7) Opp Asc (1)', and the same with the IC ('opposite the MC') and South Node ('opposite the North Node'). I've also listed the Sun/Moon and Ascendant/MC midpoints. In Trump's example, overleaf, I've listed Solar Arcs from birth to 75 years and divided them into decades, placing some key life events within the lists, too. Here's a quick guide to reading the lifetime list that follows:

1 Plu (12) Cnj Mar (12) – 28 Dec 1963
   This means Solar Arc Pluto (travelling through the 12th House) conjuncts Mars in the 12th – exact on 28 Dec 1963.
2 Asc (1) Sqr Ura (10) – 28 Mar 1965
   SA Ascendant square Uranus, i.e. Equal 10th House conjunct Uranus – exact on 28 Mar 1965. An Asc square to a planet in the other half of the chart (houses 4 to 7) indicates the Equal 4th House cusp is conjunct the planet in question.
3 MC (11) Cnj Can (11) – 23 Oct 1983
   SA Midheaven moves into the sign of Cancer on 23 Oct 1983.
4 Plu (1) Cnj Sun/Moon (1) – 30 Jun 1990
   SA Pluto is conjunct the Sun/Moon midpoint – exact on 30 June 1990.
5 Jup (4) Cnj House (4) – 4 Jan 1991
   SA Jupiter moves into the 4th House on 4 Jan 1991.
6 Moon (7) Opp Asc (1) – 8 May 2018
   SA Moon conjuncts the Descendant – exact on 8 May 2018.

Here is a Dynamic Report – calculated using Solar Fire software – of Donald Trump's Solar Arc directions (conjunctions, oppositions and squares only) from birth to age 75, along with some key life events:

Node (10) Opp Moon (4) 2 Dec 1946
Moon (4) Sqr Sun/Moon (1) 10 May 1947
Node (10) Sqr Sun/Moon (1) 28 Oct 1947
Moon (4) Opp Sun (10) 4 Apr 1948
Sat (11) Cnj Ven (11) 19 Jun 1948
Node (10) Cnj Sun (10) 22 Sep 1948
MC (9) Sqr Mar (12) 22 Dec 1948
Chi (2) Cnj Jup (2) 10 Feb 1949
Ura (10) Cnj Node (10) 14 Jun 1949
Nep (2) Sqr Mer (11) 11 Aug 1949
Mar (1) Cnj Asc (1) 17 Oct 1949
Mar (1) Cnj House (1) 17 Oct 1949
Mar (1) Cnj Vir (1) 30 Oct 1949
Mer (11) Cnj Asc/MC (11) 30 Nov 1949
Ura (10) Opp Moon (4) 2 Dec 1949

──────────── **1950s** ────────────

Ura (10) Sqr Sun/Moon (1) 28 Oct 1950
Ven (12) Cnj House (12) 18 Nov 1950
Ven (12) Cnj Leo (12) 1 Dec 1950
Ura (10) Cnj Sun (10) 23 Sep 1951
MC (10) Sqr Asc (1) 27 Apr 1952
MC (10) Cnj House (10) 27 Apr 1952
MC (10) Cnj Gem (10) 10 May 1952
Mer (11) Sqr Chi (2) 16 Oct 1952
Sat (12) Cnj House (12) 23 Nov 1952
Sat (12) Cnj Leo (12) 6 Dec 1952
Nep (2) Sqr Asc/MC (11) 28 Jan 1953
Jup (2) Sqr Sat (11) 12 Feb 1953
Sun (11) Cnj House (11) 29 Oct 1953
Sun (11) Cnj Can (11) 10 Nov 1953
Jup (2) Sqr Ven (11) 18 Feb 1955
Mer (11) Sqr Jup (2) 16 Jun 1955
Moon (5) Cnj House (5) 20 Aug 1955
Moon (5) Cnj Cap (5) 2 Sep 1955
Chi (2) Sqr Sat (11) 13 Oct 1955
Nep (2) Cnj Chi (2) 16 Dec 1955
Node (11) Cnj House (11) 7 Feb 1956
Node (11) Cnj Can (11) 20 Feb 1956
Chi (2) Sqr Ven (11) 18 Oct 1957
Nep (2) Cnj Jup (2) 14 Aug 1958
Ura (11) Cnj House (11) 8 Feb 1959
Ura (11) Cnj Can (11) 20 Feb 1959
Jup (3) Cnj House (3) 27 Jul 1959
Jup (3) Cnj Sco (3) 8 Aug 1959
• **sent to military school, autumn 1959**
Sun (11) Sqr Nep (2) 26 Dec 1959

──────────── **1960s** ────────────

Ven (12) Cnj Plu (12) 10 Jun 1961
Plu (12) Sqr MC (9) 17 Jun 1961
Moon (5) Sqr Nep (2) 16 Oct 1961
Mer (11) Cnj Sat (11) 15 Feb 1962
Chi (3) Cnj House (3) 25 Mar 1962
Node (11) Sqr Nep (2) 5 Apr 1962
Chi (3) Cnj Sco (3) 6 Apr 1962
Sun (11) Cnj Mer (11) 23 Feb 1963
Sat (12) Cnj Plu (12) 17 Jun 1963
Plu (12) Cnj Mar (12) 28 Dec 1963
Mer (11) Cnj Ven (11) 21 Feb 1964
Moon (5) Opp Mer (11) 15 Dec 1964
Asc (1) Sqr Ura (10) 28 Mar 1965
Ura (11) Sqr Nep (2) 6 Apr 1965
Nep (2) Sqr Sat (11) 16 Apr 1965
Node (11) Cnj Mer (11) 4 Jun 1965
Sun (11) Cnj Asc/MC (11) 13 Aug 1966
Nep (2) Sqr Ven (11) 22 Apr 1967
Plu (1) Cnj Asc (1) 3 May 1967
Plu (1) Cnj House (1) 3 May 1967
Plu (1) Cnj Vir (1) 16 May 1967
Asc (1) Sqr Node (10) 29 Mar 1968
• **graduates from business school, 20 May 1968; joins father's company**
Moon (5) Opp Asc/MC (11) 4 Jun 1968
Ura (11) Cnj Mer (11) 5 Jun 1968
Mer (12) Cnj House (12) 30 Jul 1968
Mar (1) Sqr Ura (10) 2 Aug 1968
Mer (12) Cnj Leo (12) 11 Aug 1968
Asc (1) Sqr Moon (4) 16 Sep 1968
Node (11) Cnj Asc/MC (11) 22 Nov 1968
Sun (11) Sqr Chi (2) 30 Jun 1969
Asc (1) Cnj Sun/Moon (1) 13 Aug 1969

──────────── **1970s** ────────────

Jup (3) Sqr Plu (12) 17 Feb 1970
Asc (1) Sqr Sun (10) 9 Jul 1970
• **president of company, c. 1971**
MC (10) Cnj Ura (10) 12 Feb 1971
Moon (5) Sqr Chi (2) 22 Apr 1971
Mar (1) Sqr Node (10) 4 Aug 1971
Nep (3) Cnj House (3) 29 Sep 1971
Node (11) Sqr Chi (2) 10 Oct 1971
Nep (3) Cnj Sco (3) 11 Oct 1971
Ura (11) Cnj Asc/MC (11) 24 Nov 1971
Mar (1) Sqr Moon (4) 22 Jan 1972
Sun (11) Sqr Jup (2) 28 Feb 1972
Chi (3) Sqr Plu (12) 17 Oct 1972
Mar (1) Cnj Sun/Moon (1) 18 Dec 1972
• **fights Justice Dept discrimination case against company, Oct 1973; hires Roy Cohn to represent him**
Mar (1) Sqr Sun (10) 13 Nov 1973

Moon (5) Sqr Jup (2) 20 Dec 1973
MC (10) Cnj Node (10) 13 Feb 1974
Node (11) Sqr Jup (2) 9 Jun 1974
MC (10) Opp Moon (4) 3 Aug 1974
Ura (11) Sqr Chi (2) 11 Oct 1974
• **announces partnership with Hyatt,
4 May 1975**
• **settles discrimination case,
10 Jun 1975**
MC (10) Sqr Sun/Moon (1) 29 Jun 1975
MC (10) Cnj Sun (10) 25 May 1976
Ven (12) Sqr MC (9) 18 Jun 1976
• **marries Ivana, 9 Apr 1977**
Ura (11) Sqr Jup (2) 10 Jun 1977
Asc (2) Cnj House (2) 26 Nov 1977
Asc (2) Cnj Lib (2) 8 Dec 1977
• **first child born, 31 Dec 1977**
Sat (12) Sqr MC (9) 24 Jun 1978
Sun (11) Cnj Sat (11) 1 Nov 1978
Ven (12) Cnj Mar (12) 28 Dec 1978
• **buys future Trump Tower building,
Feb 1979**
Mer (12) Cnj Plu (12) 22 Feb 1979

──────────── 1980s ────────────
Moon (5) Opp Sat (11) 22 Aug 1980
• **Grand Hyatt opens, Sep 1980**
Sun (11) Cnj Ven (11) 6 Nov 1980
Sat (12) Cnj Mar (12) 2 Jan 1981
Node (11) Cnj Sat (11) 9 Feb 1981
Mar (2) Cnj House (2) 1 Apr 1981
Mar (2) Cnj Lib (2) 13 Apr 1981
• **alcoholic brother dies, Sep 1981**
Nep (3) Sqr Plu (12) 22 Apr 1982
Ven (1) Cnj Asc (1) 3 May 1982
Ven (1) Cnj House (1) 3 May 1982
Ven (1) Cnj Vir (1) 16 May 1982
• **construction begins on first casino,
Jun 1982**
Moon (5) Opp Ven (11) 28 Aug 1982
Node (11) Cnj Ven (11) 15 Feb 1983
MC (11) Cnj House (11) 11 Oct 1983
MC (11) Cnj Can (11) 23 Oct 1983
• **Trump Tower opens, 30 Nov 1983**
Asc (2) Cnj Nep (2) 22 Jan 1984
Ura (11) Cnj Sat (11) 10 Feb 1984
Sat (1) Cnj Asc (1) 8 May 1984
Sat (1) Cnj House (1) 8 May 1984
• **first casino opens, 15 May 1984**
Sat (1) Cnj Vir (1) 20 May 1984
Jup (3) Opp MC (9) 23 Feb 1985
Sun (12) Cnj House (12) 12 Apr 1985
Sun (12) Cnj Leo (12) 24 Apr 1985
• **Trump's Castle opens, 19 Jun 1985**

• **buys Mar-a-Lago, 27 Dec 1985**
Ura (11) Cnj Ven (11) 14 Feb 1986
Plu (1) Sqr Ura (10) 16 Feb 1986
Moon (6) Cnj House (6) 31 Jan 1987
Moon (6) Cnj Aqu (6) 13 Feb 1987
Asc (2) Sqr Mer (11) 21 Mar 1987
Mar (2) Cnj Nep (2) 27 May 1987
Node (12) Cnj House (12) 21 Jul 1987
Node (12) Cnj Leo (12) 3 Aug 1987
Jup (3) Sqr Mar (12) 2 Sep 1987
Chi (3) Opp MC (9) 22 Oct 1987
• **publishes 'The Art of the Deal',
Nov 1987**
• **acquires Plaza Hotel, Mar 1988**
• **appears on cover of *Time*, Jan 1989**
Plu (1) Sqr Node (10) 15 Feb 1989
Plu (1) Sqr Moon (4) 5 Aug 1989
• **three Trump executives are killed in
a helicopter crash, 10 Oct 1989**
MC (11) Sqr Nep (2) 3 Dec 1989
• **Ivana discovers Marla, Xmas 1989**

──────────── 1990s ────────────
• **splits from Ivana; owes billions –
empire close to collapsing, Jan 1990**
• **Trump Taj Mahal opens, 2 Apr 1990**
Chi (3) Sqr Mar (12) 30 Apr 1990
Plu (1) Cnj Sun/Moon (1) 30 Jun 1990
Ura (12) Cnj House (12) 19 Jul 1990
Mar (2) Sqr Mer (11) 22 Jul 1990
Ura (12) Cnj Leo (12) 1 Aug 1990
Asc (2) Sqr Asc/MC (11) 5 Sep 1990
Jup (4) Sqr Asc (1) 4 Jan 1991
Jup (4) Cnj House (4) 4 Jan 1991
Jup (4) Cnj Sag (4) 16 Jan 1991
• **settles Ivana divorce, 22 Mar 1991**
Plu (1) Sqr Sun (10) 25 May 1991
• **company files for bankruptcy,
Jul 1991, and May 1992**
MC (11) Cnj Mer (11) 28 Jan 1993
Asc (2) Cnj Chi (2) 19 Jul 1993
Chi (4) Sqr Asc (1) 30 Aug 1993
Chi (4) Cnj House (4) 30 Aug 1993
Chi (4) Cnj Sag (4) 12 Sep 1993
• **marries Marla Maples, 20 Dec 1993**
Mar (2) Sqr Asc/MC (11) 5 Jan 1994
Mer (12) Sqr MC (9) 18 Feb 1994
• **debt-free, 30 Jun 1995**
Sun (12) Cnj Plu (12) 25 Oct 1995
Asc (2) Cnj Jup (2) 14 Mar 1996
MC (11) Cnj Asc/MC (11) 13 Jul 1996
Mer (12) Cnj Mar (12) 26 Aug 1996
Mar (2) Cnj Chi (2) 18 Nov 1996
Nep (3) Opp MC (9) 14 Apr 1997

- **separates from Marla, May 1997**
Moon (6) Opp Plu (12) 13 Aug 1997
Node (12) Cnj Plu (12) 30 Jan 1998
- **meets Melania, Sep 1998**
Plu (2) Cnj House (2) 1 Oct 1998
Plu (2) Cnj Lib (2) 14 Oct 1998
MC (11) Sqr Chi (2) 26 May 1999
- **divorces Marla, 8 Jun 1999**
- **father dies, 25 Jun 1999**
Mar (2) Cnj Jup (2) 14 Jul 1999
Nep (3) Sqr Mar (12) 21 Oct 1999
Mer (1) Cnj Asc (1) 26 Dec 1999
Mer (1) Cnj House (1) 26 Dec 1999

──────────── 2000s ────────────
Mer (1) Cnj Vir (1) 8 Jan 2000
- **mother dies, 7 Aug 2000**
Ura (12) Cnj Plu (12) 26 Jan 2001
Ven (1) Sqr Ura (10) 28 Jan 2001
MC (11) Sqr Jup (2) 18 Jan 2002
Asc (2) Sqr Sat (11) 4 Nov 2002
Sat (1) Sqr Ura (10) 30 Jan 2003
Nep (4) Sqr Asc (1) 18 Feb 2003
Nep (4) Cnj House (4) 18 Feb 2003
Nep (4) Cnj Sag (4) 2 Mar 2003
- **'The Apprentice' TV show airs,
8 Jan 2004**
Ven (1) Sqr Node (10) 24 Jan 2004
- **engagement to Melania, 26 Apr 2004**
Ven (1) Sqr Moon (4) 12 Jul 2004
Asc (2) Sqr Ven (11) 5 Nov 2004
Plu (2) Cnj Nep (2) 16 Nov 2004
- **company files for bankruptcy,
21 Nov 2004**
- **marries Melania, 22 Jan 2005**
Ven (1) Cnj Sun/Moon (1) 5 Jun 2005
Sat (1) Sqr Node (10) 25 Jan 2006
Mar (2) Sqr Sat (11) 3 Mar 2006
Ven (1) Sqr Sun (10) 29 Apr 2006
Sat (1) Sqr Moon (4) 14 Jul 2006
Sat (1) Cnj Sun/Moon (1) 7 Jun 2007
- **'The Celebrity Apprentice' airs,
3 Jan 2008**
Plu (2) Sqr Mer (11) 8 Jan 2008
Mar (2) Sqr Ven (11) 3 Mar 2008
Sat (1) Sqr Sun (10) 30 Apr 2008
MC (11) Cnj Sat (11) 5 Sep 2008
- **company files for bankruptcy,
Feb 2009**
- **joins Twitter, 4 Mar 2009**
Asc (3) Cnj House (3) 2 Apr 2009
Asc (3) Cnj Sco (3) 14 Apr 2009
Jup (4) Opp Ura (10) 16 Sep 2009

──────────── 2010s ────────────
MC (11) Cnj Ven (11) 6 Sep 2010
Sun (12) Sqr MC (9) 30 Sep 2010
- **joins Obama 'birther' conspiracy,
Mar 2011**
Plu (2) Sqr Asc/MC (11) 18 Jun 2011
Chi (4) Opp Ura (10) 8 May 2012
Moon (6) Sqr MC (9) 15 Jul 2012
Mar (3) Cnj House (3) 27 Jul 2012
Mar (3) Cnj Sco (3) 8 Aug 2012
Jup (4) Opp Node (10) 8 Sep 2012
Node (12) Sqr MC (9) 1 Jan 2013
Jup (4) Cnj Moon (4) 24 Feb 2013
Sun (12) Cnj Mar (12) 2 Apr 2013
Ven (2) Cnj House (2) 25 Aug 2013
Ven (2) Cnj Lib (2) 6 Sep 2013
Jup (4) Sqr Sun/Moon (1) 17 Jan 2014
Plu (2) Cnj Chi (2) 25 Apr 2014
- **company files for bankruptcy,
10 Sep 2014**
Jup (4) Opp Sun (10) 10 Dec 2014
Moon (6) Opp Mar (12) 16 Jan 2015
MC (12) Cnj House (12) 27 Jan 2015
MC (12) Cnj Leo (12) 9 Feb 2015
Chi (4) Opp Node (10) 29 Apr 2015
- **announces candidacy for President,
16 Jun 2015**
Node (12) Cnj Mar (12) 4 Jul 2015
Sat (2) Cnj House (2) 24 Aug 2015
Sat (2) Cnj Lib (2) 5 Sep 2015
Chi (4) Cnj Moon (4) 15 Oct 2015
Ura (12) Sqr MC (9) 23 Dec 2015
- **wins Super Tuesday, 1 Mar 2016**
- **clinches nomination, 26 May 2016**
- **formerly accepts nomination,
21 July 2016**
Sun (1) Cnj Asc (1) 25 Jul 2016
Sun (1) Cnj House (1) 25 Jul 2016
Sun (1) Cnj Vir (1) 6 Aug 2016
Chi (4) Sqr Sun/Moon (1) 6 Sep 2016
- **wins election, 8 Nov 2016**
Plu (2) Cnj Jup (2) 12 Dec 2016
- **sworn in as President, 20 Jan 2017**
Chi (4) Opp Sun (10) 29 Jul 2017
Moon (7) Opp Asc (1) 8 May 2018
Moon (7) Cnj House (7) 8 May 2018
Moon (7) Cnj Pis (7) 21 May 2018
Ura (12) Cnj Mar (12) 22 Jun 2018
Mer (1) Sqr Ura (10) 19 Aug 2018
Node (1) Cnj Asc (1) 25 Oct 2018
Node (1) Cnj House (1) 25 Oct 2018
Node (1) Cnj Vir (1) 6 Nov 2018
Asc (3) Sqr Plu (12) 16 Sep 2019
Ven (2) Cnj Nep (2) 27 Sep 2019

Part VI

Five Extended Essays

- Jane Fonda: The Many Faces of Personal Eve-olution
- Queen Elizabeth II: A Life of Duty in an Era of Change
- First Ladies of the United States
- The Power Degrees of the Zodiac
- Fame and Celebrity: The Addictive Commodities of Our Times

Jane Fonda: The Many Faces of Personal Eve-olution

There are some people who become a symbol of their times, and others who speak directly for their generation, but few manage to reflect successive eras in quite the way Jane Fonda has done. Each of her incarnations has uniquely mirrored the concerns and morals of its time in American history. She was a sci-fi sex bomb in the decadent, spaceflight-focused 1960s, a political idealist in the strident '70s, an exercise entrepreneur in the aspirational '80s and a media mogul's wife concerned with environmental conservation in the post-Reagan, recession-plagued '90s.

Championed by many, reviled by some, Jane Fonda has proven herself to be a resilient 'woman for all seasons' who, over the past half-century, has grown up, spoken up, fallen down and picked herself up again. And all while under America's intensely austere media spotlight, due to her roles as an outspoken feminist, Oscar-winning actress, businesswoman and daughter of an acting legend.

What do her birth chart and transits/directions reveal about this complex woman who continues to inspire and stir up the public? Befitting a chart with ten planets spread across eight (Equal) houses and eight signs, Jane Fonda has been many women in her Sagittarian quest for identity and purpose. But if on the surface her continual reinvention and image-morphing appear calculated, her true story is a universal one of personal evolution – relevant for anyone who has relinquished their voice and later found a more authentic one.

Perhaps the admiration Fonda has garnered over the years has stemmed from her refusal to live a life of false excuse – to not deny responsibility for her actions. Jane's life has been a fervent sprint in person and on film – an expedition towards becoming a complete person. She's raced ahead in the search for self-discovery while fully aware of the flaws in her character. The public has applauded her searing self-examination and stark honesty, recognizing that rare quality she possesses: integrity. As her son, Troy Garrity, confirmed at the American Film Institute tribute to her in 2014, 'She has fearlessly pursued a life to mark her existence, to prove her worth.'[1]

In true Sagittarius style, Fonda wrote in her autobiography, 'I believe that it is more joyful to embrace and be in the journey than to assume you'll ever "arrive".'[2] Fonda has embodied the Sagittarian ethos that, if change is the only constant, then we must have the courage to ensure that any such change takes place primarily in our own philosophical and spiritual development.

Three Acts

Fonda has a number of planets (plus the Ascendant and Chiron) around 0°, 28°, and 29°, and therefore in tight aspect to each other. Each time the outer planets reached these degrees by transit, much

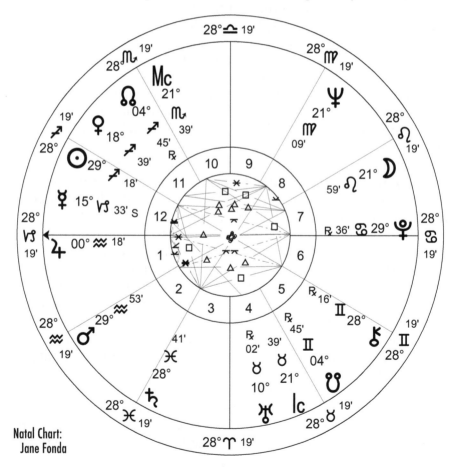

Natal Chart:
Jane Fonda

was triggered in her horoscope. Using Solar Arc directions, the years of 28–32 and 58–62 in her life will have been particularly eventful, since these planets re-aspected one another at those times. In addition, Fonda has Capricorn rising and the Sun square Saturn, so Saturn's return around ages 29 and 58 will have had greater significance.

Fonda has written that she sees her life in three 30-year acts. Here's a brief rundown from an outsider's perspective. Act I: She moved from celebrity daughter, model and acting ingénue to vinyl-clad temptress in the movie *Barbarella*. Act II: She became a peace activist and political crusader, a film producer and actress of substance, then an aerobic exercise guru who exhorted millions of devotees to new heights of physical fitness and, finally, a trophy wife who retired from acting for 15 years. Act III: She emerged as a spiritually revitalized woman in command of her true voice, writing about the issues of the younger and elder generations, rekindling her acting career and re-establishing her fitness legacy.

Jupiter and Saturn
Born into an environment both privileged (Jupiter) and emotionally isolating (Saturn), Fonda's story is that of a woman battling common problems, who had uncommon talent and made a habit of accomplishing the extraordinary. It is the saga of both Jupiter and Saturn. Looking a little deeper into the chart, we find two 'signatures' linked to these planets.

1 A Jupiter–Sagittarius–Pisces theme (Sun and Venus in Sagittarius; Jupiter rising; Mercury in the 12th House; Sun in the 12th square Saturn in Pisces): such a theme could indicate a life of exploration, learning, teaching (particularly learning while teaching); discovering faith; understanding and embracing the beliefs of others; freedom from emotional enslavement; recognizing that everything has consequence in the wider scheme; needing to impress yet being impressionable; shooting down pretence and blowing apart corruption without being a casualty of any given battle.

2 A Saturn–Capricorn–Aquarius theme (Mercury and Ascendant in Capricorn; Sun square Saturn; Jupiter and Mars in

Aquarius):[3] this could be seen in the power of the individual in society – showing what one single person can do to change the way the world thinks; respect for the outsider; alternative views on authority and hierarchy; being a conscientious objector – a rebel with a cause; moving away from people-pleasing and developing healthy boundaries without becoming aloof; overcoming early lacks to become an authority and a role model; recognizing that our need to control is what controls us; working out our conflicting impulses to both court and reject 'the System'.

Jupiter affords us much opportunity, but its journey is towards the attainment of integrity; Saturn's goal is to hold onto it. With these two planetary signatures dominant in one horoscope, there can be a number of life themes and traits: a strong moral compass and social responsibility (with 'respons-ibility' comes an ability to respond); espousing a cause and seeing it through to its end; faith born out of vision fused with wisdom born from experience; personal beliefs vs. organized religion; optimism and trust vs. pessimism and cold, hard reality; enthusiastic candour mixed with frosty reserve; a need to speak out against hypocrisy, but knowing that the System needs to change from within; searching for genuine intimacy – learning how to reach out to people and to allow them in.

Aspects and Configurations
Jane Fonda's chart has two tight aspect patterns that describe much of the drama in her life:

1 A mutable T-square: the Sun opposes Chiron, and both are in square to Saturn – with a Jupiterian emphasis (Sagittarius, Pisces).
   In Fonda's life, this has been played out in wounded, painful relationships (starting with her father), a need to prove herself, and some tough life lessons.

2 A Yod: the Sun sextile Mars forms the base, and both are quincunx Pluto on the Descendant – with a parental and Scorpionic flavour (Midheaven co-rulers Mars and Pluto, and the Sun ruling the 8th House).

Perhaps the most important addition to the Yod is Jupiter opposite Pluto (and at the Sun/Mars midpoint). This all-important opposition falls across the Ascendant–Descendant axis and speaks of Fonda's deep, evolutionary journey – mining hidden, hard-won treasures – and her social, political and spiritual metamorphoses that have also been played out through relationships. It also suggests the exaggeration (Jupiter) of key Pluto issues in her life (from the intense political enmity to which she was subjected, to her long-term bulimia and subsequent obsession with fitness).

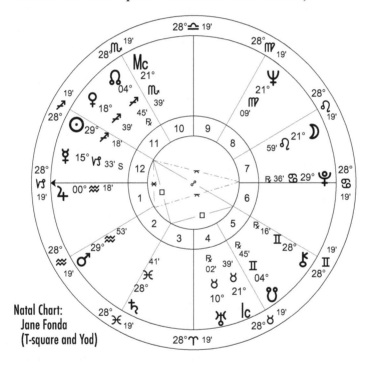

Natal Chart:
Jane Fonda
(T-square and Yod)

When social/outer planets are in tight aspect to each other and dominant in a natal chart, the times they meet again by aspect will usually prove significant in that person's life (and are known as 'recurrence' or 'resonant' transits). Jupiter and Pluto have been either conjunct or opposite one another around key times in Fonda's life: her mother's suicide in 1950; Jane's initial foray into acting in 1955–56; her 1968 political awakening, daughter's birth, and her reaction to being a sex object in *Barbarella*; the release of *On*

Golden Pond (in which she healed much of her relationship with her father) in November 1981, followed by her *Workout Book* in January 1982; her separation–divorce from Ted Turner and re-emergence in 2000–1; and receiving the AFI's Life Achievement Award in June 2014.

Exploring the Yod

In *The Yod Book*, Karen Hamaker-Zondag writes that Yods 'symbolize patterns in families that have lasted for generations',[4] and the person carrying the Yod is there to 'express ... the unspoken, repressed, or unbalanced theme of generations'.[5] She argues that people with a Yod are often restless and always searching. They find themselves stuck in stalemates and unusual, ambiguous situations in which they feel wronged, and ask 'Why did I have to go through this?' This describes much of Fonda's life journey and especially the five events analysed later in this profile.

Fonda's Yod involves two symbols of masculinity and patriarchy (Sun and Mars at the base), and all three planets are linked to power and potency (Sun, Mars, Pluto). We can see the symbolism for war heroes (Sun–Mars) and being a leader (Sun–Mars) who speaks out for social justice (Sagittarius, Aquarius) in times of paranoia, propaganda and terror (Pluto).

The Yod and Pluto's position in Cancer on the Descendant have acted like a lightning rod for some people's hatred and misplaced anger about America's catastrophic war with Vietnam. These chart factors also describe how much energy Fonda has wasted apologizing to those who were only looking for a scapegoat for the suffering caused by officialdom's huge folly.

Pluto represents the victimized and disenfranchised as well as the empowered. Fonda has always chosen to be involved with powerful men, and in doing so she has lost and betrayed her own voice in the 'disease to please' (the Sun squaring Saturn in Pisces in the 3rd House underscores this). She turned herself inside out to be loved by her father and three husbands (director Roger Vadim, politician Tom Hayden and entrepreneur Ted Turner).

Perhaps the 'buried treasure' of Pluto on the Descendant can be excavated by investigating the maternal family line (Cancer) and understanding how a certain kind of investment in others (for approval and reliance) plays a role in one's own enslavement. Each husband appeared to be heading in the direction she wanted for herself, but in each marriage Jane was swept up in their journey, supporting their vision. Fonda's natal Venus (in Sagittarius square Neptune) attracts 'search and rescue' situations, and it is closely conjunct Vadim's Saturn, Hayden's Sun and Turner's Mercury. (All three husbands also have planets/points conjunct her Saturn in Pisces in the 3rd, further suggesting that she 'lost her voice' during her times with them.)

Finally, in the Yod we also have a signature for compulsive, addictive behaviour that can, in extremis, be either self-sabotaging (Mars–Pluto) or highly empowering (Sun–Mars). Fonda's bulimia was at its most rampant from age 21 – when Solar Arc Pluto conjoined her Moon, SA Jupiter opposed her Moon and SA Mars in Pisces opposed Neptune, reflecting the addiction that possessed her – until age 36. This obsession was then replaced by compulsive exercise (Mars–Pluto). At best, the Yod also describes how she motivated people to reshape their bodies (Pluto–Descendant) through calisthenics as well as the self-esteem that sprang from doing this (Mars in the 2nd, the Sun in Sagittarius). Literally millions of followers were 'feeling the burn' through intense, transformative exercise (Mars–Pluto).

Five Key Life Events
Event 1: Her Parents' Separation; Mother's Suicide (1949–50)
Fonda's father, Henry, embodied the remoteness of her natal Sun in Sagittarius square Saturn in Pisces – he was taciturn and undemonstrative, and belittled her. In **August 1949**, he announced to Jane's mother, Frances, that he wanted a divorce so that he could remarry. Jane's SA Ascendant squared natal Uranus in the 4th, and SA Uranus squared her Moon – her home life was about to change drastically. Frances entered a psychiatric hospital in January 1950 and committed suicide on her 42nd birthday in April. Jane was told that her bipolar mother had suffered a heart attack – the girl went numb (Uranus), withdrew and created an inscrutable persona of tempered steel (Capricorn Ascendant, Scorpio on the Midheaven).

Back in August, when Frances had told Jane of the separation, the young girl vowed to 'do whatever it took to be perfect so that a man would love me'. At this time, she unwittingly fell into people-pleasing and the pursuit of perfection (both distorted reflexes of

Uranus): 'It's not that I consciously … buried [these feelings].
It's just that I'd been doing it for so long that I had begun to live
that way … I would become whatever I felt the people whose love
and attention I needed wanted me to be.'[6] Many years later, Jane
discovered that her mother had been sexually abused and had, like
her daughter, spent much of her life afflicted by the 'disease to
please'.

Around October 1950, Jane learned the truth about her mother's
suicide when she read about it in a celebrity magazine. It's
interesting to note that natal Mercury in the 12th had Solar Arc
directed to the Ascendant, and the solar eclipse of March 1950 fell
on her 3rd House Saturn. Jane kept the revelation a secret from
her brother, Peter – setting up a complicity of nondisclosure and

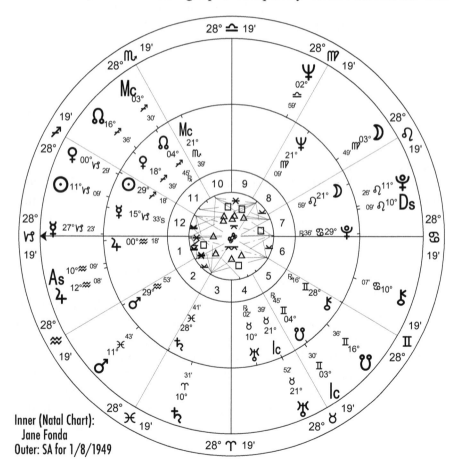

Inner (Natal Chart):
Jane Fonda
Outer: SA for 1/8/1949

denial with the rest of the family – something very foreign to her Sagittarian nature. And yet the dam had to break sooner or later …

Event 2: Jane's Political Awakening (1968)

With the Midheaven in Scorpio and its co-rulers, Mars and Pluto, so strongly involved in Fonda's chart, it's not surprising that the celebrity offspring–model–actress would morph into someone of substance and seek authenticity in her life. After conceiving her first child on **28 December 1967**, Jane began what she describes as her Second Act, the beginning of her soul-searching. Transiting Uranus in Virgo was square her Sun, and TR Neptune had just left her MC. In the nine months that followed, she became aware of the Vietnam War, she read Malcolm X's autobiography in June 1968 and gave

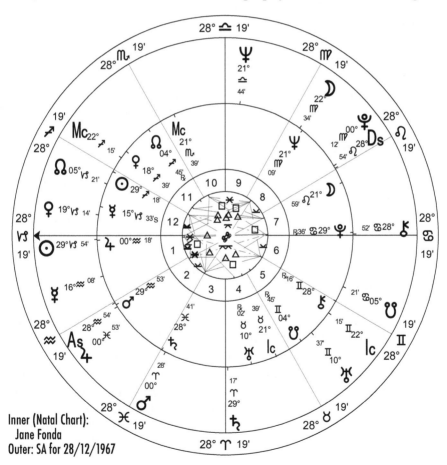

Inner (Natal Chart):
Jane Fonda
Outer: SA for 28/12/1967

birth in September. It was the beginning of her political life.[7] These events coincided with SA Mars at 0° Aries, SA Jupiter at 0° Pisces, the SA Sun opposing natal Pluto and then moving into Aquarius and conjoining Jupiter, and SA Pluto opposing Mars. As she gained in strength, her marriage to Roger Vadim weakened. In October 1969, she headed to India (her SA Ascendant was at 0° Pisces); two months later, she left Vadim, as TR Neptune at 29° Scorpio squared her Mars.

On 30 April 1970, the United States declared its intention to invade Cambodia, and for many Americans this was a wake-up call to activism. In the weeks ahead, with Neptune back at 29° Scorpio and Jupiter in Libra on Fonda's Equal 10th House cusp, the FBI and CIA began monitoring her activities (Jane Fonda's FBI file would eventually run to 763 pages). In early November 1970, following her first anti-war speech (in Ontario), she was arrested for drug smuggling and assaulting an officer (the 'drugs' were actually vitamins, and the charges were dropped) – TR Pluto in Virgo was square her Sun, and TR Neptune made its final passage to 29° Scorpio. Neptune's move into Sagittarius soon after would see Sagittarian Fonda tainted by a scandal that follows her to this day.

Event 3: 'Hanoi Jane' (8–22 July 1972)

The reason Fonda went to Vietnam, she said, was to expose the lies of the Nixon administration. Transiting Pluto stood at 29° Virgo, square her natal Sun and aspecting many points; the trip was to change her life. Although her shrill and uncompromising radio broadcasts from Hanoi were to antagonize many (as TR Jupiter retrograded back to conjoin her Sun), it wasn't until the photo of her sitting on a Vietnamese anti-aircraft gun was released as propaganda in mid February 1973 that extreme hostility was galvanized.

The political myth of Hanoi Jane grew from that date, in the month that TR Jupiter crossed over her Ascendant and returned to its natal position opposite Pluto (increasing her notoriety) and a few weeks after a lunar eclipse on her Pluto–Descendant. She was, in effect, framed and scapegoated – her actions blamed for the torture of American soldiers. Angry at the White House line, Fonda lashed out and made things worse: SA Mercury in Aquarius was square her Scorpio MC. With the SA Moon in Virgo and SA MC in Sagittarius contacting natal Chiron and Saturn that year, and SA Pluto in Virgo square the lunar nodes, it was the first of many successful efforts by the government to demonize her.

Pluto in Cancer on the Descendant is seen clearly in her chart as the vitriolic response from 'patriots' who felt betrayed by Fonda's 'traitorous' political actions and her attacks on US policy. *Current Biography 1986* described her as a 'lightning rod for America's schizophrenic rage over that undeclared and unpopular war'. (On 21 July 1972, the day she unwittingly posed on the gun, the transiting Sun was conjunct her natal Pluto at 29° Cancer, and Mercury was conjunct her Leo Moon.)

Jane's 1971 solar return (cast, as I always do, for the natal location) shows 12° Gemini rising, with Mercury at 12° Sagittarius on the Descendant (the reverse of the US Sibly chart angles), and

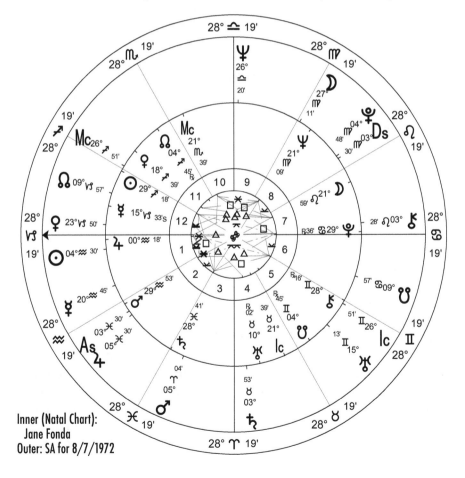

Inner (Natal Chart):
 Jane Fonda
Outer: SA for 8/7/1972

the Moon is at 18° Aquarius on the MC at 17° – both hotly political degrees for the US.

Why Hanoi? Interestingly, her natal asteroid *Hanoi* is at 0°10' Aquarius, extremely close to her all-important Jupiter–Pluto opposition. Her Moon in Leo rises through Hanoi. (With the natal Moon in Leo squaring the MC in Scorpio, there's a risk of one's concerns being dramatized and turned into a political spectacle.) In July 1972, her progressed Mars in Pisces was on the Descendant in Hanoi, and progressed Chiron in Gemini was on the MC, suggestive of the fierce (if orchestrated) opposition she would face during wartime and the inevitable damage to her professional name.

Event 4: Aerobics guru (1982)

Fonda ignited a fitness revolution and inspired home exercisers to 'feel the burn'. In doing so, she created a one-woman conglomerate of clubs, videos and books. The Jane Fonda Workout phenomenon started in late 1978 when she broke a foot filming *The China Syndrome* and decided to begin aerobics classes. The success and timeliness of the film (which made her the #1 female box office star in the world) and the launch of her Beverly Hills workout studio, both of which opened in 1979, coincided with Uranus transiting her MC in Scorpio (and SA Venus conjunct Jupiter). The phoenix had finally risen from the ashes.

In mid January 1982, *Jane Fonda's Workout Book* was published and was an international bestseller. Late April 1982 saw the release of *Jane Fonda's Workout* on videocassette, which pushed the burgeoning VCR industry into fast-forward. Not surprisingly, both events occurred under Mercury (books, videos) and Mars (exercise) Solar Arcs: SA Mercury crossed over Mars and into Pisces when the book was finished and published, and SA Mars in Aries squared Mercury at the video's release.

Event 5: Enter Ted Turner (1989–2001)

CNN boss and media mogul Ted 'Mouth of the South' Turner can be seen in much of Fonda's own chart: the intensity, the searching, the speaking up (loudly), the entrepreneurial spirit – and indeed his own horoscope reflects Fonda's Scorpio–Sagittarius side. Their relationship was built on a mutual passion for horses (Turner's Sagittarius Ascendant and Mercury are close to Fonda's Venus).

Turner arrived on the scene when Fonda was in the middle of a nervous breakdown. Months before, on her birthday in 1988, husband Tom Hayden had announced that he was in love with another woman (both Saturn and Uranus had just transited Fonda's Sun and were now in Capricorn, while her Sun–Mars–Pluto Yod aligned by SA with natal Neptune). The couple split in May 1989 (divorcing a year later), prompting both Jane's mental collapse (SA Descendant was on Neptune) and Turner's pursuit of the actress.

When Fonda and Turner married, on her birthday in 1991, as TR Pluto (natally on her Descendant) crossed her MC, it appeared to many as though she'd buried much of her former life, renounced her feminist crusades, and taken refuge as a 'Stepford wife' – her life seemingly suspended from its previous course.

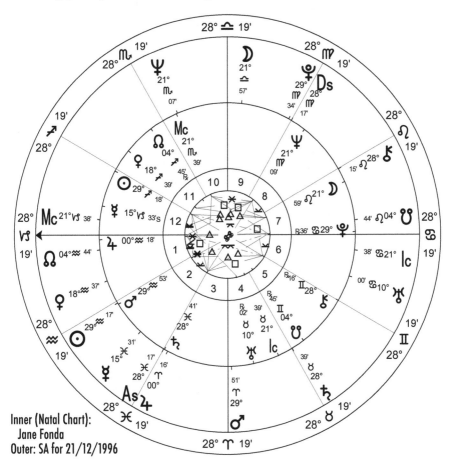

Inner (Natal Chart):
Jane Fonda
Outer: SA for 21/12/1996

What would eventually split the couple apart was Fonda's quiet move towards spirituality. It began in the summer of 1996 and developed around Fonda's 59th birthday, **21 December 1996** (bi-wheel, previous page): she intuitively knew that turning 60 would mark a profound change for her. At this time, her set of SA planets were once again around 29°/0°, prompting the ending and start of major life chapters. Also, her SA Ascendant was edging towards natal Saturn in Pisces, SA Neptune was on her natal MC, and TR Neptune would soon cross her Ascendant.

Fonda's adoption of Christianity in late 1998 was to prompt a marriage crisis the following June (she didn't tell the atheist Turner because she didn't want to be dissuaded from pursuing it during her period of discovery). There was an official parting of the ways three days into the new millennium. Turner, apparently, had already been looking for (and found) her replacement, and their divorce became final in May 2001. The couple nevertheless remain good friends and have collaborated on a number of charitable and environmental projects.

Few actors have been as swept up as Fonda was in the tumultuous social and political changes of the second half of the 20th century. She was deeply admired by many, while others cast her in the role of a hateful, anti-American hypocrite. When she combined her politics with her creative sensibilities, we saw Fonda take her acting career to stellar heights by playing women, once struck by inhibitions, panic or doubt, who transform and grow in confidence at times of crisis (the range is startling, from *Coming Home* to *The China Syndrome* and from *Old Gringo* to *9 to 5*).

In the new millennium, Jane Fonda has pulled together many strands from her past and is also writing to educate the teenage generation (*Being a Teen*) and the over-60s (*Prime Time*). She is the wiser, elder stateswoman and yet still calls for change. (For those who study Ceres, it is at 29° Aquarius, natally, plugging into Jane's Mars and the Yod.) One of the secrets of her renaissance, her continued productivity, and energy well into her Third Act? Fonda says, 'It's much more important to stay interested than interesting.'

References and Notes

1 http://www.hollywoodreporter.com/news/jane-fonda-her-afi-tribute-709817

2 All quotes from Jane Fonda, *My Life So Far*, Ebury Press, 2006.

3 In a quadrant house system, the Aquarian side comes more to the fore with the Sun joining Venus in the 11th.

4 Karen Hamaker-Zondag, *The Yod Book*, Weiser, 2000, back cover.

5 Ibid., p. 40.

6 Stretching the point a little, it's interesting to note that Jane Fonda was born on the day that Disney's *Snow White and the Seven Dwarfs* was released, and its themes of being adored/reviled, of beauty as power, and the stages of womanhood all mirror Fonda's own life – except that Snow White never looked beyond her prince for a 'happily ever after'.

7 Actress/activist Vanessa Redgrave (born 30 January 1937) was someone who aided Fonda's political awakening; their Mercury placements are one degree apart in Capricorn.

Queen Elizabeth II: A Life of Duty in an Era of Change

In the chart of Queen Elizabeth II, a fixed T-square dominates her horoscope to the exclusion of almost everything else. Mars and Jupiter in Aquarius are opposite Neptune in Leo and they square Saturn on the MC in Scorpio. In *Getting to the Heart of Your Chart*, I examine this T-square's meaning, how it reveals the major storylines in the Queen's life, and how, when triggered in forecasting, it has reflected some of her key life events. Here are a few details, followed by five major turning points in Her Majesty's life:

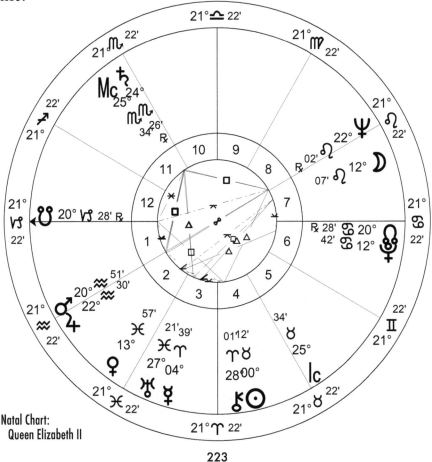

Natal Chart:
  Queen Elizabeth II

223

Mars–Jupiter in Aquarius
- Fighting for social change and modern causes; coming together during wartime; a great desire for personal freedom.
... opposite Neptune in Leo
- Glamour; a weakening of the monarchy; longing for the imperial greatness of yesteryear; royal scandal.
... both square Saturn–MC in Scorpio (the apex)
- Holding firm by holding the 'firm' together; a steely resolve; an unbending moral code; impenetrable defences and a stoic, dour public face that conceals deeper emotions; burdened by expectation; a feeling of no escape from her destiny – a dutiful job for life/until death.

Event 1: The Abdication Crisis of 1936

Elizabeth found herself directly in line to the throne because of male instability/unreliability (Mars opposite Neptune). Her uncle Edward VIII's desertion of the throne (on **11 December 1936**) and of his responsibilities (Mars and Jupiter – the uncle – opposite Neptune, both square Saturn) when Elizabeth was ten meant that her father acceded to the throne. Closeted in the confines of Buckingham Palace, she was isolated and cloistered, primed for her own sacred, religious role.

At the time, her Solar Arc Moon in Leo moved to conjunct Neptune and oppose Jupiter in fixed Aquarius. She is now locked into the role of a lifetime. Saturn was opposite Neptune in the sky, with Saturn having just stationed at the precarious mid-degree 'desertion zone' of Pisces.

It is interesting to note that Mars–Neptune also manifested in other key men of the time: Prime Minister Neville Chamberlain, whose concessions and appeasement in 1938 plunged Britain into World War II and went on to define the Princess Elizabeth's early years. Chamberlain (18 March 1869) has a Grand Trine with the same planets (Mars, Jupiter, Saturn, Neptune), while Elizabeth's uncle Edward VIII has Jupiter–Neptune trine Saturn. It took Winston Churchill, with a Mars–Jupiter conjunction and Jupiter–Neptune opposition (like the Queen herself), to lead his country to victory. Franklin Roosevelt also has the signature: Jupiter conjunct Neptune, with Neptune semi-square Mars on the MC.

The T-square is also at play for husband Prince Philip of Greece, who gave up (Neptune) his cherished naval career and position for marriage (his Moon sits at 22° Leo, exactly on his wife's Jupiter–Neptune opposition). He, Elizabeth's father and grandfather were all naval officers – Mars opposite Neptune – and even her beloved Royal Yacht *Britannia* (a giant pleasure boat designed, but never used, as a hospital ship for use in wartime) is depicted by Mars–Jupiter–Neptune. The Queen's heir, Charles (who is Venus–Neptune) can also be 'seen' in her T-square. Charles has seemed both ambivalent towards, and burdened by, his future role – and his first marriage to a glamorous 'superstar' (Jupiter–Neptune) almost wrecked his royal status.

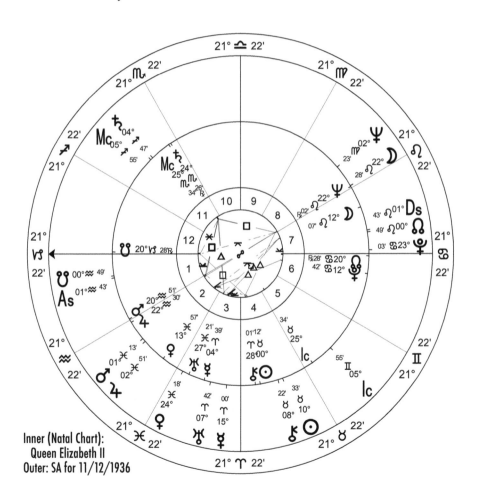

Inner (Natal Chart):
Queen Elizabeth II
Outer: SA for 11/12/1936

Event 2: Her Father's Death in 1952

Elizabeth's life changed suddenly in the early hours of **6 February 1952** when her father King George VI died in his sleep. The princess was holidaying near Nyeri in Kenya (close to her Uranus–Ascendant line).

By Solar Arc, Uranus had reached 22° Aries and tightly sextiled Jupiter and trined Neptune. SA Sun had just opposed Saturn and was now at the IC, and SA Mercury was at 29° Aries (Elizabeth was crowned a year later when Mercury moved into Taurus and crossed over her fixed Sun – the beginning of a role of a lifetime). By transit, Neptune hovered on her Equal 10th House cusp and, even more aptly for the passing of her father, transiting Pluto opposed natal Mars (both planets rule the natal MC, one part of the parental axis).

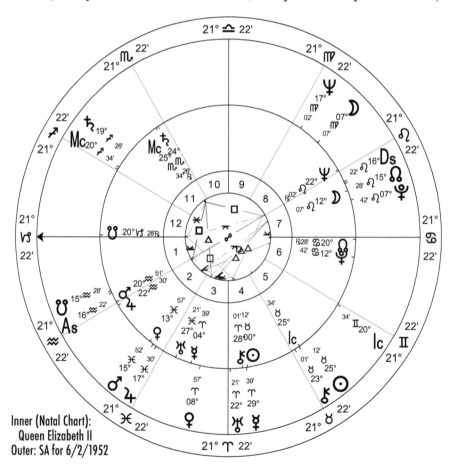

Inner (Natal Chart):
Queen Elizabeth II
Outer: SA for 6/2/1952

Event 3: The Queen's Coronation in 1953
The Government wanted the public to be an integral part of Elizabeth's coronation celebrations – to create the biggest national party ever (Mars–Jupiter in Aquarius), but tradition, pomp and ceremony would nevertheless dictate the event (Saturn–MC). The televising of the coronation on **2 June 1953** was the Palace's only major populist concession (television is known as 'the democratic medium' – Jupiter in Aquarius).

There is an exact, recorded moment for when the Queen was crowned (12:34 p.m. at Westminster) with Jupiter exactly on the MC and yet another Mars–Saturn–Neptune link (Saturn–Neptune trine Mars). In my opinion, a time of ten minutes earlier (with 9° Virgo on the Ascendant and 3° Gemini on the MC) fits better with

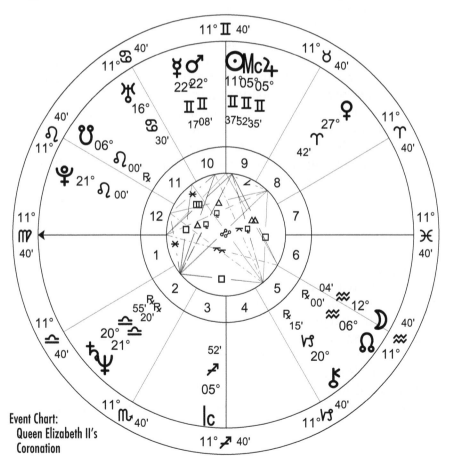

Event Chart:
Queen Elizabeth II's
Coronation

subsequent events. For instance, Diana's death and funeral in 1997 occurred at the eclipse at 9° Virgo and while transiting Pluto was almost at 3° Sagittarius.

If we use this rectified Coronation chart, it puts the SA Saturn–Neptune at 3° Sagittarius on the IC, the SA Ascendant conjunct Saturn–Neptune at 20–21° Libra (and transiting Saturn was at 19° Aries), and the SA Midheaven conjunct Uranus in the 11th at the time of the Princess of Wales's sudden demise.

Regardless of the exact time of the coronation, note the Mercury–Mars conjunction in Gemini in this chart. Mercury and the 3rd House are linked to siblings, while Mars rules the chart's 3rd House. The Queen's first immediate business was to confront the difficulty presented by her sister Margaret (herself a waspish Mercury in Virgo square Mars in Gemini) wanting to marry a divorced man, Peter Townsend. The Queen preferred to avoid the issue and bury her head in the sand (Mars–Neptune can denote an emotional ostrich). The press felt that the people's voice should be heard, and began to pry more deeply into royal affairs. Margaret's Neptune is 3° Virgo, squaring the Coronation chart's Jupiter–MC. The problem was resolved two years later, with the imperious Margaret choosing duty, status and money over marriage to a commoner. By Solar Arc, the Coronation's Mercury–Mars conjunction had moved from 22° to 24° Gemini, tying in to Margaret's natal Mercury at 24° Virgo square Mars at 25° Gemini.

By transit, there was a Saturn–Neptune conjunction in the sky (on the Queen's Equal 10th House cusp). Saturn–Neptune has proved the key to much of the Windsor saga: from the 1936 abdication to various times of war, referendums and devolution, and periods of change for the Commonwealth. Even Queen Victoria was born with Saturn in Pisces (conjunct Chiron–Pluto) square Neptune in Sagittarius (conjunct Uranus), and the House of Windsor was named in 1917 as the two planets came together. The most recent aspect (the square from Sagittarius to Pisces) occurred on 26 November 2015, 18 June 2016, 10 September 2016 – all around the degrees of the Coronation's Sun and Ascendant–Descendant, and on 23 June 2016 the UK voted to leave the European Union. The next conjunction occurs in February 2026 at 0° Aries, square grandson William's Sun in Cancer.

Event 4: Annus Horribilis

'1992 is not a year on which I shall look back with undiluted pleasure. In the words of one of my more sympathetic correspondents, it has turned out to be an Annus Horribilis,' said the Queen in a now-famous speech given on **24 November 1992**. That year, her son Andrew and toe-sucked spouse Sarah Ferguson had announced their split, her daughter Anne divorced, *Diana: Her True Story* was published and, four days before this speech, Windsor Castle had caught fire. It was also the year in which the Queen acquiesced to pay income tax (this commenced in 1993 when her Solar Arc MC moved into the commoner, everyman sign of Aquarius).

In her horoscope, it appeared to be the end of an era of respect: the MC had reached the final degree of Capricorn. TR

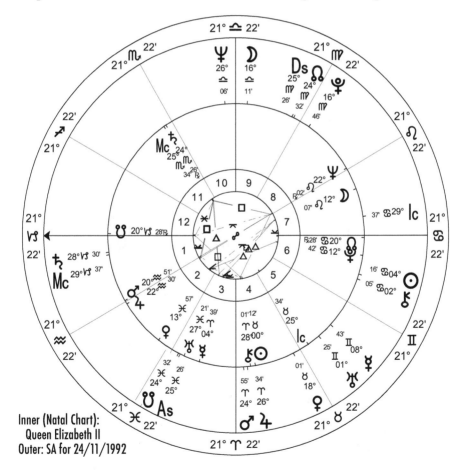

Inner (Natal Chart):
Queen Elizabeth II
Outer: SA for 24/11/1992

Saturn was opposite her Moon, and TR Uranus–Neptune squared SA Moon (on the way towards her Ascendant) – indicative of some difficult but profound domestic disturbances. Transiting Pluto was creeping towards natal Saturn–MC. (Ten years on, in February and March 2002, the Queen had another difficult year when she lost both her sister and mother within seven weeks of each other. SA Sun had reached Pluto in the 6th House of illness, and TR Uranus was square natal Saturn on the MC.)

Event 5: The Death of a Princess

Arguably, the most seismic event in post-war times for the House of Windsor was the sudden death of the Princess of Wales on 31 August 1997 in Paris. It led to an unprecedented outpouring of

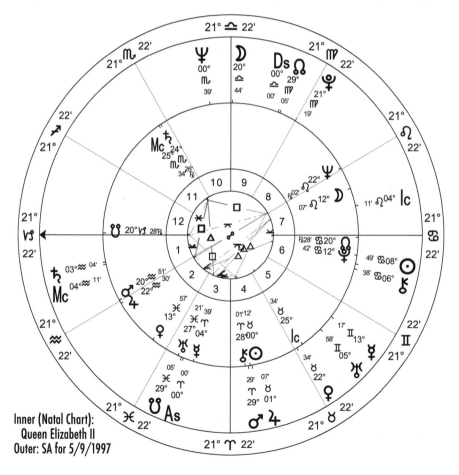

Inner (Natal Chart):
Queen Elizabeth II
Outer: SA for 5/9/1997

national grief, a wave of resentful public dissatisfaction with the monarchy and even mild rumblings of anarchy. On **5 September 1997**, it elicited an extraordinary response from the Queen, who addressed the nation and responded with sufficient emotion and respect to satiate a hitherto angry crowd.

Diana was born with her own fixed T-square around the same degrees as the Queen's. Diana's Moon at 25° Aquarius opposed Uranus at 23° Leo and both squared Venus (as the apex) at 24° Taurus. In effect, Diana's obstreperous, wilful Venus is the 'missing leg' of the Queen's T-square. Whichever way the public chooses to remember Elizabeth's reign, its ramifications on future royal generations will be unavoidably measured in accordance with Diana's turbulent impact.

Interestingly, once again a planet had aligned with the Queen's T-square: her SA Venus had reached 22° Taurus and squared her natal Jupiter–Neptune opposition – it was a crisis time prompted by her glamorous daughter-in-law. SA Neptune had entered Scorpio (the sign of Elizabeth's Saturn and MC, suggesting a dwindling of the old guard or a need to bring compassion to a rigid system) and was opposing the Sun in Taurus (a weakening of her rock-like monarchy). Mars had reached the crisis (29th) degree of Aries, and Elizabeth's Ascendant moved from 29° Pisces to 0° Aries in the sombre yet combative week prior to the funeral.

Some Final Thoughts

If we accept that a prime minister or president's chart becomes a supplementary 'national' horoscope while they're in power, we can assume a similar role for the monarch's. In the UK, we like our leaders to embody Saturn, even if a Jupiterian leader might offer more charisma and geniality. Charles lacks either signature, and has a predominance of fixity in his horoscope and 'mild' Pluto and Venus themes (Sun in Scorpio square Pluto; Moon in Taurus, Venus in Libra conjunct Neptune on the IC). If and when his son William becomes king, we'll see Jupiter at work, for he has Sagittarius rising and Jupiter strongly aspected on the MC (along with Cancer and Libra/7th House subtones).

Over the years, many astrologers have proposed dates for a change of monarch or even a move to a republic, but these dates have long passed and the monarchy is a deeply entrenched institution (our history book timelines are measured by the reigns of kings and queens). If we were to continue to speculate on a change of monarch, the horoscopes of key members would need to be considered. But the true changes will be 'hidden' in the Queen's Coronation chart and the House of Windsor's conception chart (17 July 1917, exactly thirty years before Camilla Parker-Bowles' birth). If a direct passing of the mantle from Elizabeth to grandson William were to happen (as some astrologers have suggested), it would imply an absent or physically/mentally incapacitated Charles.

The decade ahead is a conservative one. Pluto is in Capricorn until 2024, culminating in Saturn meeting Pluto at 22° Capricorn in January 2020 (an 'aftermath' aspect, which falls on the Queen's Ascendant, opposes the Suns in the Duchess of Cornwall's and the House of Windsor's charts). Uranus trudges through Taurus from May 2018 (immediately transiting the Queen's Sun and Charles's Moon) and will leave seismic cracks by the time it departs in April 2026. From 2025–6 onwards, Neptune in Aries and Pluto in Aquarius suggest a different type of royal family working in quite a different capacity.

First Ladies of the United States

The power behind the throne is the power.
– Maria Weston Chapman

Here (in a condensed version of an article I wrote for *The Mountain Astrologer)*, I've chosen to profile five First Ladies for whom we have well-sourced birth times. Each embodied her era, stamped her personality onto the role and used her position as presidential consort to influence her husband and public opinion.

Edith Wilson First Lady from 18/12/1915 to 4/03/1921

One of the more influential of the early First Ladies, Edith Bolling was the second wife of Woodrow Wilson. They were married on 18 December 1915, but befitting her Sun–Mercury opposition to Neptune, and her Venus in Scorpio opposite Pluto, there were unfounded rumours from the start that she and the president had murdered his first wife, Ellen Wilson, the previous August! And even the president's own political advisors faked love letters in the hope that Edith would flee, humiliated. But Woodrow Wilson was determined to marry the jewellery-store widow – it was a decision that would provide him with much support and constancy in the years to come.

Wilson's time in office was overshadowed by war in Europe and later by a series of strokes that left him paralysed. With Edith's Sun and Mercury (the MC ruler) opposite Neptune, and Descendant ruler Venus opposite Pluto, she devoted her life to her husband and took over his duties. As sole conduit to her husband, she effectively ran the White House and dealt with all matters of state. In doing so, she hid the extent of the president's illness from the public, declaring that he was simply suffering from exhaustion. Edith later referred to her role as a 'stewardship', and upon her husband's retirement in 1921 she nursed him until his death in 1924. Like many First Ladies, Edith devoted the rest of her own life to managing his legacy.

Chart Features
Other than the sacrificial, Neptunian signature, Edith's chart has a
strong Mars signature: Scorpio rises, chart ruler Mars culminates at
the MC, the Moon is in Aries, and the Sun's dispositor, Venus, is in
Scorpio. Aptly, Edith was considered a highly capable, formidable
First Lady, with some historians labelling her the 'First Lady
President'.

Forecasting
The given birth time is on the hour, but a birth ten minutes later
(9:10 a.m.) would place the MC by Solar Arc on Edith's Sun in
Libra at the time of meeting Wilson in **March 1915** and at their
marriage some nine months later. (The SA MC would have moved

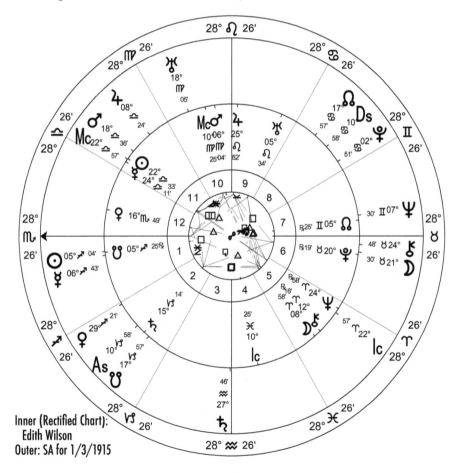

Inner (Rectified Chart):
Edith Wilson
Outer: SA for 1/3/1915

to 29° Libra when she ended her 'regency', and the couple retired.) Her husband's position was weakened (her Sun opposite Neptune) by incapacitating strokes in September–October 1919; in Edith's chart, a 9:10 a.m. birth time would put the SA Ascendant conjunct Saturn, SA Chiron on the Descendant, and transiting Saturn on her Mars–MC at this time. (To add credence to the slightly adjusted birth time, Edith's first husband, Norman Galt, had died suddenly on 28 January 1908, when her SA Uranus conjoined the MC of the rectified chart.) I've taken the liberty of using the rectified time in the bi-wheel above.

Eleanor Roosevelt First Lady from 4/03/1933 to 12/04/1945

A celebrated, imposing First Lady and accomplished politician in her own right, Anna Eleanor Roosevelt served for an unprecedented twelve years – an exact Jupiter cycle – and pulled off what no other First Lady has ever done: she played a pivotal role in the administration and forged her own career path, while also garnering widespread praise and esteem. Nicknamed the 'First Lady of the World', Eleanor was the first presidential spouse to speak at a national convention, hold press conferences and write a newspaper column.

At age 14, Eleanor had written, 'No matter how plain a woman may be, if truth and loyalty are stamped upon her face, all will be attracted to her.' In adulthood, she was fearless, courageous, bold. She worked to awaken the conscience of those she met with her passionate creed, as seen in the tireless and charismatic 'good will' conjunction of Venus in early Virgo and Jupiter in late Leo, ruling the MC and the Ascendant respectively. 'One must never turn one's back on life,' she once said. 'There is so much to do, so many engrossing challenges, so many heartbreaking and pressing needs.'

Chart Features
Once again, a focus on Libra and cardinality (plus Jupiter in Leo) reflects the First Lady's pivotal role in her husband's presidency at a time when the world was at war. Both Edith Wilson and Eleanor Roosevelt had physically incapacitated spouses (note their Neptune oppositions to the Sun and Mars, respectively). But

Eleanor campaigned openly in her husband's place (Sagittarius rising) rather than covertly (Edith's Scorpio Ascendant). 'Send Eleanor Roosevelt' was the paean cry when Americans needed their best ambassador. Blanche Wiesen Cook wrote, 'She was able to do what she did because of her understanding of community and alliances.'[1]

Eleanor's Mercury–Uranus conjunction on the Libra MC, along with Sagittarius rising, speaks of her maverick mind and firm opinions, her astute use of the media, her liberalism and outspokenness on issues of human rights, and her part in helping to draft the Universal Declaration of Human Rights which was adopted by the United Nations on 10 December 1948 (as SA Saturn conjoined natal Jupiter in Leo in the 9th).

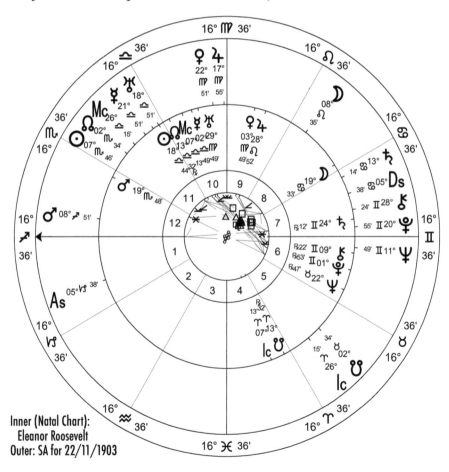

Inner (Natal Chart):
Eleanor Roosevelt
Outer: SA for 22/11/1903

Forecasting
Eleanor and Franklin D Roosevelt were engaged on **22 November 1903**, as SA Uranus conjoined her Libra Sun (SA Jupiter had already moved into the Equal 10th House). Her influence widened after FDR contracted polio in 1921; a few years later, as SA Jupiter reached the MC and the SA Moon conjoined Jupiter in Leo, she became increasingly influential in the Democratic Party.

As her husband campaigned for the presidential nomination, Eleanor had SA Pluto conjunct her Moon. FDR's sudden death in April 1945 coincided with Eleanor's SA Jupiter reaching 29° Libra – it was the end of an historic partnership.

Jacqueline Kennedy First Lady from 20/01/1961 to 22/11/1963

Jacqueline Bouvier brought style, glamour and charisma to her position as First Lady, but her primary role was that of wife and mother. She and John F Kennedy (both with Neptune on the MC) were youthful personifications of a new wave of idealism (later encapsulated in the term 'Camelot' that she used soon after his death in an attempt to lionize him). Jackie spent time restoring parts of the White House (Saturn in the 2nd is the handle of a 'bucket' chart shaping – as Mark Edmund Jones called it – and Neptune–MC) and using it to showcase the arts (Neptune conjunct a Leo MC).

Later, in her widowhood, there were years of dignified silence and hiding behind her infamous oversized dark sunglasses (Scorpio rising), as well as a controversial marriage to Aristotle Onassis that intrigued the world (Neptune–MC). She would hold positions in publishing houses (note the Sun–Mercury conjunction in the 9th, and 9th ruler Moon in the 6th trine Saturn in Sagittarius). At the age of 64, she succumbed to cancer, making her one of the shortest-lived First Ladies of the 20th century.

Chart Features
The Sun–Mercury conjunction in Leo plus Jupiter in Gemini in the 7th reflect her two marriages to world leaders (one a powerful orator and visionary president, the other an expert international trader and shipping magnate). Both the Sun and Mercury culminate at the MC when relocating her chart to Dallas, where she witnessed the horror

of her husband's being gunned down at her side. Neptune on the MC and Scorpio rising reflect the aura of mystery and the enigmatic shroud she wore for the thirty years that followed her husband's assassination. Despite showier sides to the chart (the Aries, Gemini and Leo planets), the Scorpio Ascendant and the Saturn handle suggest self-containment and a need for a privacy, respect and security.

Forecasting

Jackie met JFK, a Gemini, on **10 May 1952**, as the SA Descendant (and the North Node) reached natal Jupiter in Gemini, and the SA Moon conjoined her Descendant. They were married 16 months later as the SA Sun reached her Leo MC, and TR Saturn opposed her

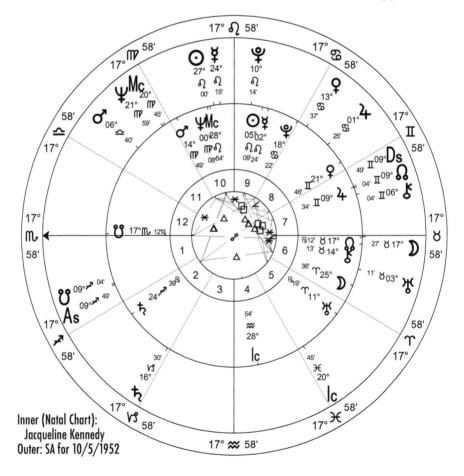

Inner (Natal Chart):
Jacqueline Kennedy
Outer: SA for 10/5/1952

Moon. When Kennedy launched his campaign for the presidency in 1960, Jackie's SA Pluto crossed over her Equal 10th House cusp. Her life would never again be the same, and any semblance of a private life was gone.

When Kennedy was murdered on **22 November 1963**, Jackie's SA Mars in Libra was approaching a square to natal Pluto, and TR Pluto was conjunct her Mars. At the same time, SA Uranus conjoined her Chiron (natally conjunct the Descendant), and the transiting Saturn–Neptune square in the sky (at 17° Aquarius and 15° Scorpio) was locked into her Ascendant–Descendant axis, prompting her withdrawal from public life.

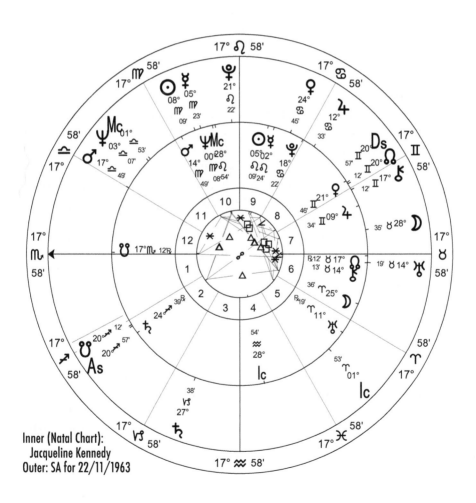

Inner (Natal Chart):
Jacqueline Kennedy
Outer: SA for 22/11/1963

Betty Ford First Lady from 9/08/1974 to 20/01/1977

Elizabeth Anne Bloomer began her time as First Lady amid scandal and uncertainty. The country was reeling from the resignation of disgraced President Nixon and was still at war in Vietnam. In her short tenure, Betty would go on to gain popularity for speaking out on every issue of the day (from equal rights to drugs and abortion) with characteristic candour – Jupiter is on the MC in Gemini.

Although she lacked the political savvy of her role model Eleanor Roosevelt, Betty gained integrity for raising breast cancer awareness following her mastectomy (weeks after she became First Lady), as well as for her courage in adversity (Sun in Aries in the 8th), talking frankly about her long battle with alcohol addiction (note the Pisces planets square Jupiter).

Chart Features
Despite the Moon and Venus embracing her Descendant (Betty and Gerald Ford were two of the most openly affectionate spouses to preside in the White House), this is a chart that speaks less of her role as spouse and more of a personal journey of self-mastery. *The New York Times* stated, 'Mrs Ford's effect on American culture may be far wider and more lasting than that of her husband, who served a mere 896 days, much of it spent trying to restore the dignity of the office of the president.'[2]

A tight Moon–Mars opposition lies at the mid degrees of mutable signs – degrees known for their precarious, fluctuating nature – and this opposition forms a T-square with Jupiter positioned at the MC. (Moon–Mars can be linked symbolically to breast surgery; and Virgo–Pisces to the habit of addiction.) Betty's Mercury (the Ascendant and MC ruler) squares Saturn–Neptune on the cusp of the 12th House, and Saturn–Neptune is the aspect to associate with sobering up and 'hard reality'.

When dedicating the Betty Ford Center (for the treatment of addiction) in 1982, George H W Bush said that Betty 'transformed her pain into something great for the common good. Because she suffered, there will be more healing. Because of her grief, there will be more joy.'[3]

Forecasting

Gerald Ford's role developed when Richard Nixon won the election on **5 November 1968**. At that time, in Betty's chart, the SA Sun moved across the Equal 10th House cusp and edged towards Jupiter. When Ford assumed the presidency in August 1974, transiting Jupiter and the mean nodes were all at 16° mutable, linking in with her pivotal Moon–Mars opposition. In October 1982, as the SA MC reached Neptune, Ford founded the Betty Ford Center near Rancho Mirage, California (where her Saturn–Neptune astrocartography lines rise).

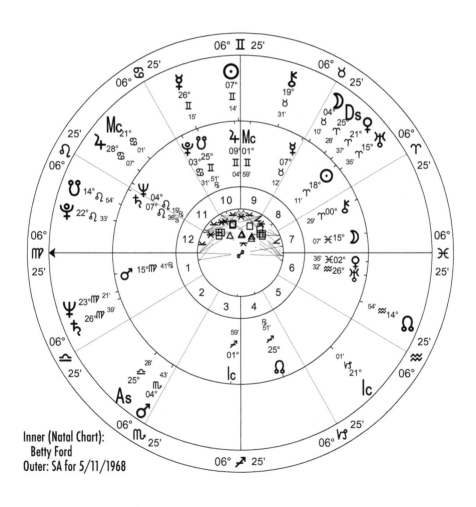

Inner (Natal Chart):
Betty Ford
Outer: SA for 5/11/1968

Nancy Reagan First Lady from 20/01/1981 to 20/01/1989

Anne Frances Robbins became Nancy Davis, an actress who would go on to act in films for MGM. She quit Hollywood a few years after marrying actor Ronald Reagan, and focused on helping him fulfil his political ambitions. With his affability and her steely determination, they were a formidable, glamorous duo – first as Governor and First Lady of California from 1967 (for eight years) and then in the White House during the aspirational, affluent Dynasty-style but politically conservative 1980s.

A seemingly fragile persona belied her immense strength as well as ambition for her husband. But criticism was particularly harsh. 'Queen Nancy' was chastised for spending money on White House china, mocked for the devoted gaze she fixed onto Ronnie and derided for her chic fashion. (Reagan's first wife, Jane Wyman, privately referred to her as 'Nancyvita', after Argentinian First Lady 'Evita' Perón.) Yet, Nancy proved to be Reagan's staunchest supporter – an invaluable asset who fiercely protected him (Cancer) and helped to eliminate the staff whose loyalty she questioned. After her husband was shot (two months into his first term), Nancy went back to astrological advice (often daily) to ensure her husband's safety and to work on changing her public image. With the help of astrologer Joan Quigley, Nancy chose to focus on the dangers of drug abuse in her 'Just Say No' campaign. The astrologer also helped Ronnie change his 'evil empire' stance on Russia and to avert scandal; Quigley later said that astrology had been the 'Teflon' in Ronald Reagan's 'Teflon presidency'.

Chart Features
When Joan Quigley judged her client's horoscope to be 'world class' in her 1990 book *What Does Joan Say?* she was referring to the stellium of planets in Cancer having just culminated at the MC. The feminine planets (Moon and Venus) rule the MC and the Ascendant respectively, but are a 'duet' (aspecting only one another), leaving Mars and Pluto at the centre of the chart's action. This power duo aspects most of the other planets/angles in the horoscope and suggests extraordinary tenacity, perspicacity and formidable resilience under pressure.

Forecasting

Nancy met Ronald Reagan on 15 November 1949, weeks before her first Saturn Return. He was president of the Screen Actors Guild, and Nancy Davis's name had mistakenly appeared on the Hollywood blacklist (at the time, TR Neptune was on her Ascendant, and SA Saturn squared Mercury on the MC). They were married on 4 March 1952, with TR Saturn near her Libra Ascendant and TR Jupiter having just crossed her Descendant.

Reagan became Governor of California on 2 January 1967, as Nancy's SA Moon (MC ruler) was on Jupiter. When Reagan launched his campaign for president on **13 November 1979**, Nancy's SA MC reached natal Jupiter. She entered the White House as SA Mercury approached her Jupiter, and the attempt on her husband's life

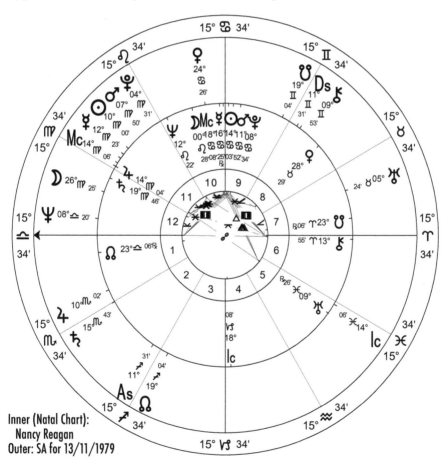

Inner (Natal Chart):
Nancy Reagan
Outer: SA for 13/11/1979

occurred with SA Mars opposing her natal Uranus, which prompted Nancy to return to astrology to avoid the unexpected.

References

1 An essay featured in *Legends: Women Who Have Changed the World*, ed. John Miller, New World Library, 1998, p. 108.

2 http://www.nytimes.com/2006/12/31/us/31betty.html?pagewanted=all&_r=1

3 Quoted in *Barbara Bush: A Memoir*, Simon and Schuster, 1994, p. 180 (of 2015 edition).

The Power Degrees of the Zodiac
Considering the Meanings of 0° and 29° in the Horoscope

'The Power Degrees of the Zodiac' was first presented at the Astrological Association of Great Britain's annual conference at Wyboston Lakes at 7.15 p.m. on 12 September 2014. A transcript was later published in *The Astrological Journal, The Astrology Quarterly* and *The International Astrologer*. It was the winner of the International Astrologer's Award for Best Article 2014–2016, presented at the ISAR Conference in Los Angeles, October 2016.

Some of the examples mentioned below are featured in greater depth elsewhere in this book, but the majority of this article has been left unchanged.

The following offers some of my own insights and observations into the first, final (and mid) degrees of the signs. I wouldn't go as far as to suggest that these are the most powerful, determining factors in a chart – but they are important ones. It's an on-going research project and I'll be using some modern-day examples – both natal charts and Solar Arc directions – that I hope will be of interest.

The Mundane Picture
On a mundane level, we know that when outer planets transit the final few degrees of a sign we say goodbye to certain events (and iconic figures) that have been at the heart of that ingress; it's the end of an era. As these planets ingress into a new sign, we can spot signposts of events to come – the mood of the new transit. The scene is set for the years ahead.

Films and music released at this time can be prophetic. Remember, for instance, the voyeuristic theme of *The Truman Show*, which was released as Neptune moved into Aquarius – and heralded the start of our fascination with (and loathing of) reality TV?

Laws passed at ingresses can herald the new planetary season. Some weeks after Uranus made its ingress into Aries, France became the first European country to prohibit the wearing in public of the niqab and burka. The planet Uranus is linked to bans and censorship, while Aries rules the face and is concerned with being the first to do things. Accordingly it was a controversial move that had both sides arguing equality – and freedom of expression. 'Bans in the name of freedom' seem to be the order of Uranus in Aries!

Neptune's move into the first degree of Pisces brought more than a whiff of scandal. There were stories about invasions. Not invasions of little green men from outer space abducting farmers and performing surgery on cows; but the invasions of privacy and the abduction of personal data. We read of leaks and infiltrations, cyber warfare and phone-hacking. Who can forget *The News of the World* scandal in the UK? Perhaps some of the biggest battles of this transit will revolve around the processing and containment of information, and in particular the collection, sale and distribution of personal data. By the end of this transit, there will be little left of personal privacy.

A few years ago, in *The Astrological Journal*, I wrote that Neptune in Pisces might be seen in:

- The increasing numbers of migrations of nomadic communities without a fixed abode.

- Telepathic forms of everyday communication.

- The erosion of drugs laws and acceptance of certain drugs for medical purposes, and a greater tolerance of euthanasia.

The transit might also link to areas ruled by its opposite sign of Virgo: diseases, viruses and plagues; the evaporation of pensions and health care provisions; and even the disappearance of an official retirement age.

0° in the Natal Chart
So, let's take a closer look at the first degree of a sign. When a planet is at 0° in the natal chart:

- There is new territory to explore. As it takes its initial steps into its new surroundings, the planet delights in discovering itself. It anticipates the new journey ahead. Embarking on this voyage, the planet appears highly eager to encounter and get a sense of *that which it will become.*

- There is a new language to learn and much work to be done; a planet at the beginning of a sign is keen to grasp that sign's essence.

- It revels in the pure, undiluted nature of the sign. There's a fresh, unstudied quality to a planet at this degree. There may also be a pioneering feel – those of us who have a planet (especially a personal planet) at 0° have something original to bring forth to the world around us.

- There is a tendency to exhibit only the sign's most familiar, obvious, prima facie, 'textbook' traits. The planet at 0° indulges in a spectrum of sign connotations and associations, but there's little deftness or experience in how to master the sign yet. The planet has grasped the initial spirit without the awareness that comes from journeying through the sign and owning its essence.

Consider a few pop culture and newsworthy examples.

There's little subtlety when the Sun is at 0° Aries. Overt, playful sexuality is one theme of this degree. The independent film-maker Russ Meyer was obsessed with low-budget sexploitation films. He directed cult X-rated 'classics' such as *Vixen!* and *Faster, Pussycat! Kill! Kill!* featuring Amazonian starlets with gargantuan, pneumatic, gravity-defying breasts, who ran around beating up men who dared to restrict their freedom. (We can see that his chart also contains Venus in Aries opposite Jupiter, Moon–Jupiter, and Mars in Sagittarius on the Descendant.)

Known for his quick wit, Meyer made comedies, live action 'cartoons' that mocked moral stereotypes, using sex to satirize American society. But many feminists hated his adolescent Arien fantasies. He was once confronted by a woman who accused him of being 'nothing but a breast man'. He responded, 'That's only the half of it.'

On a deeper level (if there is one!), the first degree of Aries is about a truthful performance, creating something stark and raw.

There's a self-obsession, and a focus on making an impact while arriving on the scene. We sense immediacy (entering the fray without a plan of attack) and the need for instant arousal and speed, as in Ayrton Senna (Sun at 0° Aries), the Formula 1 race car legend who died from massive injuries to the head while racing at 280km/h (155 mph). Sports enthusiasts still argue whether he was a reckless renegade or the number one racer of all time.

Aries is a sign associated with physicality and violence (giving or receiving), and also (somewhat paradoxically) with blind faith, naïve trust and innocence.

I have a client with the Sun at 0° Aries whose father once remarked upon both her fearlessness and childlike innocence. That's the key to the first degree of Aries. He said she could have singlehandedly taken on those in the Brixton Riots, but could've just as easily been found in the fields talking with the magical fairies and angels she believed in. She is a startling redhead who was at the forefront of many social protests and political rallies in the 1980s; someone who has fought for the underdog but is constantly too trusting and gullible in business. She gives away her time and money – and struggles to keep financially afloat. This placement defines her.

The first degree of Aries needs a clear-cut cause – now! – and sees the world in black and white terms. Not through the lens of cynicism, but through the simple polarities of good and evil, right and wrong: to 0° Aries, you're either the noble knight or the immoral charlatan.

Gemini at 0° has perhaps the lowest boredom threshold of all time and constantly needs to be 'in process' – juggling, scanning, choosing. A planet at this degree immediately sees the polarities, the contradictions, the alternatives and divisions in the world – and it's not surprising that indecision can become a major problem for the native. Its enthusiasm lies in getting other people to share information, to break the ice, to speak out and communicate. The urge to be heard, understood and in dialogue is strongest here, as is the flicker of boredom in the eyes when something newer or more tantalizing comes along.

Picture Henry VIII with Venus at 0° Gemini (suggesting fickleness and a non-committal stance in the area of women and attraction). With Venus on the MC, he was known for his numerous wives and his search for one who could deliver – literally and quickly.

A natural reporter, fact-finder and journalist, 0° Gemini is hungry for data in order to find patterns and make links. For instance, data collector Lois Rodden was born with the Sun at 0° Gemini. It wasn't just a desire to collect information and rate its accuracy, she had an interest in 'doubting' the official word – what had come before. We can see this with 0° Gemini: a rejection of what has been embedded by the previous sign (Taurus) or accepted as tradition, and a need to clarify before information-overload (later in the sign of Gemini).

But wait! All of the above are Gemini traits and themes, whatever the degree of Gemini. Nevertheless, the nature of the sign is undiluted, simplified, most obvious and raring to go when a planet is at 0°.

What of 0° Virgo? As astrologer Kim Farley often says, 'After the party of Leo, someone's got to clean up.' Someone's got to dip their toe in and check the temperature – and to look for hairs in the bath. That's usually Virgo.

At this degree, there's a determination to learn a craft and embark upon the simpler life. The understanding here is that to achieve, one must sign up to an apprenticeship, to be of service to a greater good, to have pure intentions, and to attend dutifully to the body and its needs. If 0° Leo is the degree of helping oneself to something, then 0° Virgo is the degree of 'self-help', a solo journey towards making a difference in the world. There's a belief that one's singular efforts can make a difference – if one works hard enough – and that the simple things in life are the most profound. These are the things that truly touch the soul. Bob Geldof (with Mars at 0° Virgo) saw the clarity of one man making a difference – he responded to the plight of the starving in Ethiopia. Famine relief, health, (mal-)nutrition and the overlooked are all of great concern to the earnest planet positioned at 0° Virgo.

0° in Forecasting

When a planet reaches 0° by transit, progression or Solar Arc (take your pick), there's a major shift and a new script. The planet has changed sign, element and mode. In forecasting, I predominantly use Solar Arc directions, where everything in the chart (the planets, angles, house cusps, even retrograde planets) moves forward by a degree a year.

With Solar Arc, each planet, angle or point stays at 0° for twelve months, and this sets the mood for the longer period to come. It's a portent, a signpost of what we can expect for the next thirty years; a sort of 'operatic overture' – a condensed, intensely heightened period during which we are swamped by images of this new sign and we experience issues around it. It's a year of getting to know, and beginning to work out, the essence of that sign.

An important point to remember is that when a planet ingresses into a sign, it 'speaks to' and begins to activate every planet/angle natally in that sign, regardless of the actual degree. This is the 'natal memory' – what the person knows of the sign from birth. So that initial year at 0° will have a flavour of the new sign and will be tinged by any natal positions in that sign.

A favourite example of mine that I often use is the chart of Pamela Anderson. She posed for *Playboy* when her Sun directed to 0° Leo, a sign that natally contained the over-the-top glamour combo of Venus and Jupiter in Leo. Now, we're not all going to pose for *Playboy* when our Sun's directed into Leo, but Anderson was ambitious and beautiful, and in the right place at the right time. Leo is linked to the centrefold and big blonde hair, and, being a Sun in Cancer in the 1st House, Pamela Anderson was ready to show off her weapons of mass *distraction*.

Whether the transition to a new sign is easy or fraught depends on numerous things, including the natal planets waiting in the new sign. The week after singer Diana Ross's Sun directed into Gemini, her husband announced the end of their marriage – on live TV! Her Sun (already in the 7th House) had left the safety and stability of Taurus – the sign of her Moon and Descendant – and moved into somewhat uncomfortable, unstable ground in Gemini (where Mars, Saturn and Uranus sit). Her MC had also reached the final degree of Libra – and apparently there had been a last attempt at relationship mediation but the relationship had come to an end, as did the public's perception of her fairy tale romance (natal Neptune in Libra).

The Mid-degrees in Natal Charts and Forecasting
When a planet is placed in the mid-degrees of a sign, from 14° to 16° but particularly from 14.5° to 15.5°, the planet appears to be truly ensconced in that sign's *raison d'être*. It's caught up in the

midst of living in that sign and dealing with its key issues; there's a strong feeling that things won't change for some time. It can feel like a mid-way (mid-life) crisis where there's a demand to understand the core challenges of a sign, knowing you have to keep ploughing on with no reprieve or change of scenery for a while. A Solar Arc planet in mid-Virgo, for instance, will be in the centre of chaos or bedlam for that year – snowed under with work, or perhaps dealing with health issues that throw the person off kilter.

When in a cardinal sign, the planet/angle is fully engaged in the process of moving forward, getting things done and encountering challenge and conflict. It's often a decisive period in a battle. Many people who engage in the cut and thrust of politics have personal planets at mid-cardinal degrees.

There's always a warning around Full Moons in mid-cardinal degrees – an existing conflict is exacerbated and there's no immediate solution. There was a lunar eclipse in mid-Capricorn weeks before 9/11 and there was a lunar eclipse at 15° Aries on 8 October 2014, activating so many of the charts of current politicians (including Putin, who has the Sun in Libra opposite that eclipse).

Let's consider the former UK Junior Health Minister Edwina Currie. Her Solar Arc Moon reached mid-Cancer when she 'put her foot in her mouth' and announced that most eggs in the UK were contaminated by salmonella. This caused a sudden and massive drop in egg sales and led to her resignation. The Moon and Cancer are, of course, linked to eggs and chickens and what people buy to eat daily. Her Solar Arc Mercury in Sagittarius (foot-in-mouth disease!) reached an opposition to Uranus at the time. Currie wasn't a stranger to outrageous comments, once saying that 'good Christian people don't get AIDS' and 'northerners die of ignorance and chips [fries]'.

In the mid-fixed degrees, the planet is at its most permanent, solid and durable but sometimes feels stagnant or stuck in the areas linked to that planet and sign. By Solar Arc, it can be a year of feeling stable or trapped.

In mid-mutable degrees, the planet is at its most flexible and diverse, but it's also precarious, scattered and prone to fluctuation. It can be a year of changeability, vacillation and instability.

Here's the chart for the opening of the **World Trade Center**: the Sun is at 14°54' Aries, at the heart of action, dynamic conflict and aggression. We know of the various terrorist and bomb threats over the years. On 9/11, transiting Saturn was at 14°45' Gemini, a 'testing' Saturn Return time for the building. The Twin Towers' chart has Saturn in Gemini at the most precarious of degrees – not a safe bet for a construction of that size and importance.

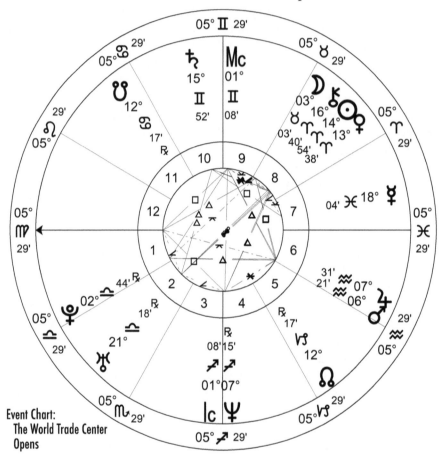

Event Chart:
The World Trade Center
Opens

And what about the Zeebrugge Ferry Disaster (in which 193 people died)? At the moment the ship capsized, 15° Virgo was on the Ascendant and the Sun was at 15° Pisces (both T-square Chiron). There's also Mars opposite Pluto, and Jupiter is at 0° Aries (the ferry's name was *The Herald of Free Enterprise*). Astrologer Dennis Elwell, who predicted a disaster and tried to warn the company, was born with Jupiter at 6° Gemini (on the chart's Moon–MC – he received press attention for his forecast). His Solar Arc Pluto had directed to 14°33' Virgo at the time. We're also reminded that the *Titanic* set sail when Jupiter was retrograde at 15° Sagittarius (there was a whole range of other disastrous aspects that day).

The Final Degree in the Natal Chart: Poised for Change
The final degree of a sign (29°, the thirtieth degree) in the natal chart is the end of an era. Known as the anaretic degree (or 'degree of fate'), it's often given a negative spin and ancient astrologers awarded the malefics (Mars and Saturn) rulership over the final degrees of the signs. Some horary practitioners observe that the querent can do nothing to affect the outcome; it's too late to have control over the situation – it's a fait accompli.

Whereas the 0° planet is taking initial steps on the road ahead and is in the process of envisioning, discovering and mapping out its journey, the planet at 29° senses the end of a familiar path.

- We will encounter some of the most challenging facets of that planetary placement.

- There's a feeling of inevitability and 'fatedness'; there's no going back; situations are irreversible or irretrievable. There may also be a fascination with that which happened before we were born that cannot be undone – a lifelong mission to come to terms with the circumstances we've been saddled with at birth.

- There's a knowingness about the dynamics of the sign; by now the planet is a seasoned player – it's earned its stripes – and is skilled in that sign; and equipped to deal with issues linked to it. With a natal planet or angle at 29°, we were born to finish the job of that sign; to display (eventual) mastery over its issues.

Some examples follow.
The need to take risks – to put oneself on the line – defines 29° Aries. This might mean tap-dancing on a window ledge or walking the high-wire with no net. At 29° Aries, the person may reach crisis point and make a decision without much forethought. Having been through Aries, a planet now basks in its devil-may-

care spontaneity – before it has to slow down in Taurus. The degree of 29° Aries exalts in continuing to be childlike regardless of the perils, mishaps or accusations of selfishness. It can also employ force and is no longer afraid of (or deterred by) violence. There's a skill in promoting a cause and getting people enthused by one's adventures and battles.

Australian astrologer Anne Button has done much work on what she calls the 'potent and insatiable anaretic degree' – a degree that demands closure and has an insatiable/craving feeling to it. She refers to that planet being in a 'liminal' space. This is a disorientating place of transition, waiting and not knowing – when you have left the tried and true (the comfort zone) but have not yet been able to replace it with anything else. It's about learning to navigate and live with the ambiguity and haziness of being in an in-between place.

The judge in the Oscar Pistorius case delayed the verdict (11 September 2014) – and left everyone in total Scorpionic suspense. She was waiting for Mars to reach the final degree of Scorpio the next morning (!) where it conjoined Pistorius's Sun. His is a chart of a do-or-die man who knows nothing but full-on intensity and extreme behaviour in his fight against all odds. (It's interesting to note that the Moon was at 29° Scorpio on 3 May 2007 when it was discovered that Madeleine McCann had been abducted. She has not yet been found.)

Another master of the game, **Billie Jean King**, the tennis legend, has the Sun at the final degree of Scorpio. Let's take a look at her chart (pictured opposite). Firstly, though, the Moon is at 0° Libra – she was an early advocate for equal prize money for women athletes, and in the 1970s became an American figurehead of the struggle for female equality. Yet, King is someone who hates confrontation and, with her Moon–Neptune conjunction, was never quite comfortable with the feminist ideology of the time, which she felt could be intolerant and doctrinaire.

With a planet at the final degree of Scorpio, there may be: lifelong compulsions; a steely will, tunnel vision and total intensity one-on-one; an unflinching focus on the final, ultimate goal (be that victory or an obsession with death and endings); an ability to execute under pressure; an all-or-nothing, fight-to-the-death, winner-take-all philosophy; authenticity; emotional inscrutability; and an innate understanding of the relationship between power, money, sex, politics and gender. (I often think Scorpio should go into one of the 3 Ps: Politics, Psychology or Prostitution!)

The Sun at 29° Scorpio reveals Billie Jean's impact on gender politics, as well as the influence she has had on sponsorship (Scorpio – other people's money) and prize money in the women's game.

This Sun placement was not without heavy personal consequences: she had to keep her (homo)sexuality hidden. The newly founded women's tennis tour and her own livelihood depended on this being kept secret.

The final degree of Scorpio knows how to play the game – to suss out the competition and devise a strategy. When King agreed to participate in a Battle of the Sexes tennis match (20 September 1973), she needed nerves of steel to beat hustler Bobby Riggs, who

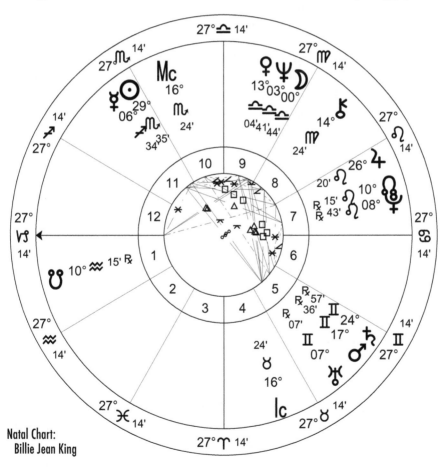

Natal Chart:
Billie Jean King

had just defeated the women's number one player, Margaret Court. The match had 30,000 spectators and 40 million at home in front of their televisions. It divided America into men for Bobby and women for Billie Jean. On that night, Venus and Mars were in opposition and in mutual reception: what a perfect planetary set-up for a 'battle of the sexes'! Venus was in powerful, premeditated and poker-faced Scorpio. It stood less than 1° opposite Mars in solid but slow Taurus, which had turned retrograde the day before. King stayed focused and made Riggs look old and slow. She won in straight sets!

Scorpio is a politically savvy sign that experiences (and is adept at handling) crises and extremes. With King's Sun at the final degree of Scorpio, she knows that the buck stops with her. She was born (Sun) to take control (Scorpio) and complete (29°) a Scorpio theme.

Not surprisingly, at the time of this sports circus extravaganza, King's Sun had directed to 29° Sagittarius (natally the Sun is square Jupiter in Leo). It was an over-the-top, surreal spectacle befitting Sagittarius: one loud night of high drama, hyperbole and publicity on the world stage. It would overshadow the lifelong sporting achievements of both athletes. The win over Riggs would give King and her cause the professional credibility she craved (the Sun directed from Sagittarius to Capricorn soon after). In victory, King slew myths about women and weakness. She hit the first sporting strike for gender equality and freedom of choice (natal Moon at 0° Libra); her win sounded a death knell (her natal Sun at 29° Scorpio) to many male chauvinists who had perpetuated the myth of sexual inequality.

Back to 29° Sagittarius – it can be larger than life, with a gift for seeing the big picture. Think of Judy Garland's emotional, histrionic performances that packed a punch in your gut – designed to capture an audience's love. She had the Moon at 29° Sagittarius.

But 29° Sagittarius can also be the breadth and height of indiscretion. If you want something to go out with a whimper or pass unnoticed, please don't do it when a planet has directed to this degree of Sagittarius!

When Sarah Ferguson offered an undercover journalist 'cash for access' to her former husband in April 2012, her SA Mercury had reached the final degree of Sagittarius. What a gaffe that action proved to be! Hopefully, a final one. And the Solar Arc was all the more potent since natal Mercury rules her Midheaven (her reputation) and comes from a conjunction with Neptune in Scorpio in the 12th House.

With her natal MC at 29° Scorpio, **Heidi Fleiss** was the reigning million-dollar madam of Hollywood and the keeper of the town's most intimate secrets in her infamous 'black book'. (We can speculate that Charlie Sheen's name was on half the pages – with his MC on her Ascendant–Venus conjunction in Aquarius! Interestingly, documentary-maker Nick Broomfield made a fascinating film about Fleiss and his Sun is also on this conjunction.)

With a 29° Scorpio MC and the Sun in Capricorn, Heidi's story is about control – her need for absolute control. Although she never wanted to be famous or exposed (Scorpio prefers to keep control in the boardroom, not flaunt it on the stage), she was one of the most

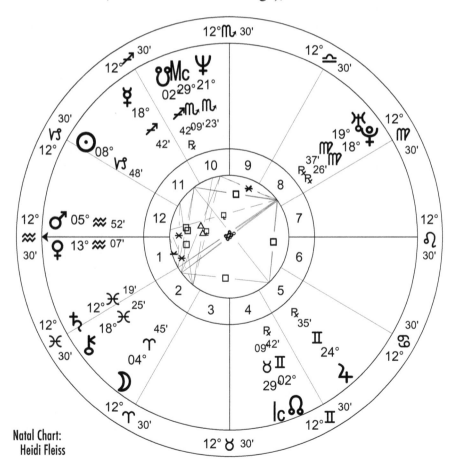

Natal Chart:
Heidi Fleiss

influential madams in the US – and all before her Saturn Return. Her power extended to playing matchmaker to the richest men in the world, pairing them with women tailored for their every fantasy. But like a good Capricorn businesswoman, Fleiss took a 40 per cent cut of their earnings. On her slowest night, she made $10,000.

Her arrogant and cocky persona proved to be her downfall. With Mercury in Sagittarius square Uranus–Pluto in the 8th, she once boasted, 'I took the oldest profession on earth and I did it better than anyone on earth.' When her SA MC was at the end of Sagittarius, her high-profile case ended because her conviction for pandering was overturned – she got lucky temporarily. But she later served twenty months inside for tax evasion when the MC had directed into Capricorn. And then it really was over. She said, 'I had the party, did the party, threw the party, was the party. I'm partied out.'

Gender, sex and secrets are all on the agenda in Scorpio, particularly in the final degree, where there's a mastery of anything covert, underground, clandestine. As Quentin Crisp wrote, 'The war between the sexes is the only one in which both sides regularly sleep with the enemy.' Another expert in the battle of the sexes is Germaine Greer, with Mars at 29° Scorpio in the 10th House and co-ruling the MC. Mars closely trines Pluto.

Billy Tipton was a jazz musician who married four times. Not until his post-mortem was it revealed that Billy was really a woman – someone who had lived life as a man so as to be accepted as a musician in the 1930s and 1940s. This revelation left his wives and three adopted sons bewildered – they hadn't had the slightest suspicion that their dad was female. Tipton's Ascendant ruler is Venus and it's at 29° of inscrutable Scorpio. It's also closely trine Neptune on the MC, which in itself is a placement of speculation and mystery. 'Is he or isn't she?'

When Martin Bashir secretly interviewed Diana, Princess of Wales, it was to become the most astonishing, shattering and indiscreet royal interview of all time. Transiting Pluto was at 29° Scorpio when they taped the conversation. When it aired two weeks later, Pluto had moved into less-than-cautious Sagittarius. The Princess's ploy backfired and set the scene for the dismantling of her public life, it established her global notoriety as a loose cannon, and even foreshadowed the tragedies that lay ahead. (Diana died when her Solar Arc Moon reached 29° Pisces: it was the finale of her domestic drama, the warped fairy tale, and the start of some major speculation surrounding her demise. In addition, when she was laid to rest, she became the Lady of the Lake. Incidentally, the Queen's Solar Arc Ascendant was at 29° Pisces, too.)

To get a final feel for the last degree of Scorpio as a 'hotly political' one, consider the chart for **Margaret Thatcher's resignation** (below). Facing the humiliation of defeat in a leadership contest and a lack of support from colleagues, the three-time Prime Minister signed her resignation statement at 7:35 a.m. on **22 November 1990**. The Sun was rising on the Ascendant at 29° Scorpio – it was the end for a leader who had wielded total Scorpionic control. Thatcher never recovered from her party's betrayal, branding it 'treachery with a smile on its face'. The degree of 29° Scorpio was fitting –

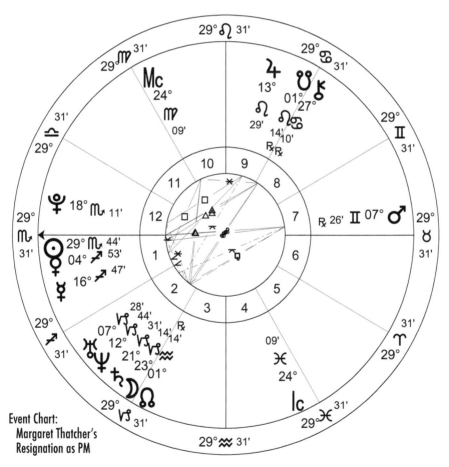

Event Chart:
Margaret Thatcher's
Resignation as PM

it was the end of her 'acid reign' – eleven ruthless, controversial years in power. (John F Kennedy's assassination on the same date in Dallas in 1963 also occurred when the Sun was at 29° Scorpio.)

With 0° Leo there's an interest in (and desire for) celebrity or in revelling in one's own world of creative adventures, and relishing the discovery/realization that Leo can create. Sometimes the desperation for recognition, the spotlight and personal glory is palpable (think of Madonna – Venus at 0° Leo – and her blonde ambition). But, by the final degree of Leo a planet or angle has developed style, star presence, élan, and demonstrates a natural ability to deal (and mix) with celebrity. There's authority and respect – the final word on advice, on knowing what's best for us – but a warning of egomania and excessive pride. While 0° Leo has an instinct to demand attention, 29° Leo has a natural ability to command it.

And what of 29° Pisces, the final degree of the zodiac? Pisces is occasionally and unfairly branded the dustbin of the zodiac. The final degree of Pisces is about 'rest cures, religion and pills', as the Sondheim song goes. Pisces is the true survivor, and 29° Pisces has seen it all. The first client I ever had with the Sun at 29° Pisces had come through addictions, gurus, religions, self-help quick-fixes and 101 other ways to escape the mundane world and connect to something higher. He'd tried everything and had been everything.

Pisces at 29° recognizes that we are all made of the same magic (although its opposite sign, Virgo, might call it 'dirt'). It's the talent to save, rescue and pour energy into addressing the needs of the forgotten and disenfranchised. Think of singer-turned-saint Bono, who has his MC ruler Mars at 29° Pisces. Saving people (Pisces) in crisis situations (29°).

That final degree is not always a blessing – it's also the degree of those who feel duped by people or have experienced major betrayal. One woman (a Sun Pisces with Pisces MC) discovered that her record company had siphoned off her royalties when her MC moved to 29° Pisces. She launched an attack and filed a lawsuit when the MC moved into 0° Aries. It was a dirty fight and took eight years of her life and reputation. She finally won the lawsuit and rights to her royalties when her Sun moved to 0° Taurus, suggesting she was now moving to a firmer financial foundation.

Evangelists ('messengers of good news') usually have strongly Jupiterian and Neptunian charts (or their signs prominent). They are missionaries who sell and promote their vision of God, rescuing and offering redemption. With Mars at 29° Pisces, evangelist **Jim Bakker** (chart below) saw himself as the ultimate visionary: he had a Jesus complex and felt crucified and betrayed by those who sought to curtail his brand of selling God on TV. His was 'prosperity theology': make money, give it to us and then you'll be happy and go to Heaven. In short, the donation box got bigger than the message and the Gospel.

On **19 March 1987**, Bakker fell from grace and resigned from his ministry as his Solar Arc Sun reached 29° Aquarius. Soon after, the Sun entered Pisces and he was truly crucified (most famously

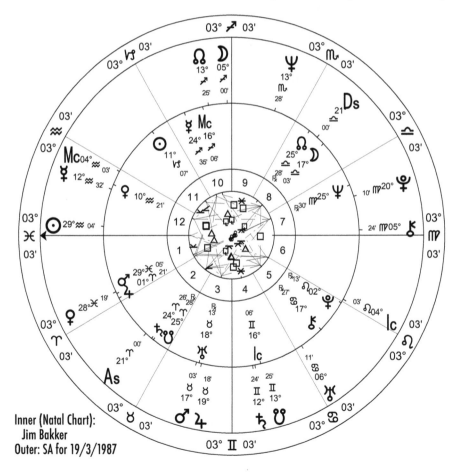

Inner (Natal Chart):
  Jim Bakker
Outer: SA for 19/3/1987

bound in chains and humiliated in front of the world's media). He was handed a 45-year prison sentence for mail fraud.

At the final degree of Virgo, there's consideration for the underprivileged (knowing what it's like to feel small, degraded or overlooked), and an ability to deal with crisis issues around health and safety. Along with 29° Capricorn, here we have the control freak who has already considered every angle, whether it's the diet, schedule, route or other people's habits. At 29° Virgo, there's a finicky attention to detail, to getting it right, being faithful to one's word, ensuring contracts and agreements are drawn up with every 'T' crossed, etc. There's an obsession with precision and sculpting (e.g. creating the body beautiful); perfecting a craft; finishing the apprenticeship. Often there's a need for an unpretentious, understated (sometimes solitary) life – feeling content in the rhythms of regular life.

Remember Jack Nicholson (with the Moon at the final degree of Virgo) in *As Good As It Gets* as the obsessive-compulsive novelist who avoids the cracks in the road and eats at the same table in the same restaurant every day? That phrase 'as good as it gets' should be a mantra for all those final-degree Virgos to enjoy life now.

In UK politics, we had the Labour Party's 'Red Queen', **Barbara Castle** (chart opposite). As a Libran, her Venus placement at 29° Virgo assumes greater importance: her concern was Libran and Virgoan – a concern for care, safety and addressing the ills and injustices of society. She was put in charge of the Department of Employment and Productivity (Virgo), radically reformed pensions (pensions are, aptly, what you get at the end – 29° – of your working life), higher pay for nurses and increased benefits for old and disabled people. She brought in seat belts for cars and the breathalyser law, and ensured Child Benefit was paid to the mother rather than through the father's pay packet. Castle was chief architect of the Equal Pay Act (following the famous Dagenham women's strike at the Ford plant, as TR Uranus crossed over her Mercury and later Venus). When the film *Made in Dagenham* was released, Jupiter was conjunct Uranus at 29° Pisces. It recently transpired that Castle drew up a dossier on VIP paedophiles but the document was confiscated for 'national security reasons'.

George W. Bush's Solar Arc Ascendant was at 29°59' Virgo (the sign of his natal Mars) at the time of 9/11. It was the crisis of his life

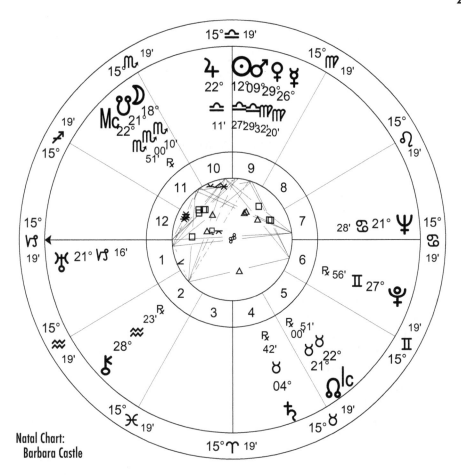

Natal Chart:
  Barbara Castle

and yet the moment he'd been waiting for. The Ascendant would then move into Libra (where his Moon, Jupiter and Neptune are placed), giving rise to a new script on a wave of nationalistic fervour and patriotism (Moon–Jupiter); an attempt to put the wrongs to rights and bring the terrorists to justice (Libra).

29° in Forecasting

What of the final degree in forecasting? Here are some observations:

- It's the end of a chapter. We're poised for change, but before we jump into a new field of experience (and perhaps an unknown scenario) we must deal with a crisis of sorts …

- It's a year when some of the most challenging aspects of the sign demand to be seen and resolved. It's the end of the line – can we meet the demands before moving on? It's the end of a thirty-year era and often coincides with an intense twelve months (the final degree) that 'packs a punch' – a time when exaggerated manifestations of that sign appear as life events.

- We can truly make our mark by wrapping up long-term endeavours.

Positively, that which has been mastered – skills that have been acquired – can be put to good use in these twelve months. This is where the last degree can truly come into its own. It can be a year of distinction or simply concluding a long period of endeavour.

In 1997, intrepid British politician Mo Mowlam worked to restore an IRA ceasefire in Northern Ireland and persuaded various sides to participate in the peace process – all during a time when she was fighting a brain tumour. Mowlam was instrumental in the signing of the Good Friday Peace Agreement on 10 April 1998, when her SA Saturn had reached 29° Libra. She retired from Parliament two years later. In hindsight, it's clear that her historic work had been completed at this time. It proved to be her legacy.

Woody Allen's Ascendant reached 29° Libra when he began a relationship with his partner Mia Farrow's adopted daughter, Soon-Yi. It was still at 29° Libra on **13 January 1992** (bi-wheel opposite) when Farrow discovered nude pictures Allen had taken of Soon-Yi. The affair became public that August (as his SA Ascendant moved into Scorpio), along with very damning accusations against him from Farrow of child molestation. The degree of 29° Libra is linked to the last-chance attempts to keep a relationship in balance before war breaks out; the final attempt at a diplomatic solution. Sometimes it works, sometimes it doesn't.

The final degree of Scorpio is the crisis degree of the crisis sign. In forecasting, it is a tough, profound period, 'a dark night of the soul' before we see the light of day in Sagittarius. A student of mine had her MC Solar Arc to 29° Scorpio when a family member was bullied online into committing suicide. Prince Harry's SA MC was at this same degree when Diana was killed, as was Marlon Brando's when his troubled daughter killed herself.

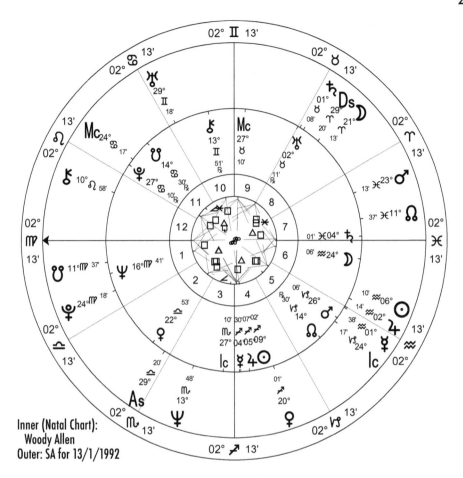

Inner (Natal Chart):
Woody Allen
Outer: SA for 13/1/1992

No Turning Back: When Scripts Change

Finally, here are a few examples of events when planets and angles directed to either 0° or 29°.

Superman Christopher Reeve: his natal Moon–Mars in Sagittarius suggests his love of horse-riding and competitive horsemanship. When he was thrown from his horse, at an event on 27 May 1995, he was left paralysed: a quadriplegic and unable to breathe on his own. Note the tight natal quincunx from Mars to Uranus (for his chart, see page 152). By Solar Arc, Mars had reached 0° Aquarius, and Uranus was at 0° Virgo, starting a very new script in his life. By transit, Mars was at 0° Virgo quincunx SA Uranus at 0° Aquarius – a remarkable repetition of planetary aspects. (Chiron, so often associated with horses and motorcycles, had directed to the Descendant and another link to horses, Jupiter, had directed to square Mercury.)

Gordon Brown waited a long time to see his dream of premiership come true. When he became Prime Minister, his Solar Arc MC had finally reached his Sun, a classic leadership measurement and a Solar Arc year of a memorable change in status. At 0° Pisces, perhaps he was destined to play out the role of patsy. Three years later, Brown called an election. I'm assuming he did this without an astrologer: transiting Pluto was on his MC and his Sun had directed to 29° Aries and his MC ruler Saturn to 29° Scorpio – it was time for another big script change. (See pages 100–1 for more details.)

Political defeats and resignations are fascinating astrologically. Americans won't have forgotten **Gary Hart's** resignation due to the rumours of an extra-marital affair (famously on a boat called *Monkey Business*) on **8 May 1987** (bi-wheel opposite), just 26 days into his presidential campaign. Only days before, he'd dared the press, 'Follow me around … If anybody wants to put a tail on me, go ahead. They'll be very bored.' They weren't!

Natally, Hart has a tight square from Mars in Libra to his MC in Capricorn (warning of sexual pursuits damaging his civic reputation). By Solar Arc, his MC had reached 29° Aquarius and his Mars 29° Scorpio – both crisis degrees. The Moon had entered Leo, bringing much attention to his daily life and domestic set-up.

And whatever happened to labour union leader Jimmy Hoffa? Well, don't ask me, but his chart at the time of his disappearance (30 July 1975) certainly describes the end of a chapter: Solar Arc Ascendant at 29° Aries, and the Moon–Saturn at 29° Cancer (plus Pluto at 0° Virgo). Perhaps, as some have suggested, he met a violent, Aries end in a deadweight Moon–Saturn home/coffin at the bottom of the sea (Cancer).

Can They Talk!
Let's end with the degree that likes to have the final word: 29° Gemini. Here we have the multi-tasker, adept at technology or language or making connections. The difficulty lies in finishing things off – they try to juggle too much and are weighed down by chronic indecision – and then they drop the ball.

The final degree of Gemini disperses the information (or says their piece) and then leaves others to handle the aftermath, just as

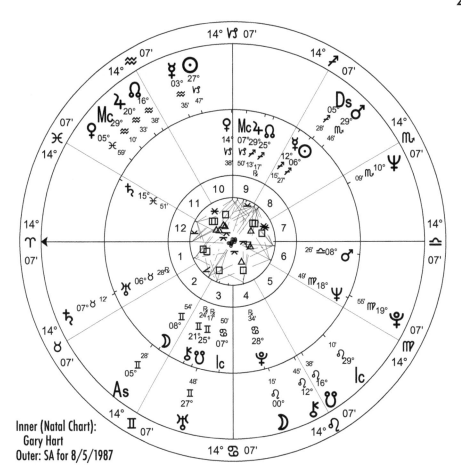

Inner (Natal Chart):
Gary Hart
Outer: SA for 8/5/1987

whistleblower Ed Snowden did (Sun at 29° Gemini), avoiding the conflict and consequences (characteristic of the mutable signs). Interestingly, his Sun had Solar Arc directed to the degree of the US's natal Pluto when he released the classified documents.

Someone else more than able to drop a Gemini bomb was age-obsessed **Joan Rivers** (chart overleaf), born with Mercury and Venus at the final degree of Gemini. Whether she was talking about her body, what the famous are wearing or quipping that Michelle Obama was transgender, Joan Rivers was the wisecracking witch who spelled it with a 'b'. In fact, one person roasted her with the line, 'Joan, you've been called "bitch" more times than a white guy serving a life sentence.'

Rivers died without having the final word, so I'm giving it to her now. Well, sort of.

Picture it, *The Tonight Show*, the mid-80s. Joan is guest host. She's interviewing actress Joan Collins, herself a Gemini (possibly with Aries rising, too) and both are monuments to malice. Suddenly she turns to Joan Collins and says, 'OK, Joan, of all the husbands you've had, who was the best lover?' Joan Collins replied, 'Yours, darling.'

It was the only time Joan Rivers was struck dumb and lost for words.

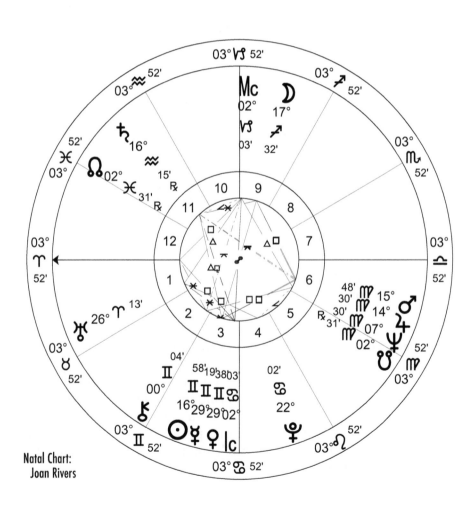

Natal Chart:
Joan Rivers

Fame and Celebrity:
The Addictive Commodities of Our Times

We live in a society defined, driven, saturated and obsessed by celebrity – a culture that sees fame as the highest embodiment of success and a population that covets it as the ultimate symbol of achievement. This article is about the psychology and pathology of stardom, and the all-consuming cult of celebrity today. We will pay particular attention to Jupiter and Neptune in both natal and mundane astrology.

The word 'fame' originates from the name of the eavesdropping, gossiping goddess of Greek mythology, *Pheme* (meaning 'rumour'), who granted renown, gossip or scandal to mortals (she was *Fama* in the Roman pantheon, and nowadays we sue for de*fama*tion). Fame is defined as 'the state of being known or recognized by many people because of [one's] achievements, skills, etc.'[1] The 'etc.' now covers countless alternative avenues of expression.

In ancient times, only athletes and conquerors were afforded celebrity status. ('Fame,' Socrates wrote, was 'the perfume of heroic deeds.') However, no longer is fame dependent on or the byproduct of some extraordinary accomplishment, such as a scientific breakthrough, technological discovery or act of heroism. Nor is it simply awarded for performance talent or sporting prowess. These days, anyone can be famous for almost anything (from videotaping sexual escapades with the powerful to perpetrating a gruesome crime) as long as the media play along and rouse public interest. And in order to maintain this 'fame', starlets must flaunt their stardom and sell out – or cash in on their popularity – for as long as they're in vogue.

Society's need for heroes has been replaced by the public's desire to get in on the act and have a stab at making the Big Time. Later in his life, Andy Warhol, considered the father of modern fame, changed his original prophecy, 'In the future, everyone will be world-famous for fifteen minutes,' to a more cynical prediction: 'In fifteen minutes, everyone will be famous.' This seems ever more prescient, considering the nature of modern-day fame where bland ambition has become a surrogate for burgeoning talent. The public's appetite for celebrity is as insatiable as ever but, since Neptune's journey through democratic Aquarius, stardom has been downgraded and its currency devalued.

At the time of the 1962 great conjunction in Aquarius, Professor Daniel J Boorstin wrote 'From Hero to Celebrity: The Human Pseudo-Event', a seminal, prophetic essay on fame. He highlighted the shift from the hero as a big man distinguished by his achievements to the celebrity as a big name marked out by his image or trademark. He observed: 'Two centuries ago when a great man appeared, people looked for God's purpose in him; today we look for his press agent.'[2]

Astrological Signatures
There is no simple or single astrological formula for fame (or success, for that matter). Perhaps before the 20th century, the astrological signatures for honour, distinction and eminence were easier to determine in people's lives. For instance, the Sun, Jupiter and the Midheaven/10th House can all be linked to the carving-out of a distinguished reputation and societal recognition of individual achievement. Nowadays, though, fame and stardom are not always linked to venerable traits or to a particular skill set.

Many in the public eye are OPPs (a term coined by Donna Cunningham for 'Outer-Planet People') – they are those who have Uranus, Neptune or Pluto strongly positioned and aspected in their horoscopes. Although OPPs shape or personify the Zeitgeist in various and specific ways, the birth charts of those who have achieved fame are as varied as the celebrities themselves. What emerges from studying the charts of the famous is not an ability to predict their fame but rather a capacity to assess the quality of these individuals – and with this quality we can forecast their motivations, passions, drives and character. If we think in terms of 'planetary types' (a Pluto type, for instance, is defined as someone with a stand-out, heavily aspected or prominent Pluto and/or with planets/points in Scorpio or the 8th House), we can see that the Plutonic celebrity will display different conduct, make a specific type of impact and have different needs and drives compared to a Saturnian, Uranian or Neptunian star. Even if a 'famous chart' cannot be defined, what's clear is that, once the celebrity is famous, their chart comes to the fore, and their traits become more apparent, magnified and scrutinized.

Jupiter and Neptune: Fame and Phenomena

While the Sun and Leo are the pair most often linked to fame and prominence,[3] it is Jupiter, the King of the Gods, that reveals the measure of our desire and hunger for renown, success and public recognition. Astrologically, Jupiter symbolizes the need to be elevated, to be 'great' and to be seen as important. It is also linked to promotion, advertising, broadcasting and exhibition – all components of the celebrity machine. When Jupiter is strong in the horoscope, as the Gauquelins' research revealed, the native commands respect and craves distinction, influence, glory and power. At its best, Jupiter can be generous, philanthropic and benevolent.[4]

Celebrity bestows gifts and advantages (Jupiter), and the famous are exalted, praised, pampered and overindulged – they and their desires become larger than life. Stars are seldom disagreed with and rarely need to experience delayed gratification. Being famous is a free pass for getting away with the most self-centred, outlandish behaviour. One face of Jupiter is personified in this demanding kind of diva (or divo) – the charismatic yet monstrous celebrity who makes outrageous, over-the-top demands. The Jupiterian type can quite easily 'go Hollywood' and exhibit a superior attitude dispensed from a high altitude.

> Fame is a perversion of the natural human instinct
> for validation and attention.
> – Heathcote Williams

Fame attracts petulant, prideful egocentrics – Jupiter at its worst. The Jupiterian is the fame-seeker who feels entitled to such elevation and greatness but may secretly pursue celebrity to compensate for inner feelings of inadequacy or smallness. Once fame has been achieved, research suggests that the celebrity may struggle with a toxic mix of monumentally high self-regard, delusions of grandeur and low self-esteem. A need for reassurance through omnipotence then manifests as compensation for insecurities and human shortcomings.

> Fame is like a river, that beareth up things light and swollen,
> and drowns things weighty and solid.
> – Francis Bacon

While Jupiter represents the desire for fame, Neptune is the filter through which fame is advertised and spread, with the celebrity being a product packaged and cued up to be sold for mass consumption. Neptune also describes that intangible something that celebrities possess and project – the X factor that elicits an emotional response (be it devotion, love or obsession) from the public. Astrologically, Neptune is the magical aura that surrounds the super-famous and helps them to transcend their achievements; it's the 'high' they feel when receiving applause. It's also the fan 'mania' – the gossip, scandal and global attention they attract – and the yearning and projection experienced by the non-famous.

Whether we follow celebrities or wish to be a star in our own right, fame is highly seductive and addictive – we are narcotized by its allure (Neptune). Its elusive quality ensures that we continue to hanker after this lucrative aphrodisiac. Eternal Neptune and its sign, Pisces, are linked to the dream and hope that everyone will know our name and the longing to 'live forever'. The famous are remembered – indeed, immortalized.

Celebrity Creators: The Tabloids

Celebrity is a consequence of media attention and the media provide us with daily, sometimes hourly, access to stars who have an image and product to sell. The media and, in particular, tabloid newspapers are Neptunian in essence. Tabloids have the ability to sell celebrities or tarnish their reputations with speculation and innuendo (Neptune). As the public's interest in the famous grows ever more fickle, the media ruthlessly pursue and manipulate anyone with a sellable story and then dispense of those who become unfashionable. Every season is hunting season.

> People who read the tabloids deserve to be lied to.
> – Jerry Seinfeld

One of the events that heralded a new wave of media in the United Kingdom was the launch of the *Daily Mail* on 4 May 1896, soon after the Neptune–Pluto conjunction in sound bite, media-savvy Gemini. A horoscope (pictured below) calculated for 6.00 a.m. in London (around the time that the paper would have first been available to purchase) shows the Moon in human-interest Aquarius (the *Mail* would later portray itself as the paper of the people) and Mercury at 1° Gemini, an area of the zodiac that I link to gossip, hearsay and the 'It Girl' phenomenon. Jupiter had just entered Leo, while Mars in mid-Pisces squared Neptune exactly: the *Mail's* readers were offered entertainment and competitions rather than reportage. The line between hard news and celebrity news was beginning to blur.

The *Mail's* relaunch in the mid-1930s (aiming a radical political voice at a mass audience of working-class readers – Aquarius) further changed the face of the British tabloid press. The newspaper was

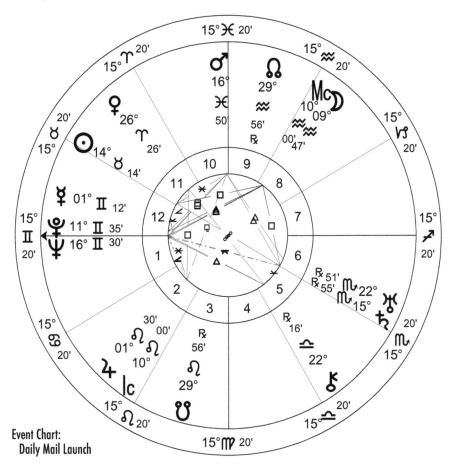

Event Chart:
Daily Mail Launch

repackaged, content was simplified further and news stories with attention-grabbing headlines focused on the sordid and sensational. (These days, it is still celebrity-focused but better known for its moralistic and conservative tone – note that the Sun in Taurus is opposite Saturn.)

In the US, the Saturn–Neptune conjunction of November 1952 coincided with the tabloid *Confidential* hitting the news-stands (during the same Uranus–Neptune square that defined the McCarthy era of Communist witch hunts). Some months later, in April 1953, the *National Enquirer* was bought out by Generoso Pope, Jr. (born 13 January 1927, with Jupiter – note his name! – in Aquarius opposite Neptune in Leo, and a Mercury–Pluto opposition), who revamped it into its current salacious format.

The Fame Cult

Andy Warhol (chart opposite) is often credited with creating the modern cult of celebrity; he was born with the Sun rising in Leo square Jupiter on the MC, and Venus–Neptune also in Leo. Venus–Neptune is also the aspect to associate with manufactured pop idols and popular culture. Warhol grew up in Pittsburgh, Pennsylvania and every Sunday worshipped at a Byzantine Catholic church full of saints' icons. Later, he would replace saints with celebrities as gods for worship and sell celebrity as the new opiate of the people.

Warhol's artwork and films reflected the commerciality and superficiality of life. He often said, 'Look at the surface of my work; there's nothing else.' But there was more to it than that. His evocative Pop Art, particularly his screen-printing technique (churned out at his studio, The Factory), became a symbol of the burgeoning consumer society, an assembly line of products and images, with celebrity as the new religion. Warhol captured the Zeitgeist of celebrity culture and advertising, and delighted in obscuring the boundary between image and reality.

The Price of Fame

Fame is an anesthetic to the reality of life. Like Neptune, fame is an amorphous, shapeless entity – it has no tangible characteristics, no emotions, no value system. Yet, there is a belief (Jupiter) and an illusion (Neptune) that something magical will happen to us if we become famous. As in the Cinderella fairy tale, we're plucked out of obscurity, all our troubles evaporate and we become idolized. We marry our prince (or princess) and then expect to live an idyllic life happily ever after.

However, fame is also notoriously transient. When the public loses interest, as it inevitably does, this is disorientating (Neptune) and makes it tougher for the celebrity to return to a regular life and work. For some, once fame has been tasted, it is impossible to give up the narcotic. For others who disappear from the limelight, there's an assumption from the public and press that they're missing their fame (hence invitations to appear on Neptunian shows like *Where Are They Now?* and *UnSung*) – that they're desperate to cling on to past stardom lest they become someone who is remembered for having been forgotten.

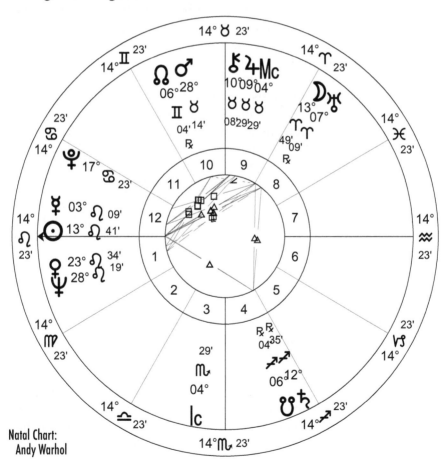

Natal Chart:
Andy Warhol

I think that when you're famous every weakness is exaggerated.
– Marilyn Monroe

Does fame destabilize the personalities of those who become famous, or do unstable people pursue fame? This may be almost impossible to ascertain, but the downside of fame is reflected in the astrological natures of Jupiter and Neptune, too. Fame is an uncharted terrain to all, at first. How do celebrities hold on to their sense of self? There's disorientation (Neptune) over the loss of anonymity, and a feeling of separation when friends don't know how to treat them. Celebrities may be unsure how to handle or even trust the entourage who wish to fulfil their every whim. With public recognition comes over-familiarity and a loss of privacy. Becoming famous is like selling our soul to the public – we belong to everyone (for as long as they want us), and everyone thinks they know us. In order to escape the intrusion, the famous become guarded, hire security in an attempt to be more untouchable, and retreat into an isolated world, becoming refugees from reality (Neptune).

Ironically, the famous must sell the illusion of intimacy in order to win over the public, but in attaining public acclaim, personal freedom is curtailed; fans presume a false bond and acquire a sense of entitlement. So, how can the celebrity reconcile the need to please the public (whose support pays for their lifestyle) with a growing contempt for the intrusive fans and paparazzi? If they don't play to the crowd and keep the ovations coming, the younger, fitter, hungrier wannabes are waiting in the wings for their chance. And how can the celebrity attempt a balancing act with the media, hoping to be left alone yet still have their product or agenda publicized?

This was highlighted in the life of Princess Diana, the most photographed and hunted celebrity of the 20th century: chart ruler Jupiter squares Neptune in her chart, and Neptune trines her Sun–Mercury in the 7th House. Madonna, on the other hand, was always hungry for fame and has succeeded by using the media to manipulate her image and reignite her notoriety over the decades. The *Desperately Seeking* (attention) performer has a Jupiter–Neptune conjunction in a square to Venus at 0° Leo. Her ex-husband Sean Penn loathed the paparazzi when he was married to her: he has Mercury square Neptune, while Mars in Gemini on the Descendant suggests the violent outbursts and fistfights with photographers who pursued him. With a Sun–Uranus conjunction in Leo, Penn rejected (Uranus) his celebrity status to focus on creative pursuits and social activism.

That Certain Something: Jupiter–Neptune in Combination

What of those celebrities who are born with both Jupiter and Neptune strong or in aspect to each other? Together, these planets symbolize the selling and morphing of an artist into a titanic phenomenon. It is interesting to note that America is the land of fame and celebrity, and the US Sibly chart shows Sagittarius rising, with Jupiter conjunct the Sun and Venus, plus an elevated Neptune.

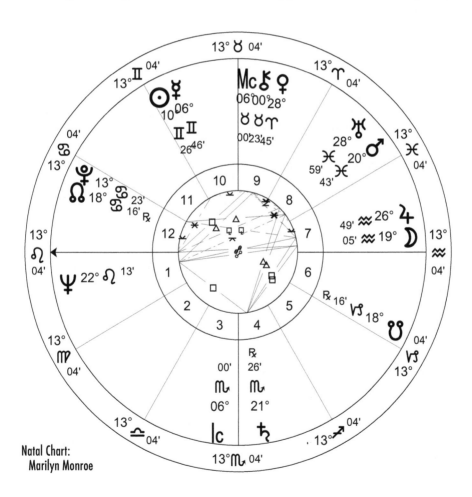

Natal Chart:
  Marilyn Monroe

Many of the most enigmatic celebrities, such as Whitney Houston, Elizabeth Taylor and Marilyn Monroe, have charts that combine the essences of Jupiter and Neptune. These three women suffered from relentless press hounding and fell from elevated positions (Jupiter) when their addictions, scandals and vulnerabilities were revealed and sold to the media (Neptune). Whitney Houston's battle with addiction dominated tabloid headlines for two decades (she has Neptune as the apex of a T-square and a dominant Jupiter). Elizabeth Taylor enchanted audiences with her beauty and her diamonds, and the media chronicled her roller coaster life of excess, addiction, health crises and marital breakdowns. Taylor's chart has a Jupiter–Neptune signature: the Sun–Mercury–Mars conjunction in Pisces opposite Neptune, Sagittarius rising, and the Moon exactly square chart ruler Jupiter. **Marilyn Monroe's** chart (previous page) has the Moon conjunct Jupiter in the 7th House opposite Neptune, and she was sold as the ultimate glamour goddess, despite her emotional and mental fragility.

Although the charts of Madonna, Michael Jackson and Prince are dominated by Pluto (suggesting that they pushed buttons and were instrumental in truly shaping their generation), these performers were all born around the Jupiter–Neptune conjunction of the late 1950s. Singer Celine Dion (with a strongly Aries chart) has the Jupiter–Neptune square, as do other key players involved in the movie *Titanic*. Garth Brooks, another artist who has also sold more than 100 million albums, was born with the Sun conjunct Jupiter, Mercury and Venus – all square Neptune.

What happens when Jupiter and Neptune meet in the sky? Susan Boyle became a worldwide media phenomenon during the 2009 Jupiter–Neptune–Chiron conjunctions in the 'ordinary person' sign of Aquarius (the same period that saw the start of the TV show *Glee*, the world's most popular instant messaging service WhatsApp, and the deaths of three media icons of their time: Michael Jackson, Farrah Fawcett and Walter Cronkite).

The 1971 Jupiter–Neptune conjunction in Sagittarius heralded the soft-rock and easy-listening music genres as well as the re-emergence of the singer–songwriter as poet – the direct, unaffected, and searingly honest storyteller. With a natal Moon in Sagittarius opposite Jupiter, Carole King 'happened' to record her *Tapestry* album in January 1971, during the Jupiter–Neptune conjunction. It was released a few weeks later (as she approached her first Saturn Return, and Solar Arc Neptune squared her natal MC), and by June it was on its way to becoming a cultural phenomenon. *Tapestry* was a symbol of a gentler era of Sagittarian hope and faith, and has since sold more than 25 million copies.

The Birth of Reality TV

As an outer planet transits through a sign, issues around that sign of the zodiac and its polar opposite are triggered. Aquarius is a sign linked to someone who is an equal member of the crowd, whereas its opposite sign, Leo, is seen as the special individual who stands out as the chosen one. Neptune's transit through the Air sign of Aquarius between 1998 and 2012 heralded the age of social media and also saw the development of the 'everyman' (Aquarius) celebrity (Leo) – a herd of talented and not-so-talented ordinary people thrust into the spotlight, courtesy of Facebook, YouTube and voyeuristic talent or reality TV shows like *Big Brother*, *The X Factor*, *Dancing with the Stars* and the *Idol* franchise.

During this transit, which began with the fitting release of the ingenious satirical movie *The Truman Show*, we watched two Leo–Aquarius spectacles that continue to this day: ordinary people becoming famous and the famous appearing to be ordinary by being deglamorized and put through their paces. Favourites (Leo) were picked from the group (Aquarius), and reality shows and their 'stars' became more bankable than Hollywood films and actors.

Remember My Name: The Selling of Neptune

As Neptune sojourns through its fourteen-year stay in each sign, the types of aspiration and glamour associated with that sign are sold to the previous Neptune generation(s) via music, fashion, film and TV. Neptune in Capricorn (1984–98) sold the upwardly mobile, entrepreneurial spirit to the Neptune in Sagittarius generation (1970–1984). To remain in control of their product (Capricorn) and envision their future (Sagittarius), wannabes were instructed to train in the arts and work at their craft. They could have it all if they worked hard enough. The equation was aspiration + perspiration = success. Numerous performing arts schools opened during the Neptune in Capricorn era.

The Neptune in Aquarius period (1998–2012) sold its previous generation a different dream. At the time of writing this, the Neptune in Capricorn group (born 1984–98, spanning Madonna's emergence as a 'Material Girl' all the way to the Spice Girls' promotion of 'Girl Power') is between 19 and 34 years of age. This generation was sold the Aquarian dream that anyone could be famous and stand out from the crowd. When asked what they wanted to be when they grew up, members of this generation are likely to have answered 'Rich and famous', as though it were a viable career option. No one in this generation of narcissistic entitlement wanted to settle into a humdrum job. As they mature, though, they are realizing they can't all be pop stars, models and WAGs (footballers' 'wives and girlfriends').

Neptune in Aquarius also brought us social media and social networking.[5] Here, the celebrities appear more accessible, and the wannabes can brand themselves as 'legends' in a self-absorbed environment where even the most mundane (or private) of happenings can be shared, followed and commented on. **Chris Crocker** became an instant Internet celebrity when his histrionic 'Leave Britney Alone!' monologue went viral (another Neptune term) on **10 September 2007** and received more than four million views in two days. TR Neptune was close to his MC, TR Jupiter was approaching his Sun, and TR Pluto was on Solar Arc Mercury in Sagittarius.[6] Many criticized his ambiguous gender and his decision to live as a girl, which he did for three years. With Venus–Neptune in Capricorn and Mars–Pluto in Scorpio, Crocker has since used his celebrity to challenge both prejudice in the LGBT community and gender stereotypes in society.

> To be popular, one must be a mediocrity.
> – Oscar Wilde

We now have the 'sella-brity', with nothing to celebrate and everything to sell. Since Neptune's sojourn through Aquarius, fame has been democratized, but it is operated on a conveyor belt of endless, interchangeable nine-minute wonders, an oversaturation of D-list celebrities and contestants on reality shows. A few years ago, now-notorious publicist Max Clifford (born with Sun–Mercury in Aries square Jupiter) offered his Top Ten Tips to Becoming

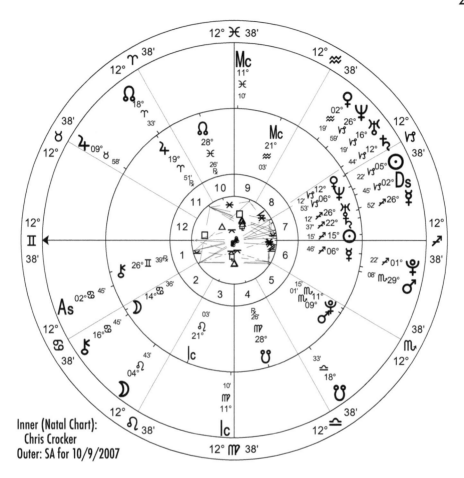

Inner (Natal Chart):
Chris Crocker
Outer: SA for 10/9/2007

Famous,[7] which included appearing on a reality or talent show, dating a celebrity, flaunting your body and shooting a homemade sex video.

The current all-consuming desire for success has made 'ambition' and 'fame' dirty words, linked to the ruthless ambition and the tell-all media personalities of British 'It' girls like Katie Price (born at a Full Moon with the Sun at the start of Gemini) and the American Kardashian family: Kim (Neptune rising in Sagittarius, and Jupiter–MC), Khloé (Sun–Mercury–Venus opposite Jupiter, and Moon opposite Neptune), and Kourtney (Sun square Jupiter, and Neptune–MC). Half-siblings Kylie and Kendall Jenner have Mars-themed charts. Overleaf, you'll find their charts, plus their mum, Kris's, too.

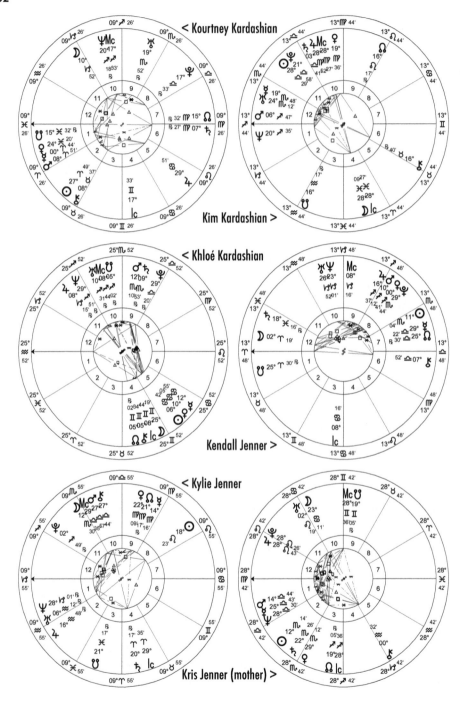

< Kourtney Kardashian

Kim Kardashian >

< Khloé Kardashian

Kendall Jenner >

< Kylie Jenner

Kris Jenner (mother) >

Fame is just obscurity biding its time.
— Carrie Fisher

It's now estimated that modern celebrity lasts around fifteen months. No one who has experienced fame walks away the same person. For a few, it's a form of therapy – a vindication and compensation for past grievances or a chance to give back generously. For many, it gives power and wealth and grants them entry into a secret world of luxury and ease. For most, fame annihilates any hope of having a normal life. The major Hollywood studios of yesteryear would cultivate and look after their stars, but there is little protection for the famous now. Jodie Foster, who has lived her life in the spotlight, wrote of the media's increasingly mercenary attitude:

> In my era, through discipline and force of will, you could still manage to reach for a star-powered career and have the authenticity of a private life … you could stand up and say, 'I will not willfully participate in my own exploitation.' Not anymore. If I were a young actor or actress starting my career today in the new era of social media and its sanctioned hunting season, would I survive? … I would quit before I started. If I had to grow up in this media culture, I don't think I could survive it emotionally.[8]

It's sometimes argued that tabloids and the paparazzi are scapegoats, merely surrogates of the public will (Neptune). We hear cries advocating 'the freedom of the press', but celebrities are rarely given freedom *from* the press. A loss of anonymity usually results in a loss of privacy. It's also said that to be photographed is to permit an intimacy, even though most photographs of celebrities are rarely taken with the subject's consent.

I have enemies I've never met. That's fame!
— Tallulah Bankhead

The famous must come to terms with what the Aussies call the 'Tall Poppy Syndrome' (the media build up the celebrities and then chop them down). This is the dark, paradoxical side to celebrity: the media's simultaneous exaltation and persecution of the famous.

Remember the *Flashdance* phenomenon of 1983? More than 20 million copies of the soundtrack and 10 million singles of the title track were sold, and $200 million were raked in at the box office. Transiting Neptune was at 27°–29° Sagittarius. For a short time, the film turned star Jennifer Beals (Sun at 27° Sagittarius) and composers Giorgio Moroder (Moon at 27° Sagittarius) and Irene Cara (Sun at 27° Pisces, Descendant at 28° Sagittarius) into worldwide sensations.

After starring in the 1980 Alan Parker film *Fame* and singing its rousing, anthemic title song, **Irene Cara** was already strongly associated with the youthful, modern-day strivings for success – note her MC in Pisces in a Grand Trine with the Moon and MC ruler Neptune, while also squaring its co-ruler Jupiter. The movies *Fame* and *Flashdance* inspired a generation to train in the performing arts and, befitting Cara's Sun and MC in Pisces, these films merged drama, music and dance with the inspirational theme of making your dreams happen. But when Cara's enormous success made her a victim of industry greed, she sued for unpaid royalties (in mid May 1985), only to find herself blacklisted by industry chiefs – her reputation tarnished by rumour (Pheme) – and facing the wrath of media moguls who did their best to bury her professionally.

At the time of discovering the theft (**in early 1985**, bi-wheel opposite), Pluto and Jupiter – both tied natally to her MC–IC axis – had Solar Arc directed to oppose and square her natal Sun. SA Neptune was conjunct natal Jupiter, and her MC had reached 0° Aries, too. It became an eight-year battle to finally win the rights to her royalties and reclaim her good name.

In 2004, when Cara was asked for her advice to future generations of 'Fame' hopefuls, she offered a heartfelt plea that reflects the Piscean nature of her own chart:

> I wish I could assure them that they will be loved and cherished for the human beings they are and not merely for the talent they may possess. I wish I could say that they will be protected from hateful journalists [who criticize out of envy] and not out of any honest judgement of the work … I can only hope and pray that they will find the inner strength to persevere and never allow other people to define them or write their story … [to] find the will to sing their song another day.[9]

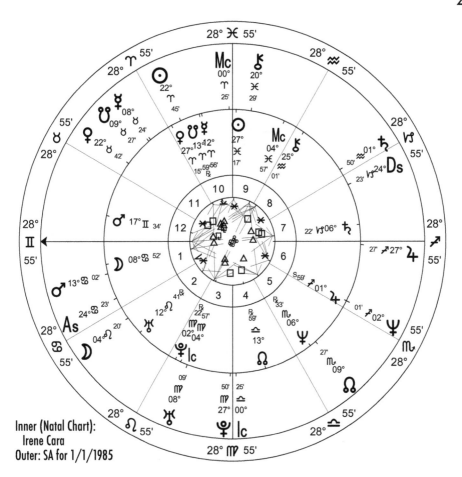

Inner (Natal Chart):
Irene Cara
Outer: SA for 1/1/1985

References and Notes

1 http://dictionary.cambridge.org/dictionary/english/fame
2 Daniel J Boorstin, *The Image: A Guide to Pseudo-Events in America*, Penguin, 1962, p. 55. (My thanks to Richard Swatton for introducing me to this text.)
3 The solar/Leonine journey is a personal quest of self-discovery. The solar/ Leonine type attempts to express its unique, inner sense of self through creative output; it veers off course when it hankers after applause or needs centre stage, the glare of the spotlight, or elevation from the group (Aquarius).

4 A strong Jupiter is also found in the charts of those who benefit from fame by association: celebrity friends and fortunate contacts. And Jupiter is also associated with the public's need to cast judgement. TV shows like *The X Factor* have become a cattle market for public opinion, offering viewers weekly popularity contests. The non-famous are now 'armchair emperors' who condemn or champion the contestants with a thumbs-up or thumbs-down. For more on Jupiter, see my article, 'Jupiter: A New Take on an Old Con Artist', in *The Mountain Astrologer*, October/November 2011, which is also published in *Horoscope Snapshots* (Flare, 2014).

5 Six influential social networking websites created during this transit have prominent Neptune aspects (along with some expected Mercury–Uranus connections): Facebook (4 February 2004) was born during a Sun–Neptune conjunction in Aquarius square the nodal axis; MySpace (1 August 2003) has Sun–Venus opposite Neptune; LinkedIn (5 May 2003) has Sun–Mercury square Neptune in Aquarius; and YouTube (14 February 2005), Twitter (21 March 2006), and Friends Reunited (incorporated 24 February 2000) all have Venus–Neptune in Aquarius. And aptly, Wikipedia (15 January 2001) began with Mercury–Neptune in Aquarius. The rise of photo-led and image-sharing sites such as Pinterest, Instagram, Vine and Flickr coincided with Neptune's move into pictorial Pisces.

6 Crocker and Britney Spears have their Mercurys conjunct as well as their Suns, and his Ascendant had Solar Arc directed to 2° Cancer – Britney's MC degree – by the time of the infamous broadcast.

7 http://news.bbc.co.uk/1/hi/entertainment/6168077.stm

8 http://www.thedailybeast.com/articles/2012/08/15/jodie-foster-blasts-kristen-stewart-robert-pattinson-break-up-spectacle.html

9 Cited in Jeff Guinn and Douglas Perry, *The Sixteenth Minute: Life in the Aftermath of Fame*, Penguin, 2005, pp. 102–103.

Further Reading

Borkowski, Mark. *The Fame Formula*. Pan, 2009.

Brayfield, Celia. *Glitter: The Truth About Fame*. Chatto & Windus, 1985.

Evans, Andrew, and Wilson, Dr Glenn D. *Fame: The Psychology of Stardom*. Vision, 1999.

Evans, Jessica, and Hesmondhalgh, David. *Understanding Media: Inside Celebrity*. Open University Press, 2005.

Gritten, David. *Fame: Stripping Celebrity Bare*. Penguin, 2002.

Orth, Maureen. *The Importance of Being Famous*. Henry Holt, 2004.

Additional Data

The charts presented in the profiles section have the data and source listed in their essays. The following are from other sections of the book (with a page reference noting when their charts are first mentioned and in bold if a chart wheel has been included). Untimed data are from reliable online sources or biographies.

Page   Name, date, time and zone, place (co-ordinates). Source (data collector).

60   **Boy George**, 14/06/1961, 02:50 GDT, Bexley, England (51N26, 0E08). George quoted his baby book on Twitter (Sy Scholfield).

60   **David Bowie**, 8/01/1947, 09:00 GMT, Stockwell, London, England (51N28, 0W07). From various biographies, including his ex-wife's; copies on file. (Gary Lorig quotes Bowie personally for 09:30.)

67   **Charles Kennedy**, 25/11/59, 02:15 GMT, Inverness, Scotland (57N27, 4W15). Birth certificate (Caroline Gerard).

105   **Bill Gates**, 28/10/1955, 21:05 or 22:00 PST, Seattle, Washington, USA (47N36, 122W20). From the book, *Hard Drive, Bill Gates and the Making of the Microsoft Empire* by James Wallace and Jim Erickson, which gives 'shortly after 9:00 p.m.'. Cindy Rempel quotes Gates for 22:00.

117   **Donatella Versace**, 2/05/1955, 05:00 MET, Reggio di Calabria, Italy (38N06, 15E39). Birth certificate (Grazia Bordoni).

188   **Brigitte Bardot**, 28/09/1934, 13:15 GDT, Paris, France (48N52, 2E20). Birth certificate (Michel and Françoise Gauquelin).

189   **Ed Gein**, 27/08/1906, 23:30 CST, North La Crosse, Wisconsin, USA (43N51, 91W15). Birth record (G.S. MacEwan).

189   **Martina Navratilova**, 18/10/1956, 16:40 MET, Prague, Czechoslovakia (50N05, 14E26). From her to Frank Clifford.

192   **Roseanne**, 3/11/1952, 13:21 MST, Salt Lake City, Utah, USA (40N46, 111W53). From her, quoting her birth certificate (Aggie Damron; Donna Hennen).

192   **Coretta Scott King**, 27/4/1927, 16:00 CST, Marion, Alabama, USA (32N38, 87W19). Birth certificate (Janice Mackey and Jessica Saunders).

193   **Christine Keeler**, 22/02/1942, 11:15 GDT, London, England (51N30, 0W10). Cyrus Abayakoon vouches for the accuracy of the data.

193   **Karen Silkwood**, 19/02/1946, 21:50 CST, Longview, Texas, USA (32N30, 94W44). Birth certificate (Ed Steinbrecher).

194   **John DeLorean**, 6/01/1925, 12:00 EST, Detroit, Michigan, USA (42N20, 83W03). Birth certificate (Michel and Françoise Gauquelin).

194   **Rodney King**, 2/04/1965, 07:00 PST, Sacramento, California, USA (38N35, 121W30). Birth certificate; copy on file (Lois Rodden).

195   **Arthur Scargill**, 11/01/1938, 14:00 GMT, Barnsley, England (53N34, 1W28). Richard Llewellyn quotes the National Union of Mineworkers, of which Scargill was President (David Fisher).

195   **Lee Harvey Oswald**, 18/10/1939, 21:55 CST, New Orleans, Louisiana, USA (29N57, 90W05). From Oswald's mother (T. Pat Davis).

196   **Tony Blair**, 6/05/1953, 06:10 GDT, Edinburgh, Scotland (55N57, 3W13). Birth certificate (Caroline Gerard).

196   **Imelda Marcos**, 2/7/1929, 05:30 AWST, Manila, Philippines (14N35, 121E00). Birth certificate; copy on file (Sy Scholfield).

197   **David Koresh**, 17/08/1959, 08:49 CST, Houston, Texas, USA (29N46, 95W22). From his mother (Joyce Mason).

197   **Patty Hearst**, 20/02/1954, 18:01 PST, San Francisco, California, USA (37N47, 122W25). Birth certificate (Janice Mackey and Jessica Saunders).

198   **Bob Dylan**, 24/05/1941, 21:05 CST, Duluth, Minnesota, USA (46N47, 92W06). Birth certificate; copy on file (Bob Garner).

198   **Richard Pryor**, 1/12/1940, 13:02 CST, Peoria, Illinois, USA (40N42, 89W35). Birth certificate (Michel and Françoise Gauquelin).

199   **Billie Holiday**, 7/04/1915, 02:30 EST, Philadelphia, Pennsylvania, USA (39N57, 75W10). Birth certificate, as quoted in *Wishing on the Moon* by Donald Clarke; copy on file (Frank Clifford).

199   **Michael Moore**, 23/04/1954, 12:45 EST, Flint, Michigan, USA (43N01, 83W41). Birth certificate, quoted by Moore (Edith Hathaway).

208   **Jane Fonda**, 21/12/1937, 09:14 EST, Manhattan, New York, USA (40N46, 73W59). Birth certificate; copy on file (Lois Rodden).

213   **Roger Vadim**, 26/01/1928, 21:00 GMT, Paris, France (48N52, 2E20). Birth certificate (Didier Geslain). (Autobiography gives 22:00.)

213   **Tom Hayden**, 11/12/1939, 02:00 or 14:00 EST, Detroit, Michigan, USA (42N20, 83W03). From him '2 a.m. or 2 p.m.' (Ed Steinbrecher).

213   **Ted Turner**, 19/11/1938, 08:50 EST, Cincinnati, Ohio, USA (39N10, 84W27). Birth certificate; copy on file (Frank Clifford).

223   **Queen Elizabeth II**, 21/04/1926, 02:40 GDT, Mayfair, London, England (51N31, 0W09). Official announcement from the Home Office (Cyril Fagan).

224   **Neville Chamberlain**, 18/03/1869, Birmingham, England (52N30, 1W50). Online sources.

224   **King Edward VIII**, 23/06/1894, 21:55 GMT, Surrey, England (51N10, 0W20). Official bulletin (Cyril Fagan).

224   **Winston Churchill**, 30/11/1874, 01:30 GMT, Woodstock, England (51N52, 1W21). Father's letter, as quoted by son Randolph in *Winston S Churchill, 1874–1900* (Sy Scholfield).

224   **Franklin D. Roosevelt**, 30/01/1882, 20:45 LMT (+4:55:44), Hyde Park, Dutchess County, New York, USA (41N47, 73W56). Mother's diary, as quoted in *Sara and Eleanor: The Story of Sara Delano Roosevelt and Her Daughter-in-Law Eleanor Roosevelt* by Jan Pottker.

225   **Prince Philip**, 10/06/1921, 21:46 EET, Mon Repos, Corfu, Greece (39N36, 19E56). Official bulletin.

225   **Prince Charles**, 14/11/1948, 21:14 GMT, London, England (51N30, 0W10). Buckingham Palace records; copy on file.

228   **Princess Margaret**, 21/08/1930, 21:22 GDT, Glamis Castle, Scotland (56N36, 3W00). Birth certificate (Joanne Clancy).

228   **Queen Victoria**, 24/05/1819, 04:15 LMT (+0:00:32), Kensington Palace, London, England (51N30, 0W11). Official royal bulletin as transcribed in *The Times*, 26/5/1819, p. 2 (Sy Scholfield).

231   **Diana, Princess of Wales**, 1/07/1961, 19:45 GDT, Sandringham, England (52N50, 0E30). From Diana to her astrologer-friend Debbie Frank, and from Diana's mother to Charles Harvey. (Birth times and anecdotes given later by Diana appear to have been 'red herrings'.)

232   **Camilla, Duchess of Cornwall**, 17/07/1947, 07:00 GDWT, Denmark Hill, London, England (51N28, 0W05). Biography *Camilla: The King's Mistress* by Caroline Graham (HarperTorch, 1995), p. 1. Date and place confirmed by Sy Scholfield from her *Times* birth notice.

233   **Edith Wilson**, 15/10/1872, 09:00 LMT (+5:24:20), Wytheville, Virginia, USA (36N57, 81W05). Her autobiography, *My Memoir* (The Bobbs-Merrill Co., 1939). The chart presented is for 09:10.

235   **Eleanor Roosevelt**, 11/10/1884, 11:00 EST, New York, New York, USA (40N43, 74W00). Family register; copy on file (Joan Negus).

237   **Jacqueline Kennedy**, 28/7/1929, 14:30 EDT, Southampton, New York, USA (40N53, 72W23). From her to Frances McEvoy via a mutual acquaintance (Frances McEvoy).

241   **Betty Ford**, 8/04/1918, 15:45 CWT, Chicago, Illinois, USA (41N51, 87W39). Birth certificate; copy on file (Tom and Thelma Wilson).

242   **Nancy Reagan**, 6/07/1921, 13:18 EDT, Manhattan, New York, USA (40N46, 73W59). Birth certificate (without a birth time) printed in *Nancy Reagan: The Unauthorized Biography* by Kitty Kelley; time from *Fly Away Home* by John Weld, p. 187 (his mother Deborah Lewis had cast a chart for a 17-year-old Nancy); copies of both on file.

247   **Russ Meyer**, 21/03/1922, 09:35 PST, Oakland, California, USA (37N48, 122W16). Birth certificate; copy on file (Frank Clifford).

248   **Ayrton Senna**, 21/03/1960, 02:35 BZT, Sao Paulo, Brazil (23S32, 46W38). Birth certificate (Marcello Borges).

248   **Henry VIII**, 28/06/1491 (7/07/1491 Gregorian calendar), 08:45 LMT (+0:00:00), Greenwich, England (51N29, 0E00). Birth record (Martin Harvey).

249   **Lois Rodden**, 22/05/1928, 00:27 MST, Lang, Canada (49N56, 104W23). From Rodden, rectified from mother's recollection of 'after midnight'.

251   **Edwina Currie**, 13/10/1946, 23:30 GMT, Liverpool, England (53N25, 2W55). From Currie's secretary in January 1988 (David Fisher).

251   **World Trade Center**, 4/04/1973, 15:00 EST, Manhattan, New York, USA (40N46, 73W59). *The New York Times*, 28 March 1973, p. 93 (Sy Scholfield).

252   **Zeebrugge Ferry Disaster**, 6/03/1987, 18:28 CET, Zeebrugge, Belgium (51N20, 3E12). Online sources.

252   **Dennis Elwell**, 16/02/1930, 23:44 GMT, Stourbridge, England (52N27, 2W09). From him to Garry Phillipson, rectified by Elwell from his parents' recollection that he was born 'late at night'.

254   **Oscar Pistorius**, 22/11/1986, 10:30 EET, Sandton, Johannesburg, South Africa (26S07, 28E03). Date and place from his autobiography *Blade Runner* (Random House, 2009, p. 1). Time from Pistorius's aunt to Philippe Lepoivre, 'between 10h30 and 11h30'; 'most correct estimate would be 10h30 – morning'.

254   **Billie Jean King**, 22/11/1943, 11:45 PWT, Long Beach, California, USA (33N46, 118W11). Birth certificate (Doris Chase Doane).

256   **Judy Garland**, 10/06/1922, 06:00 CST, Grand Rapids, Minnesota, USA (47N14, 93W31). Note from birth registry (Edwin Steinbrecher); copy on file. Same on birth certificate quoted in *Contemporary American Horoscopes*. Scott Schechter's thorough biography *Judy Garland* (Cooper Square Press, 2002) gives '5:30 a.m.'; copy on file.

256 **Sarah Ferguson**, 15/10/1959, 09:03 GMT, London, England (51N30, 0W10). Buckingham Palace records; same from her to her astrologer Penny Thornton.

257 **Heidi Fleiss**, 30/12/1965, 09:05, Los Angeles, California, USA (34N03, 118W15). Birth certificate; copy on file (Frank Clifford).

257 **Charlie Sheen**, 3/09/1965, 22:48 EDT, New York, New York, USA (40N43, 74W00). From him to Linda Clark, quoting his birth certificate. Sy Scholfield quotes Sheen's interview stating he was born at 22:58.

257 **Nick Broomfield**, 30/01/1948, London, England (51N30, 0W10). Online sources.

258 **Germaine Greer**, 29/01/1939, 06:00 AEST, Melbourne, Victoria, Australia (37S49, 144E58). From her (Tiffany Holmes).

258 **Billy Tipton**, 29/12/1914, 02:00 CST, Oklahoma City, Oklahoma, USA (35N28, 97W31). From news clippings (Joan McEvers).

258 **Panorama** (BBC TV series) **Interview with Princess Diana**, 5/11/1995, 19:00 GMT, Kensington Palace, London, England (51N30, 0W08). From the BBC documentary 'Princess Diana: Behind the Panorama Interview'. (The show was broadcast on 20/11/1995, 21:40 GMT. Sy Scholfield quotes *The Times*, 20 November 1995, p. 43.)

259 **Margaret Thatcher's Resignation**, 22/11/1990, 07:35 GMT, Downing Street, Westminster, London, England (51N30, 0W09). http://www.margaretthatcher.org/document/108254 (Frank Clifford).

260 **Bono**, 10/05/1960, 02:00 GDT, Dublin, Ireland (53N20, 6W15). From him, 'two on the dot' (Ed Steinbrecher).

261 **Jim Bakker**, 2/01/1940, 11:00 EST, Muskegon Heights, Michigan, USA (43N12, 86W15). Birth certificate; copy on file (Genevieve Edwards).

262 **Jack Nicholson**, 22/04/1937, 11:00 EST, Neptune, New Jersey, USA (40N13, 74W01). From him to Mark Johnson. Fredrick Davies in *Signs of the Stars* quotes Nicholson for 11:20 a.m. His birth certificate was filed in May 1954 and has no time of birth; copy on file. New York is sometimes stated as his birth place.

262 **Barbara Castle**, 6/10/1910, 14:30 GMT, Chesterfield, England (53N15, 1W25). From her to the Astrological Association (David Fisher).

262 **George W Bush**, 6/07/1946, 07:26 EDT, New Haven, Connecticut, USA (41N18, 72W55). Hospital records; same on birth certificate (Kim Castilla).

264 **Mo Mowlam**, 18/09/1949, Watford, England (51N40, 0W25). Online sources.

264 **Woody Allen**, 1/12/1935, 22:55 EST, Bronx, New York, USA (40N51, 73W54). Birth certificate; copy on file (Lois Rodden).

264 **Marlon Brando**, 3/04/1924, 23:00 CST, Omaha, Nebraska, USA (41N15, 95W56). Birth certificate (Michel and Françoise Gauquelin).

266 **Gary Hart**, 28/11/1936, 14:25 CST, Ottawa, Kansas, USA (38N37, 95W16). Birth certificate (Marion March).

266 **Jimmy Hoffa**, 14/02/1913, 06:52 CST, Brazil, Indiana, USA (39N31, 87W08). Birth note from registry; copy on file (Ed Steinbrecher).

267 **Ed Snowden**, 21/06/1983, 04:42 EDT, Elizabeth City, North Carolina, USA (36N18, 76W13). Birth certificate; copy on file (Eric Francis Coppolino).

268 **Joan Rivers**, 8/06/1933, 02:00 EDT, Brooklyn, Kings, New York, USA (40N38, 73W56). From Rivers on a talk show in March 1997 (Shelley Ackerman).

268 **Joan Collins**, 23/05/1933, morning, Paddington, London, England (51N32, 0W12). Online sources. Her second autobiography *Second Act* (1996) states 'morning', Fredrick Davies used 3 a.m. for a reading, while *Hollywood Sisters* (1989) by Susan Crimp and Patricia Burstein gives 7 a.m. A private source close to Frank Clifford states that Collins was a client and is unsure of her birth time other than 'morning'.

274 **Generoso Pope, Jr**, 13/01/1927. Online sources.

274 **Andy Warhol**, 6/08/1928, 06:30 EDT, Pittsburgh, Pennsylvania, USA (40N26, 80W00). From the biography *Famous for 15 Minutes* by Ultra Violet; copy on file.

276 **Sean Penn**, 17/08/1960, 15:17 PDT, Burbank, California, USA (34N11, 118W18). Birth certificate; copy on file (Aaron Fischer).

278 **Elizabeth Taylor**, 27/02/1932, 02:30 GMT, Golders Green, London, England (51N34, 0W12). Birth report; copy on file (Sy Scholfield). (Taylor and her mother both gave out a time of 2 a.m.)

278 **Marilyn Monroe**, 1/06/1926, 09:30 PST, Los Angeles, California, USA (34N03, 118W15). Birth certificate; copy on file (Bob Garner).

278 **Michael Jackson**, 29/08/1958, 19:33 CDT, Gary, Indiana, USA (41N36, 87W21). From him to his astrologer, Chakrapani Ullal; same from nephew Taj Jackson on Twitter 'straight from the birth certificate' (other times exist).

278 **Prince**, 7/06/1958, 18:17 CDT, Minneapolis, Minnesota, USA (44N59, 93W16). Birth certificate; copy on file (Frank Clifford).

278   **Susan Boyle**, 1/04/1961, 09:50 GDT, Bangour Hospital, Blackburn (West Lothian county), Scotland (55N54, 03W35). Birth certificate (Caroline Gerard).

278   **Carole King**, 9/02/1942, 23:42 EWT, Brooklyn, Kings, New York, USA (40N38, 73W56). Birth certificate, as quoted by King (Ruth Elliot).

280   **Chris Crocker**, 7/12/1987, 16:58 EST, Bristol, Tennessee, USA (36N36, 82W11). From him online (Sy Scholfield.)

280   **Max Clifford**, 6/04/1943, Kingston upon Thames, England (51N25, 0W19). From the book 'Max Clifford: Read All about It' by Max Clifford and Angela Levin (Random House, 2012), p. 16.

281   **Kim Kardashian**, 21/10/1980, 10:46 PDT, Los Angeles, California, USA (34N03, 118W15). Birth certificate (Alexander Angel).

281   **Khloé Kardashian**, 27/06/1984, 22:55 PDT, Los Angeles, California, USA (34N03, 118W15). Birth certificate (Viktor E).

281   **Kourtney Kardashian**, 18/04/1979, 03:15 PST, Los Angeles, California, USA (34N03, 118W15). Birth certificate (Viktor E).

281   **Kylie Jenner**, 10/08/1997, 17:25 PDT, Los Angeles, California, USA (34N03, 118W15). Birth certificate (Viktor E).

281   **Kendall Jenner**, 3/11/1995, 15:38 PST, Los Angeles, California, USA (34N03, 118W15). Birth certificate (Viktor E).

281   **Kris Jenner**, 5/11/1955, 02:47 PST, San Diego, California, USA (32N43, 117W09). Birth certificate (Viktor E).

284   **Jennifer Beals**, 19/12/1963, Chicago, Illinois, USA (41N51, 87W39). Online sources.

284   **Giorgio Moroder**, 26/04/1940, 02:45 MET, Ortisei, Italy (46N34, 11E40). Birth certificate; copy on file (Grazia Bordoni).

284   **Irene Cara**, 18/03/1959, 10:41 EST, Bronx, New York, USA (40N51, 73W54). From her to Lynn Rodden, quoting her birth certificate.

286   **Britney Spears**, 2/12/1981, 01:30 CST, McComb, Mississippi, USA (31N15, 90W27). From her and her mother to Barry Street of The Astrology Shop (Covent Garden, London).

More About Author Frank Clifford

Data Collector An astrologer and palmist since 1989, Frank Clifford began data collecting with Lois Rodden, contributing to and editing her magazine *Data News* and book *Profiles of Women* (1995). Frank's first book, *British Entertainers*, was published in 1997 and updated in 2003. Frank's database of celebrity data is on the Solar Fire program as *The Clifford Data Compendium* (1997, 2000) and on Astro-Databank. In 2009, he produced *The Astrologer's Book of Charts*, an eclectic collection of 150 horoscopes and worksheets for students. The collection of charts and essays, *The Book of Music Horoscopes*, followed in 2018.

Publisher Back in 1996 Frank founded the imprint Flare Publications, and since then he has edited/published two dozen titles on astrology and palmistry, including *Astrology in the Year Zero*, *The Contemporary Astrologer's Handbook*, a revised edition of *The Twelve Houses* and many of his own titles (including *Horoscope Snapshots: Essays in Modern Astrology*). In 2010, Flare went into partnership with Faber & Faber to release its e-books. Flare has also been instrumental in bringing astrology books and authors to the Chinese market.

Media Astrologer Over the years, Frank's media work has ranged from the sublime to the ridiculous – from being interviewed for documentaries about *Little Britain* and Danny Boyle's feature film *Sunshine*, guesting on Radio 4's *The Inconstant Moon*, and working with the Oxford University Press and Universal Studios ... to being asked by *The Sun* to locate a then-missing Saddam Hussein! Frank has also combined his work as a consultant astrologer with that of Sun sign columnist for *Marie Claire* (UK), *Quick and Simple* (Hearst, US), the celebrity weekly *Reveal* (UK) for three years, and *Candis* (UK) for twelve years. He has also been profiled in various broadsheets and tabloids (including *The Guardian*, *The Daily Express* and *The Independent*), and has been featured on TV and radio. For many years, Frank wrote columns in *The Astrological Journal* and the *ISAR Journal*, and continues to write for *The Mountain Astrologer*. In 2013, Frank became the magazine's first guest editor and has since edited more than half a dozen issues.

Palmist Frank is also a well known palmist and consultant (with *The Guardian* dubbing him the 'palm reader to the stars'), and his book

Palmistry 4 Today (published in five languages) is considered *the* modern textbook on the subject. Frank's second book on palmistry, *Palm Reading* (Hamlyn, 2003, Flare 2018), is a unique guide with profiles on love, work and personality. Cards of these profiles were published in 2007. Most years Frank organizes a palmistry conference, which brings together some of the top hand analysts in the country.

Teacher/Speaker Back in early 2004, Frank bought and began running the popular London School of Astrology (www.londonschoolofastrology. co.uk) and continues to organize certificate and diploma classes, seminars and residential courses in astrology and palmistry. Regarded as the students' choice for studying astrology in the UK, the LSA prides itself on hosting seminars and classes by some of the world's most accomplished astrologers. Frank also set up an annual Astrology Student Conference (www.astroconference.com) with Wendy Stacey. He has lectured in over a dozen countries (across Europe, Asia, Australia, Mexico and the US), given keynote lectures at most international astrology conferences, and for some years was a regular guest tutor on a psychology course at the London Metropolitan University. Along with Noel Tyl and a few others, Frank has helped popularize and promote the forecasting method of Solar Arc directions through his teachings and writings.

Frank has also given stand-up comedy talks/roasts at some astrological conferences (including Norwac, the AA and FAA conferences). Frank made his first trip to China in December 2012, where the press dubbed him 'the Dean of the Harry Potter School', and lectured at the Science Museum in Shenzhen. He returned in 2016 to speak to a bank as well as a business school at Guangzhou's prestigious university. He has since joined forces with New Moon in China to create online astrology courses in Mandarin.

In 2012, Frank was honoured by his peers with The Charles Harvey Award for Exceptional Service to Astrology. In 2016, the ISAR membership voted his work on the power degrees of the zodiac 'Best Article 2014–2016', and Frank was nominated for a Regulus Award for Professional Image at the 2018 UAC in Chicago.

In recent years, Frank has written shorter volumes including *The Midheaven: Spotlight on Success* and *Dialogues*. The next phase sees the publication of a student textbook/teaching manual, *Birth Charts*, plus new online courses with the LSA and New Moon.

Palmistry 4 Today

This acclaimed, fully illustrated textbook offers immediate access to the mysteries of the hand. In 4 easy-to-follow-steps, this innovative, fully revised and expanded edition presents: The Palm Detective; Timing Techniques; Love, Health and Career; and Palmistry in Action.

'An excellent book, well written and well illustrated, guaranteed to get the beginner hooked on palmistry from page 1; the practitioner could learn a lot from it too. Thoroughly recommended.' – *Prediction* magazine

'It's easy to read, packed with interesting information, beautifully presented and very well illustrated. It's honest and open, too, which I love the most... It's very modern and there are lots of really nice concepts here and much to learn.' – Lori Reid, leading palmist

Getting to the Heart of Your Chart: Playing Astrological Detective

This volume is designed to help astrologers identify, prioritize and then synthesize the components, themes and storylines of any horoscope. Packed with original ideas and observations, this textbook includes innovative sections on: the five themes found in any chart; the seven major assessments; and how to judge planetary influence. Includes dozens of biographies and over 150 horoscopes demonstrating astrology in action.

'A book I could only have dreamed about when I began studying astrology and stumbled my way forward ... Frank's insights are so informed that even well-experienced astrologers will enjoy and learn from this book.' – Mary Plumb, *The Mountain Astrologer*

'The author's ability to create an immediate rapport draws one into reflective engagement right from the opening page.' – Anne Whitaker, *The Mountain Astrologer*

Horoscope Snapshots: Essays in Modern Astrology

In 18 engaging essays, discover: the deeper sides to your Sun sign; how your Sun, Moon and Ascendant differ; the real nature of Jupiter; parental significators; vocational indicators; and the role of Pluto in America.

'Entertaining as well as educational... Fascinating and fun to read.' – *Dell Horoscope*

The Midheaven: Spotlight on Success

The Midheaven (MC) is associated with success, achievement and recognition. It has much to say about our reputation and public image, as well as early parental messages and ambitions. This absorbing volume offers many original insights from the author's years of research. (Mini-book)

'This excellent punchy guide to the Midheaven cannot be bettered... A delicious concentrate of accessible astrology.' – Victor Olliver, *The Astrological Journal*

www.frankclifford.co.uk

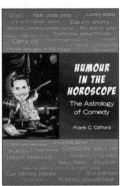

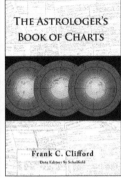

Two international
astrologers examine
(in four new essays):
potential traps for the
counselling astrologer;
Mercury in consultation;
the transformational
potential of astrology;
and the tools to use
when preparing for a
chart analysis.
(Mini-book)

This sparkling and
entertaining guide on
your Mars and Venus
signs – written by two
top media astrologers –
is packed with practical
advice and astrological
insights into your
relationship needs,
passions, turn-ons and
turn-offs.
(Mini-book)

Which signs and planets
link with which types of
humour? With the help
of numerous horoscopes,
Frank Clifford has
put together a unique
volume of charts,
observations and wicked
one-liners that well and
truly hit the astrological
funny bone.
(Mini-book)

From Dolly to Dali,
Nixon to Manson,
George Galloway
to Greta Garbo,
Christine Keeler to
Monica Lewinsky. 150
accurately timed and
sourced horoscopes and
worksheets. Includes
new data. Charts
presented in both
Placidus and Equal.

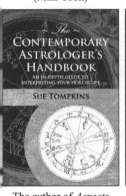

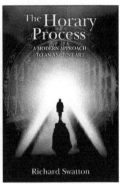

The author of *Aspects
in Astrology* presents an
authoritative guide to
chart interpretation with
an in-depth exploration
of the planets, zodiac
signs, houses and
aspects. Included are
biographies and step-
by-step instructions for
synthesizing the main
horoscope factors.

From an award-winning
psychological astrologer
comes the definitive
book on the astrological
houses. This edition
of the best-selling
handbook remains a firm
favourite among students
and professionals. With
a new foreword by Dr
Liz Greene and tribute
essays from astrologers.

Faye Blake (formerly
Faye Cossar) shows
how to create a
vocational profile,
which enables you
and your clients
to: identify talents,
blocks and style;
create a CV, website
and logo; define
goals and awaken life
purpose and passion.

A clear guide to
learning the craft of
horary astrology and
preparing for judgment.
Sections include:
horary as a magical
art; the divinatory
attitude; signification
and rulership; the art of
timing; and how to use
horary methods on natal
charts.

www.flareuk.com

The London School of Astrology

– the students' choice in contemporary astrological education –

• Accredited Foundation courses for beginners in central London
• Accredited Diploma courses for those with more experience
• Saturday seminars, Summer School courses and other events
• Short courses in tarot and palmistry (modern hand analysis)

• **New online astrology and palmistry courses for all levels**

Learn astrology, palmistry and tarot in a fun, supportive environment
with the UK's most experienced, professional astrologers/tutors/writers

To find out more
Visit our website **www.londonschoolofastrology.co.uk**
Email: admin@londonschoolofastrology.co.uk

Telephone: 020 8402 7772

Self-knowledge, spiritual development, vocational training

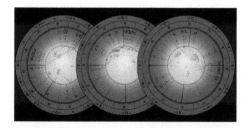

Lightning Source UK Ltd.
Milton Keynes UK
UKHW010753101218
333747UK00015B/1318/P